CAMANACHD!

CAMANACHD!

The Story of Shinty

Roger Hutchinson

Birlinn

This edition first published in 2004 by
Birlinn Limited
West Newington House
10 Newington Road
Edinburgh EH9 1QS

www.birlinn.co.uk

First published in 1989 by Mainstream Publishing, Edinburgh

ISBN 1 84158 326 X

British Library Cataloguing-in-Publication Data
A catalogue record for this book is
available from the British Library

Typeset by Hewer Text Limited, Edinburgh
Printed and bound by the Cromwell Press, Trowbridge, Wiltshire

A-màireach bidh Bhliadhn' Ur againn,
'S a rìgh! gur beag mo shunnd-sa rith';
Mi ceangailt' aig an stiùir aice,
'S na siùil a' falbh nan stròicean.

'S gur iomadh fear is aithne dhomh
'S a chaman ùr fo achlais
Dol dh'ionnsaigh na Cloich Glaise,
Ged tha mise tarraing ròpa.

(Tomorrow we'll have the New Year. Oh Lord, little
is my joy for it; me being tied to the helm
and the sails going to tatters.
And there's many a one I know, with a new
caman under his arm, making his way to the
Clach Ghlas while I'm pulling on a rope.)

        – Angus Lamont, Lagnancruach, Tiree
         born c. 1844 died c. 1888

Contents

Preface to Second Edition

Fifteen years ago, introducing the first impression of this book, I wrote about my gratitude to the township of Ballachulish for giving me my first sight of the game called shinty. That was in 1976. Earlier this year, twenty-eight winters later, I drove again through Ballachulish and on the same patch of grass boys were still playing shinty. That is called staying power.

So I am grateful to Ballachulish, as to all the shinty playing parishes of Scotland past and present. But this new preface must in fairness be devoted to another district.

The first edition of *Camanachd!* was published in 1989. It was received by the shinty world with what I now know to be typical generosity. Nowhere was that more apparent than in my home territory of Skye. Within a few weeks of publication I was invited to make a speech to open the annual sale of work for Skye Camanachd at the Gathering Hall in Portree. I knew it would be a formidable experience. Only the degree was unexpected.

That hall was packed with Sgiathanaich. From all corners of the island they had come, young and old, to show their support for something which transcended sport. They were engaged in an act of affirmation. From the stage I looked over a friendly ocean of faces. This, I thought, is a great sleeping institution.

The next year it woke up. In 1990 Skye Camanachd, organised by a brilliant young manager and staffed by a sensational squad of players, fought its way past Kingussie and Fort William to the final of the Camanachd Cup, where they met Newtonmore on a flawless after-noon in Lochaber.

And as the revised appendix to this edition shows in a few stark letters and numerals, Skye won. It was comfortably the greatest day in the island's sporting history. Nobody who experienced that Camanachd Cup Final will forget the passion. Chris Tyler, the *West Highland Free Press*'s cartoonist, characteristically captured its spirit with a cartoon showing a queue for the ferry at Kyleakin (in those pre-bridge days). On the slipway Chris sketched a notice which read: 'Will the last person leaving Skye please remember to turn off the lights'. How many Sgiathanaich were there in Fort William? Four thousand? Six thousand? Eight thousand? All of them, it seemed, spilling out of the stadium and around the grassy knolls . . . On that day the great beast of history revived itself and slouched into our present. On that day it was suddenly possible to see and feel the atmosphere of the Great Games between Strathglass and Glen Urquhart in the 1880s. On that day all that shinty has meant and still means to Scotland came alive.

So the acknowledgements and the thanks of the first preface still stand. Some of them with a little sadness, as they feature great men who are no longer with us. But one more should be added – this book, now more than ever, owes a debt to Skye Camanachd, to all of its officials, coaches, supporters and players, past, present and future.

Roger Hutchinson, Isle of Raasay, 2004

Preface to First Edition

I first encountered the game of shinty less than fourteen years ago. I would shortly be taking up a job which involved reporting sport at the *West Highland Free Press* and, driving north through Ballachulish, I came across a group of boys using what I now know to be junior camain on a patch of worn ground before the council houses. This, I was told, was the old game itself. It was still the major winter sport in large parts of the Highlands and even on one or two islands. There were great stories about its history. I asked to see a book which would tell me more, but was told that apart from the excellent, energetic *Shinty Year Book* no such publication was in print. Shortly afterwards Donald MacKinnon, who was then the manager of Skye Camanachd, put a good deal of time and effort into helping me research some of the last hundred years of shinty in Skye and Wester Ross. Although nothing, apart from a couple of newspaper articles and a whetted appetite, came directly from those investigations, Donald planted the seeds of this book.

While I was researching the story of shinty it was suggested to me that I might be tempted to see it as a long and venerable tale which is slowly coming to an end. This shocking notion had hardly crossed my mind. Being immersed, however briefly, in the fascinating history of the sport has blinded me to its present failings. Where others see a depressing indictment of standards when Kingussie romp to another high-scoring win, I see merely another great team following in the footsteps of Cowal, Newtonmore, Caberfeidh, Kyles Athletic and their own forebears. Where others point to administrative frailty I can see nothing worse than a continuation of good and hard-working people doing their best for a game which has never had the easiest of lives. I am not, therefore, poised to presume to prescribe for the future

well-being of shinty; and this book teaches no lessons unless they are
those which we may learn from the past.

Many people have helped with *Camanachd!*, but I must give particular thanks to John Willie Campbell, Alister Chisholm, Jack Richmond, Willie Batchen, Sorley Maclean, Archie MacDonald, Professor
Norman MacDonald, Toby Carter, Andrew Sherwood and Fraser
Gordon; and to all of the club secretaries who responded to my
enquiries; while making it clear that none of them are to be repre-
hended for any omissions or defects in the finished product, for which I
am solely responsible.

I am lucky enough to live within walking distance of Sabhal Mòr
Ostaig, the Gaelic College, and the Clan Donald Centre in Skye. Both of
their excellent libraries laid the foundations for the research of this book.
The people who work at both places were helpful, interested and
encouraging to a fault. In particular, Alan Boyd at the Sabhal Mòr
patiently offered Gaelic translation and Rab MacDonald Parker
gave me unstinting access to the remarkable collection of Highland
literature which has been amassed in Armadale.

Nobody can write about the history of the caman in Ireland without
drawing on Art Ó Maolfabhail's *Cáman: 2,000 years of Hurling in Ireland.*
Reverend J. Ninian MacDonald's loving little work *Shinty: A Short
History of the Ancient Highland Game* (1932) was invaluable, as was the
thesis which Muirne Campbell submitted to the Celtic Department of
the University of Aberdeen in 1970, and, of course, the aforementioned
Shinty Year Book.

The first rough draft of the history of shinty was written by reporters
and correspondents attached to the *Inverness Courier, Northern Chronicle,
Oban Times, Ross-shire Journal, Press & Journal, Badenoch Record,* and
Strathspey Herald. I am indebted to them, and to the *West Highland Free
Press,* a younger newspaper than most of the others but one which lost
no time in realising that the good health of the game of shinty is as
important a Highland issue as any other.

Finally, I would like to thank the Scottish Arts Council for help in
researching this book.

Roger Hutchinson, Skye, 1989

1

Out of Ireland

'The hero's flame rose from the crown of his head.'

Swift, sea-going curraghs from the north-east coast of Ireland first shipped the caman and the ball, with Christianity and the Gaelic language, to Scotland.

Of this there is little doubt. We may not know exactly when, as few records of trade or of war or of friendship and intermarriage between the Pictish kingdoms of Scotland and the Gaelic civilisation of Ireland exist. But we know that at the beginning of the sixth century a taskforce of Irish Gaels established a foothold in Argyllshire, probably on the peninsula of Kintyre, which points like an arthritic finger towards County Antrim, and that they claimed their settlement to be part of the kingdom which they named Dalriada. We know that a few, soon to be beatified, priests set sail with their disciples shortly afterwards on shallow vessels of wood and hide to spread the word of God amid the druidical settlements which lay beyond Dalriada. We know much of these priests and attendant monks. They were adept seafarers and fishermen, farmers, builders and writers. They were young, strong and stubborn. Beneath a strictly old-fashioned tonsure, which denuded the scalp from temple to temple, and to which the Caledonians would adhere for fifty years after the Synod of Whitby had agreed upon a new form of shaven head, (thereby defying King Oswy and ignoring Rome), stood men who may not have been precisely warrior priests but who were certainly muscular Christians, proud of a faith and a way of life which had stood firm while the rest of Christian Europe all but collapsed before a wave of barbarian fire and pagan riot. And we know that these sixth-, seventh- and eighth-century followers of Barr, Maolrubha and Columba played an outdoor sport using a small ball and a long stick which curved at the striking end, and that they called this game *camanachd*.

No single nation or culture can claim for itself alone the invention of such a game. The recreational striking of a ball with a stick occurs throughout recorded history. Many such ancient sports have passed through the centuries to have the modern world trim their thorns, oversee them with constitutional ruling bodies, standardise and articulate their rules, and present them, neatly attired, to society.

Nor can it be suggested that the running, driving, stick-and-ball game is a product strictly of the European genius. The following description dates from the 1930s:

> We children played and ran along the beaches. [In the high mountains] I had never known such wide open spaces, such flat ground for running . . . [and] there were many new games to learn. By far the most popular and interesting of these was . . . played with . . . bent sticks and a ball . . . The object of the game was to drive the other party of players as far east or west as we could. We usually played against a neighbouring village and when we were lucky we would drive them miles along the beach far beyond their village and the game would only stop when the sun set. The boys were in the forefront of the game, hitting the ball with their sticks. But the girls had the privilege of being allowed to catch the ball with their hands . . .

The game took place on the shores of New Guinea. The ball was a 'hard, round *koae* seed' and the stick a bent cane. It would be pointless to suggest here even the slightest colonial influence, when the claims of the Raj to have educated the peoples of India and Pakistan in their twentieth-century eminence in international hockey look increasingly embarrassed and threadbare as evidence accumulates of a similar game being played throughout the sub-continent long before the arrival of the cutters of the East India Company.

But to say that a European genius for games is not unique is not to deny that the genius exists. The countries which surround the Mediterranean Sea and skirt the north-eastern Atlantic Ocean have in the past two thousand years colonised and administrated between them most of the peoples of the world. Their talent for exporting and imposing their own idea of order, off and on the field of sport, has been matched by their appetite for the riches and the habits of those peoples. When the Khans of Persia traded spices with the infidel and presented to him an exhibition of horseback riding which involved striking, while at full gallop, a round object with a mallet, they could not have forseen that the game would subsequently have been seeded throughout Asia, adopted as a favoured pastime of the aristocracy in Great Britain and Argentina and would finally, sanitised and christened 'polo', be reintroduced to its country of origin, to *their* country, where it had long been dead, by officers of the army of Queen Victoria.

The journeys of different sports across land and sea, in the cargo-holds of merchant ships and the kit-bags of colonial travellers, are never easy to trace down through the centuries. The journey taken by the game which Scots now know as shinty, the Irish as hurling and the children of immigrant Canadians – whose fathers transformed it into the international sport of ice-hockey – as camag, shinny or shinny-hockey, is a largely unrecorded odyssey. To make order of the earlier centuries of its life is to place down and stare hopefully at such fragments of literature, folklore and carvings in stone as constitute the merest scattered pieces of a jigsaw the size of a continent.

The ancient Greeks were familiar with an organised game involving a bent stick and a ball. There is in Athens a carved panel which dates from the fifth century BC. It shows two figures facing each other, crouched, with their sticks crossed over the ball which lies between

Who can claim to have invented such a game? This Athenian carving dates from the fifth century BC. *The sport's origins (and its fate) are unknown. (National Museum of Greece)*

them. Behind stand the cameos of other players and a man without a stick but with one hand raised, presumably giving the signal to commence play.

This game may have travelled south with the Celts of central Europe who perambulated around the continent in the centuries before Christ, or it may have been collected by them, another small item of hand luggage, as they paused in Hellas before shifting again, slowly westwards. Whether they adopted the game, or introduced it and stayed for long enough to pose for a curious Athenian sculptor, little further evidence of it was deposited before the Celtic people reached the last staging post and looked out over an ocean which even they could not, for the time being, contemplate crossing. *Pelota* may be a relic of Celtic culture in northern Spain, but it does not resemble camanachd. *Hurnussen*, in Switzerland, used a bent stick and a ball but was not, apparently, a team game. *Sautreiben*, in Germany, was a team game, but the stick was short and straight and its elementary rules were closer to rounders.

Only in the small, weather-torn islands at the end of the world did a game develop which obviously resembled that unambiguous scene etched on to the base of a pedestal in an Athenian gymnasium. The resemblances are so pronounced and, given the vacuum between the Athenian republic and the pre-Christian fiefdoms of Great Britain and Ireland, so strange that the observer might be startled into insisting upon a connection. 'With what ease', writes Patrick Leigh Fermor, 'populations moved about in ancient Greek lands, in the world conquered and Hellenized by Alexander, the wide elbow room of Rome and the Byzantine Empire! Undocumented, free and unregimented, people wandered where they liked between the Thames, the Danube, the Euphrates and the upper Nile – anywhere, in fact, that was free of the Barbarian menace, and often beyond.' But no evidence exists as to how so frivolous an idea might have been flipped across such a waste of time and space, and the observer might be best advised to think of bent canes and *koae* nuts on the sands of New Guinea and consider parallel evolution.

If this it was, it did not remain parallel for very long. The Athenians shortly had other things to occupy their minds, such as invading Spartan galleys and upstart Macedonians intent on destroying the city state, and the elegant little game with the curved stick and the ball slipped out of their history without leaving so much as its name behind. Beset, at the time, by lesser problems, the people of the numerous kingdoms of old Ireland gave their game a basic form and a name – camanachd – which have lasted to the present day.

Gaelic literature is the oldest literature in Europe, north of the Alps. Writers in this ancient and venerable language and the bearers of its verbal heritage demand respect when they tell us of the history of their race. When the *Book of Leinster (An Leabhar Laigneach)* was composed in the twelfth-century AD, its contributors were using a language which had a pedigree longer than that of the language used by Winston Churchill when, 800 years later, he described the *History of the English-Speaking Peoples*.

The *Book of Leinster* records the first-ever game of camanachd to be celebrated in print as taking place on the first day of the sixth week in summer, in the year 1272 BC. It was an unpleasant affair. As part of a lengthy military engagement between the Fir Bolg and their persistent invaders, the Tuatha Dé Danaan, twenty-seven of the latter engaged a select from the former in a pre-battle game of camanachd. The Fir Bolg won, and promptly fell upon their opponents and slew them. An exchange of messengers between the respective kings then agreed the chivalric rules and itinerary of the battle proper (it was to be fought with equal numbers on each side during any given engagement, to the disappointment of the Fir Bolg king, who possessed the larger army) and the two forces set to.

The Tuatha Dé Danaan eventually battered from the Fir Bolg the right to settle in Ireland and one of their kings, Lugh, received pagan deification. In his mortal life, which was some time before the tenth century BC, Lugh is credited with being a patron of public sports. As well as introducing chess and the horsewhip to Ireland, he started the annual Tailteann Fair, which always featured camanachd, in memory of his foster-mother. Following his death and subsequent apotheosis, the pagan harvest festival of Lunasa, the beginning of August, was named after Lugh. Aonach Tailteann, the first day of August Tailteann Fair, died with Roderick O'Conner, the last king of Ireland, at the end of the twelfth-century AD, and was revived in 1924 – when once again, as we shall see, it featured a remarkable pan-Celtic camanachd competition. The name of Lugh, a powerful one in pre-Christian Europe, followed his spirit into immortality, forming the base of such distant settlements as Loudun, Lyons, Leiden, and Leignitz. 'Free and unregimented, people wandered where they liked . . .'.

The game of camanachd, the shout of young voices on damp fields and the sharp crack of contact, echoes down the centuries from a host of annals and legends which were born in Ireland in those turbulent years before and after the dawn of the first millennium, AD. Many of these tales have entered the banquet hall of international folklore. Moen, the great king of Leinster – a province which was to become the nursery of camanachd's Irish offspring, hurling – was born dumb. Despite the earnest attentions of the philosopher, poet and harpist of his dead father's court, the young prince entered manhood as a mute and was consequently subject to the regency rule of his uncle. Fortunately the lad played games and one auspicious day he received a vicious knock on the shin from another player's caman. Moen's anguished yelp ('This has happened to me!' he is reputed to have barked) broke the silence. 'Labraid Moen, labraidh Moen,' ('Moen speaks') his colleagues observed. The name Moen was quickly forgotten and the name of Labhraidh, The Speaker, King of Leinster, entered history.

But it is from the saga of Cuchullin, the first and the greatest of the Homeric Gaelic legends, that we gain a proper understanding of the importance of this field sport in the vibrant Celtic civilisation of what the Romans came to know, and despair of, as Ultima Thule.

Cuchullin, the Ulster traveller and warrior who left his name to lie fittingly upon the most momentous mountain range in Britain, the black soaring pinnacles of Skye, won his first triumphs and his earliest reputation with a caman and a ball. There are countless versions of the boyhood deeds of Cuchullin, but as those which find their way into print grow progressively more whimsical as they grow more distant from their source, it is as well to return to the two earliest manuscript recordings of the story, *Leabhar na h Uidhre* and *An Leabhar Laighneach*. Both date from the twelfth-century AD, but there are some years between them, and the latter draws strongly upon the former. The cynical modern reader might be interested to learn that twelfth-century calligraphers did not regard themselves as being entirely fools. Appended to the later version of Cuchullin's story, in *An Leabhar Laigneach*, is the comment: 'I who have written this story, or rather this fable, do not accommodate my belief to certain things in this story or fable. Some things in it are devilish illusions, some are figments of the imagination, some appear true, some the opposite, and some are from the delight of foolish people.' Another appendix, presumably from a different source, wishes more positively 'A blessing on everyone who remembers the Táin honestly in this form and does not alter it'.

And so, with a hint of intellectual discord in a candle-lit medieval sanctum, the 'devilish illusion' or the honestly remembered tale of the first great player of camanachd was passed down to us.

Cuchullin was brought up bearing the name of Setanta in his parents' house by the sea on the plain of Muirtheimhne (modern Dundalk) during the time of Christ. Throughout his childhood he heard tales of the youth of Eamhain and of their king, Conchubhar, whose days of monarchy involved rising early, settling the affairs of state 'and thereafter dividing the day into three': 'The first third of the day is spent in watching the youths playing games and camanachd, the second in playing board games, and the last third of the day is spent in consuming food and drink, to the lulled music of minstrels and musicians, until sleep comes on them all.'

Setanta asked his mother for permission to join the youths of Eamhain, but she at first refused, insisting that he should wait until a champion of Ulster could accompany and protect him. 'I think it too long to wait for that,' replied the child, and set off on foot.

He took his caman of bronze and his ball of silver; he took his little javelin for casting and his toy spear with its end sharpened by fire, and he began to shorten the journey by playing with them. He would strike the ball with the caman and drive it a long way from him. He would throw his javelin and he would cast his spear, and he would rush after them and catch them before they touched the ground.

He went to the youths of Eamhain without the bond of their protection. And no one used to go to them in the playing field until they had given him the bond of their protection. He did not know this. There were thrice fifty youths at their games on the green of Eamhain. The boy went on to the playing field in their midst and caught the ball between his legs when they cast it, nor did he let it go higher than the top of his knee nor lower than his ankle, and he pressed it and held it close between his two legs, and not one of the youths managed to get a grasp or a stroke or a blow or a shot at it. And he carried the ball away from them over the goal.

'The boy defies us,' said Follamhain mac [son of] Chochubhair. 'Attack him, for he is of the Ulstermen, and let them not make it a habit to join your games without putting themselves under your protection and safeguard.'

They cast their thrice fifty camain at the boy's head. He lifted his single caman and warded off the thrice fifty sticks. Then they cast the thrice fifty balls at him. He warded off the thrice fifty balls.

Then a transformation came over him. You would have thought that each rib of hair had been driven into his head, so upright did it stand. You would have thought that a spark of fire was on the tip of each bristle. One eye closed until it was no wider than the eye of the needle. The other eye opened until it was as wide as the mouth of a mead goblet. He bared his jawbone to his ear. He opened his lips until his gullet became visible. The hero's flame rose from the crown of his head.

Then he set upon the youths.

At about this point King Conchubhar made his daily visit to the green at Eamhain,

. . . and saw something which astonished him: thrice fifty boys at one end of the field and a single boy at the other end, and the single boy winning victory from the thrice fifty youths. When they played the hole game (*cluiche poill*) and when it was their turn to cast the ball and his to defend, he would catch the thrice fifty balls outside the hole and none would go past him. When it was their turn to defend and his to drive, he would fill the hole with all their balls and they would not be able to prevent him.

Conchubhar took in the young Setanta, who soon found himself invited to a feast in the king's honour, hosted by a smith called Cullin. The smith was in the habit of releasing a fierce watch-hound to protect his grounds, which he did immediately after the king's arrival at his table. Setanta, arriving late, was set upon by the dog and, armed only with his caman and ball, was obliged to kill it by driving the ball into its jaws.

The smith, vexed, demanded to know how his dog would be replaced. Setanta swore that he would rear another animal of equal merit and that until then he himself would serve as the smith's guardian. A druid approved the settlement and added that the boy should thereafter be known as Cullin's dog – *Cuchullin*. When the boy commented that he was quite happy being called Setanta, the druid replied: 'Do not say that, for all men in the world will some day have the name of Cuchullin on their lips.'

These tales cannot be carbon-dated. They may predate the birth of Christ, or they may be as young as the twelfth- century: their value is undiminished. In *cluiche poill*, they provide the earliest clues as to the origins of golf. They suggest a rudimentary form of organised play. The tactic of Cuchullin shielding the ball between his legs was not known to the earlier *Leabhar na h Uidhre*, it is an embellishment of the composers of *An Leabhar Laighneach*. The latter, however, with their expressed concern about diabolic influences on parts of the story, omit the graphic description of Cuchullin's epileptic fury at being assaulted by 150 caman-wielding strangers.

The references to a bronze caman and a silver ball, a detail found only in *An Leabhar Laighneach*, are seminal: throughout the Irish and Scottish fables which were to follow, shinty equipment was rarely made of wood alone. Different qualities of metal, from base and functional to precious and oranmental, were used in the sporting equipment as well as in the brooches, javelins and chariots of the design-conscious Celts to signify the social standing, or the personal promise, or the spiritual worth of the user. This was a culture which embossed, inlaid and patterned most intricately its lowliest items of everyday household use.

The habit died slowly. As late as the eighteenth-century, camanachd challenge matches took place between the men of County Wexford and those of Cornwall. Hearing of this, William III ordered an exhibition game to be played in London between twenty-one Irishmen and twenty-one Cornishmen. The match was organised by Sir Caesar Colclough, a Wexford landowner. The Irishmen won (although any slight satisfaction that might have been gained from this reversal of the result at the Boyne was short-lived: Sir Caesar and his squad of players drowned off the Hook lighthouse on their return voyage) and the ball, the match-ball, was plated with silver, as was only suitable and traditional for a game of camanachd which involved the presence of royalty.

These glittering allusions are to be found, transferred without effort, in the oral folklore and the traditions of Gaelic Scotland. In the summer of 1889 and the spring of 1890 the Reverend J. MacDougall busied himself collecting folk tales in Argyllshire. He encountered a native of Ardnamurchan, one Alexander Cameron, who was working on the road between Duror and Ballachulish. Cameron related some of the tales of Fionn mac Cumhaill. He told how Fionn heard of a dream of a sleeping giant with an infant cupped in his hand. On the floor by the giant two boys played with camain of gold and a ball of silver and a huge deer-hound suckled two pups.

MacDougall was told another story: of an old king from across the Irish Sea who had two sons from two wives, and whose present wife favoured her own son by giving him a caman of gold and a ball of silver, while the child of the first marriage had to make do with a wooden caman and a wooden ball. Limited as he might have been by such humdrum equipment, the first son nonetheless excelled at the game, and after inflicting one particularly heavy defeat on his half-brother he was taunted and told that his lack of a golden caman was a mark of parental disapproval. When this was brought to the attention of the king he redressed matters by giving his first son a caman of gold and a ball of silver, but the stepmother, angered, promptly refused him permission to play any more with her boy. The lad found a new playmate: a deer-hound bitch from within the castle walls.

The wild colours and myriad devices of these stories speckle the tapestry of Irish and Scottish Gaelic culture. They established beyond doubt that from what is generally known as the Dark Ages (although they were not so dark in the far north and west of Europe) onwards, the game of camanachd was the only outdoor sport worthy of reference. They suggest that the history of the game could go back many more centuries in time, that if we are to give even a small amount of credence to these 'honestly remembered' tales then this is the oldest organised team sport still extant in an original form in the western world. The stories show us the game of camanachd as a legacy of the age of chivalry: a hard, skilful, mannered and courteous sport whose practitioners would be applauded as much for gallantry as for dexterity, as much for defeat philosophically taken as for magnanimity in victory – standards which set most of the current values of modern Scottish shinty. The tales describe the game as a training for young men on the threshold of adult life (which pre-dates another much-abused contemporary notion of sport) and as a good preparation, or even an acceptable substitute, for the waging of war.

Thus, when John Francis Campbell struck out from his English legal practice in the middle of the nineteenth-century to compile his famous and influential *Popular Tales of the West Highlands*, he was soon able to cement in print what he must already have guessed: that the game which he had played as a boy on his father's Islay estate had a substantial and colourful pedigree.

It was not entirely unique in the early years of the nineteenth-century for a laird's son to spend his formative years previous to Eton, university and society life playing shinty and speaking Gaelic with the sons of his father's tenants and employees, but it was no longer commonplace. Campbell was one of the lucky ones: his father insisted on such a background. In this way Walter Frederick Campbell left at least some part of the West Highlands and Islands to his inquisitive son, for he was never able to leave the land and feudal superiority of Islay to John Francis. Bankruptcy, which hovered at the shoulder of many a Highland landowner of the time, took care of that. Campbell recalled of his youth:

> As soon as I was out of the hands of nursemaids, I was handed over to the care of a piper . . . I learned to be hardy and healthy and I learned Gaelic. I learned to swim and take care of myself, and to talk to everyone who chose to talk to me . . . I worked with the carpenters; I played shinty with all the boys about the farm; and so I got to know a good deal about the ways of Highlanders by growing up a High-lander myself.

Campbell's *Tales* were, for their time, uniquely well-informed. In compiling the classic story of Conall Gulban he was given by 'old men in Scotland, widely separated and who cannot read, who know the story' the same heroic metaphor for Gaelic Scotland's revenge on the ugly Scandinavian hordes who raided the western seaboard from the eighth to the thirteenth-centuries, drawn in the image of a shinty-playing champion, a roguish, feckless but indomitable wielder of the caman. In Barra, Dunoon, Beauly, Colonsay, South Uist and Benbe-cula, Campbell heard with only minor deviations the same story of Conall Gulban's arrival in the lonely north, Scandinavia, the realm of Lochlann. He recorded the event – honestly remembered, we may be sure – as follows:

> The lads of the realm of Lochlann were playing shinny on a plain, and Gealbhan Greadhna, the son of the King of Lochlann, working amongst them. He did not know who they were, but he went to

where they were, and it was the Prince of Lochlann and his two scholars, and ten over a score; and the Prince of Lochlann was alone, driving the goals against the whole of the two-and-thirty scholars.

Conall stood singing 'iolla' to them, and the ball came to the side where he was; Conall struck a kick on the ball, and he drove it out on the goal boundary against the Prince of Lochlann. The prince came where he was, and he said, 'Thou, man, that came upon us from off the ocean, it were little enough that would make me take a head off thee, that we might have it as a ball to kick about the field, since thou wert so impudent as to kick the ball. Thou must hold a goal of shinny against me and against the two-and-thirty scholars. If thou get the victory thou shall be free; if we conquer thee, every one of us will hit thee a blow on the head with his shinny.'

'Well,' said Conall, 'I don't know who thou art, great man, but it seems to me that thy judgement is evil. If every one of you were to give me a knock on the head, you would leave my head a soft mass. I have no shinny that I can play with.'

'Thou shalt have a shinny,' said Gealbhan Greadhna.

Conall gave a look round about, and he saw a crooked stick of elder growing in the face of a bank. He gave a leap thither and plucked it out by the root, and he sliced it with his sword and made a shinny of it.

Then Conall had got a shinny, and he himself and Gealbhan Greadhna went to play. Two halves were made of the company, and the ball was let out in the midst. On a time of the times Conall got a chance at the ball; he struck it a stroke of his foot and a blow of his palm and a blow of his shinny, and he drove it home.

'Thou wert impudent,' said Gealbhan Greadhna, 'to drive the game against me or against my share of the people.'

'That is well said by thee, good lad! Thou shalt get two shares of the band with thee, and I will take one share.'

'And what will thou say if it goes against thee?'

'If it goes against me with fair play there is no help for it, but if it goes against me otherwise I may say what I choose.'

Then divisions were made of the company, and Gealbhan Greadhna had two divisions and Conall one. The ball was let out in the midst, and if it was let out Conall got a chance at it, and he struck it a stroke of his foot, and a blow of his palm, and a blow of his shinny, and he drove it in.

'Thou wert impudent,' said the Prince a second time, 'to go and drive the game against me.'

'Good lad,' said Conall, 'thou shalt get the whole company the third time, and what wilt thou say if it goes against thee?'

'If it goes by fair play I cannot say a jot; if not I may say my pleasure.'

The ball was let go, and Conall got a chance at it and he all alone; and he struck it a stroke of his foot, and a blow of his palm and a blow of his shinny, and he drove it in.

'Thou wert impudent to go and drive it against me the third time,' said the Prince.

'Thou shalt not say that to me nor to another man after me,' said Conall, and he struck him a blow with his shinny, and knocked his brains out. Then he looked contemptuously at the others; he threw his caman from him, and took his departure.

Although the Irish claim Conall Gulban to have been an Irishman (his exploits are, of course, as much a part of Irish as of Scottish Gaelic legend) and the great-grandfather of Columba (which would have placed him firmly in the fifth century AD), it seems likely that the story dates from the Middle Ages. Conall's name is certainly not to be found in manuscripts until the end of the seventeenth-century, when it crops up in Argyll and in Munster.

But quibbling over the centuries is a sterile exercise. Just as the mystical tales of Cuchullin contain practical pointers to the evolution of the game of golf out of camanachd, so Conall's choosing of an elder branch for his caman is based firmly on reality. In the Uist version of the tale the elder branch does not make an appearance. There are few trees of any description on Uist, and at this juncture in the Hebridean version of the story Conall is obliged to wish for his grandfather, who appears holding an iron caman which he presents to the young man with the oblique, muttered warning: 'Bad, bad, thou has wished too soon.'

Most of all, in the cautionary tale of Conall Gulban there is to be found the witty challenge of the Gael to all the spoilt princes; the teaching of an uncompromising (and in this instance all too final) lesson to a petulant poor loser; the cheerful, spirited independence of mind which is still to be found in the people and, more miraculously, still to be found in their game.

If it was the unqualified success of Columba's apostolic – and, let it be said, colonising – mission to the northern Picts of Scotland which incidentally resulted in camanachd becoming that country's national sport, then it is ironical that a sad, fatal incident on the field of play was largely responsible for the saint finally quitting Ireland.

Columba had fallen out with the High King of Ireland, Diarmaid mac Cerbuill, over Diarmaid's ruling that Columba had acted improperly in transcribing a borrowed book without its owner's permission. Feelings were running high enough between the court and the cloth in the year AD 563 when a young prince, the son of a king of Connaught who was being held hostage by Diarmaid, fell into a fierce argument during a game of camanachd with the son of one of Diarmaid's courtiers – an argument which he settled in the manner of Conall Gulban, by striking the other boy on the head with his caman and killing him. The young prince fled to Columba for sanctuary, but Diarmaid ordered him to be forcibly removed from the proud and resentful priest and put to death. For the last time in Ireland, Columba lost his temper. Swearing vengeance, he gathered his belongings and twelve followers, pushed a coastal curragh out off the Derry shore and made for Dalriada, where his relative, Conaill, was king. Within the year Columba was in Iona, refusing even to look upon Ireland, and within the millennium Scotland was Christian and Gaelic-speaking.

No curse fell upon the game of camanachd in Ireland following this bitter incident. The last 1,400 years have seen hurling, its first-born son, find a level of popular acclaim and public patronage which excites envy and admiration from across the water. During the past century hurling has been assisted into the modern age by the establishment of the Irish Hurley Union in 1879, the dedicated, nationalist Gaelic Athletic Association in 1884, and of course, not least by the release of the twenty-six counties from colonial rule in 1921. Its role as a part of every Irishman's birthright has, in fact, been ratified by the state.

It was not always so. Edward III's famous edicts in 1363 and in 1365 – when, fearful for his supply of practised archers to fuel the Hundred Years War, he forbade 'useless games, which can be of no profit, under pain of imprisonment for those attending or taking part' – specified handball, football, cockfighting and *cambucam* (the edicts were in Latin). Localised Irish versions of the edicts were issued in 1366. The Statutes of Kilkenny were wonderfully precise and, most notably, made the first official reference in Ireland to hurling (as opposed to camanachd):

> Whereas a land which is at war requires that every person do render himself able to defend himself, it is ordained and established that the commons of the said land of Ireland, who are in divers marches of war, use not henceforth the games which men call hurlings with great clubs of a ball on the ground, from which great evils and maims have arisen, to the weakening of the defence of the said land, and other games which men call coitings, but that they apply and accustom themselves to use and draw bows and throw lances and other gentle games which appertain to arms, whereby the Irish enemies may be better checked by the liege commons of these parts; and if any do or practise the contrary, and of this be attaint, that he be taken and imprisoned, and fined at the will of our lord the King.

There is no mention of cock-fighting or of football in this momentous sentence, although the reference to 'coitings' may suggest that the placid old village-green pastime of quoits was regarded by the authorities in fourteenth-century Ireland as almost as much of a time-waster as the iniquitous hurling. Their allowance that there was such a body as 'liege commons' and therefore, by implication, their opposites – disloyal citizens – also indicates that the authors of the Statutes of Kilkenny knew full well that their order had as much chance of being properly respected on the fields of Leinster and of County Down as did its equivalent in the islands of the Hebrides or the straths of the Great Glen.

For a long time hurling developed in Ireland – originally, it appears, in Leinster – side by side with camanachd. The latter was the winter game, adapted to the hard, frosted ground; the former its summer variant, using a larger, softer ball, shorter and thicker clubs, and more aerial play. As far as English observers of the Irish scene were concerned, the two were homogenous and the name of hurling was used to describe either or both of them, it being easier to employ and the finer points of difference between the two games being, in any case, irrelevant to the outsider.

An early nineteenth-century hurling gathering in Ireland – 'At some of these gatherings two thousand have been present.' (National Library of Ireland)

By the seventeenth-century hurling had established the higher profile in the southern states of Ireland, at least in the eyes of the literary beholder. An Englishman named John Dunton, who opened a bookshop in Dublin in 1698 and gained some reputation in Ireland as a poet and a playwright, has left us a description of the summer sport which illustrates colourfully and lucidly both the differences and similarities between a hurling meet and the game of camanachd as it was played then and now in Ireland and in Scotland.

I may say something to you of the sports used among the Irish on their holidays. One exercise they use much is their hurling, which has something in it not unlike the play called Mall.

When the cows are casting their hair, they pull it off their backs and with their hands work it into large balls which will grow very hard. This ball they use at the hurlings, which they strike with a stick called commaan and about three foot and a half long in the handle. At the lower end it is crooked and about three inches broad, and on this broad part you may sometimes see one of the gamesters carry the ball tossing it for 40 or 50 yards in spite of all the adverse players; and when he is like to use it, he generally gives it a great stroke to drive it towards the goal.

Sometimes if he miss his blow at the ball, he knocks one of the opposers down: at which no resentment is to be shown. They seldom come off without broken heads or shins in which they glory very much. At this sport one parish sometimes or barony challenges another; they pick out ten, twelve, or twenty players of a side, and the prize is generally a barrel or two of ale, which is brought into the field and drunk off by the victors on the spot, though the vanquished are not without a share of it too.

This commonly is upon some very large plain, the barer of grass the better and the goals are 200 or 300 yards one from the other; and whichever party drives the ball beyond the other's goal wins the day. Their champions are of the younger and most active among them, their kindred and mistresses are frequently spectators of their address. Two or three bagpipes attend the conquerors at the barrel's head and then play them out of the field. At some of these gatherings two thousand have been present together.

A seventeenth-century Scot would have recognised more than he found foreign at such a meeting. The size of the ball and the width of the striking end of the caman may have been unfamiliar, but the form of the game, the size of the pitch, the knocks cheerfully taken, the crowd, the pipes and the barrel of ale all clearly sang of home.

Hurling continued to attract the most attention and, as the years went by, the most players, but its parent – the old game of camanachd – took an unconscionable long time about dying in Ireland. Strong bonds with Gaelic Scotland outside the Pale, particularly in the north-east of the country, where hurling was slow to establish a monopoly and where the old game continued to thrive, helped it on its increasingly unsteady way.

A fifteenth-century grave slab in Inishowen, County Donegal, carries a relief engraving of a broadsword, a ball and a caman. Far from being a hurling stick, the caman could easily be employed in a modern shinty match. The inscription on the stone says that it was made not to the memory of an Irish knight, but in honour of Manas mac Mhoireasdain of Iona. Mac Mhoireasdain's identity, his reasons for being in Ireland and, presumably, for dying there, are not revealed. But the man whose fondness of his broadsword was obviously matched only by a liking for the game of camanachd could have been a *gall-oglaigh*, one of the thousands of foreign mercenaries who were invited by Irish noblemen to help defend their lands against the Anglo-Norman invaders. Most of these 'galloglasses' (as Shakespeare called them, using the vulgarism of his time) came from the north-west Highlands and Islands of Scotland. Their surviving names – MacSweeney, MacDougall, MacDonald, MacRory – led the late Professor Eoin MacNeill to conclude that almost all of these men, who for three centuries helped to maintain the

The fifteenth-century grave slab of Manas mac Mhoireasdain of Iona – a Galláglach at least as fond of his caman as of his broadsword? (Commissioners of Public Works, Dublin)

independence of large parts of Gaelic Ireland against a formidable enemy, were 'from the Norse kingdom of Argyll and the Hebrides'.

The bond between these cousins was indeed strong. It had hardly been weakened by the passage of centuries and a few miles of treacherous sea. Small stories as well as great legends indicate its strength. In 1539 a young chieftain of Mull, Murdoch of Lochbuie, found himself obliged by an ambitious uncle to flee for his life from Scotland and his inheritance. He escaped to Ireland, where his prowess in a shinty match attracted the attention of the Earl of Antrim, who gave Murdoch of Lochbuie protection and patronage until he was ready to return, in triumph, to Mull.

But in 1602 the bond was torn from seam to seam. The final English conquest at the battle of Kinsale signalled the end of the truly heroic resistance of Gaelic Ireland. Many *gall-oglaigh* and their families lost their lives in the years which followed; almost all lost their Irish homes and estates; those who limped home were never to return, or ever again to send their sons and clansmen to fight the lost battle of their Irish kin. As it turned out, the Scottish Highlander was to have battles of his own to fight in the ensuing years. To the year 1602, says Eoin MacNeill, 'may be assigned the beginning of the severance of the old relations, and the break-up of the old community of interests, which had existed for centuries between Ireland and the West Highlands. That movement away from Ireland was further encouraged when the West Highlands become not merely Protestant, but for the most part strictly Presbyterian as well.'

A small undertow in the tidal rip of this turbulent part of Scottish and Irish history was the game of camanachd. It was left, understandably unnoticed in the clamour of the time, to fend for itself on either side of the Irish Sea.

In Ireland the winter game gave way slowly to hurling. It faded from the scene like any dying language or culture – almost imperceptibly. Indeed, it has been claimed that as late as the great famines of the middle of the nineteenth century, camanachd, the game known in Scotland as shinty, the game with the elegant, longer driving stick and skilful, intricate ground play, was enjoyed by more participants in the whole of Ireland, particularly in the rural outlying areas, than was hurling. It certainly did survive well into the nineteenth and, in some remote spots, into the twentieth century. In the north its survival was possibly assisted by those less-welcome visitors from Scotland who crossed paths with the retreating *gall-oglaigh*: the Protestant planters in Ulster. In 1812 William Shaw Mason conducted an amateur survey of around 200 Irish parishes. He sent questionnaires to ministers of the Church of Ireland, and summarised the replies into a three-volume *Statistical Account* of the country. In Holywood, near Belfast, Shaw Mason recorded:

> Among their other amusements, the game of *shinny*, as it is called by some, and *common* by others, is worthy of note. *Common* is derived from a Celtic word 'com' which signifies 'crooked', as it is played with a stick bent at its lower extremity somewhat like a reaping hook. The ball, which is struck to and fro, in which the whole amusement consists, is called *nag*, or in Irish *brig*. It resembles the game of golf in Edinburgh. Christmas is the season when it is most generally played. It prevails all through Ireland, and in the Highlands of Scotland. Nor is it confined to any sect, and Dissenters and Romanists seem to be equally attached to it.

And from the parish of Ballintroy, on the north coast of County Antrim, from where the low hills of Kintyre are plainly visible, Shaw Mason was told:

> We have no particular customs except that on Christmas Day and on the first of the year, a great concourse of people assemble on the strand, at White-Park, to play *common* or *shinny*. This formerly was frequented by young and old, and the amusement generally ended by drinking whiskey and broken heads: but of late years, only young people appear on these occasions, and the day concludes without any drunkenness or riot.

These early nineteenth-century Church of Ireland ministers may not have been aware of the history of the sport being practised in their parishes, or of its estranged twin, which was behaving at the time in an identical manner across the Irish Sea. But some of them recognised the difference between their game and the increasingly popular intruder from the south, hurling. The minister to Ardstraw, County Tyrone, informed Shaw Mason:

> There are no patrons nor public sports [here], except playing at *common*, as it is called; this diversion resembles hurling in the south;

but since the institution of the yeomanry, it has been seldom practised. The ball they play with is a small wooden one, which they strike with sticks inflected at one end. In the south of Ireland, the curve of the hurl is broad, and the ball large, and of a soft substance, covered with leather. Formerly they spent here eleven days successfully at Christmas time in this exercise, now they idle only one; a manifest proof of the increase of industry.

As late as 1875 a history of the County Down was claiming that the main sport in that area was 'cammon, that is, the shinty of Scotland'. The camain used by Dublin's Trinity College Hurley team in 1879 and 1880, their team photographs show us, were roughly fashioned shinty, not hurling, sticks.

But shinny, cammon, or camanachd was never to have a ruling body in Ireland, never to be properly constituted, never given rules, annual general meetings, fund-raising committees, secretaries, government grants, sponsors, the serious attention of the media, or any of the stuff of life for a sport which wished to survive in the twentieth-century.

The Gaelic Athletic Association (GAA) was formed in Dublin in 1884 as an avowedly nationalist organisation. It was dedicated above all other things to preserving and fostering the sports of old Ireland. It spurned, as it still spurns, sports with the taint of colonial import, such as hockey or association football. And the game of hurling was seen by the Gaelic Athletic Association as the true embodiment of the spirit of Eire on the playing field. There were good reasons for this. Hurling was strongest in the Catholic, nationalist south. The game even had a small historical political record: as early as 1667 we hear of a subversive meeting of hundreds of 'Irish Papists' at Clanwilliam, near Kilnamanagh, 'under pretence of a match at hurling'.

The patriotic, political implications of this uniquely Irish game were identified by the Gaelic Athletic Association. Three years after Gladstone came out in favour of Home Rule, two English members of his Liberal Party arrived in Dublin to address a meeting in favour of independence. They were met at the railway station by a thousand young members of the Gaelic Athletic Association bearing hurling camain on their shoulders.

In 1891 the funeral cortège of Charles Stewart Parnell, the man who had persuaded Gladstone of the political justification and historical inevitability of an independent Ireland, was led through the streets of

Dublin by thousands of GAA members carrying hurleys draped in black cloth. In 1903 a solemn procession of young men, hurleys on their shoulders, commemorated the centenary of the execution of Robert Emmet in the Irish capital city. As the poet and historian Art Ó Maolfabhail writes: 'From that day forward wherever in Ireland the broad caman, now the caman of the GAA, was seen, it was regarded as a symbol of defiance of English rule in Ireland.'

The symbol was given added potency in 1917 when the English actually went to the trouble of banning the carrying of the hurling caman in public. This prohibition succeeded, of course, in elevating the simple bent stick to an unprecedented level of popularity in Ireland. When Eamonn de Valera arrived in Tipperary he was greeted by a forest of camain. And the political power of the hurling caman persists to the present day. In 1971 a party of Republican women were arrested while demonstrating outside Belfast courts of law. They were charged with possessing offensive weapons – hurling camain.

In all of this agitation the old game, the one played by Cuchullin and Conall Gulban, Lugh and Columba, the game with the longer, more graceful stick and the small, hard ball was all but forgotten. By the end of the nineteenth century camanachd was, ironically, occasionally referred to in Ireland as 'the Scottish game'. Officials of the GAA could have been forgiven for assuming that it was in fact a Scottish import to their country, an unwelcome corruption, like singing 'The Sash' and holding Orange Day parades on Irish soil.

Starved of oxygen, camanachd died in republican Ireland in the early years of the twentieth century and hurling was left alone to carry the standard. The cousins and offspring of the game had, of course, taken root elsewhere. Command performances for George III were not the only time that hurling was witnessed in the parks of London – hurling matches frequently took place in the fields behind the British Museum in the eighteenth century. When, in the middle of that century, the men of Hambledon in the Hampshire South Downs began to refine and develop the game of cricket, they could not keep a straight bat. They used a short, thick stick, broad and curved at the striking end: a hurling caman in all but name. Even English recorders of the history of hockey concede that 'in Britain, hockey under the name of hurling, shinty or bandy, is attested first in Ireland'.

Bandy, or *bando* or *cnapan*, in fact last saw daylight in Britain as the

Welsh branch of the family. Once the game was common throughout southern Britain, from the fens of East Anglia to Kettering (where it is recorded on third-century stone) and the Midlands. It was played on ice as well as on *terra firma*, and was certainly the game referred to by Thomas Becket's secretary in 1160 when he wrote of 'many young men' playing on the frozen fen, 'as swiftly as a bird flythe in the aire, or an arrow out of a cross bow. Sometimes two run together with poles and hitting one another eyther one or both doe fall, not without hurt. Some break their arms, some their legs, but youth desirous of glorie, in this sport exerciseth itselfe against the time of warre.'

As the bent root of 'cam' has been preserved in Ireland through the women's stick game camogie, so bandy lives on, curiously, as the name of an indoor eleven-a-side stick game which is played chiefly in Scandinavia, on ice. In Britain, bandy faithfully followed another breed of indomitable Celts into the hills of Cymru. During the last century it was hugely popular in Wales, and so common that several Englishmen could not help referring to the game which they saw played by 'the common sort' in Irish meadows as 'bandy'. In the springtime of 1777 a travelling Englishman, James Price, asked a Welshman in the countryside of Glamorgan why the surrounding area was so stripped of ash and elm:

'Alas,' said he, 'do you observe those vast crowds of people before you drawing towards the sea?'

'Yes,' said I, 'I suppose there is a wreck on the coast.'

He informed me otherwise and said that they were going to a great bandy match to be played this day on a particular sand near the seashore where many thousands of people, men, women and children, will be assembled to see the sport; that it is the sixteenth match played this spring.

My companion further informed me that the inhabitants of a dozen or more parishes are in uproar and mind little beside these matches. Tis computed there are in each of these parishes upwards of a hundred gamesters including young boys who are initiating, that each gamester furnisheth himself with three bandys.

If we add three more which are destroyed by unskillful bending and the great number broke by thumping, thwacking and breaking each other's heads, not a bandy returning from some of these matches, it will make six hundred in every parish annually.

The bandy stick was indeed made preferably of ash, and the ball of yew, boxwood or crabapple, although Glamorgan coalminers were known to improvise with a pick handle and a ball of rags. Bandy was groping towards some form of organisation and structure in the middle of the nineteenth century when elementary restrictions were imposed on the number of players in each team (between twenty and thirty), the pitch was designated as 200 yards and the goals ten yards wide. But rugby union and association football arrived in Wales in time to halt the defoliation of the county of Glamorgan and to send this ancient game spinning into the void arm in arm with its neighbour from the Isle of Man, *cammag.*

Early cricketers found it hard to keep a straight bat: this is cricket on the Artillery ground, Finsbury, in 1743. (Marylebone Cricket Club)

Welsh bandy, Manx cammag and Irish camanachd would have to wait on the Elysian Fields for their cousin from the far north. From the weather-torn shores of the Minch to the lush rolling south of Scotland, shinty, shinny, camanachd, cammon, cammock, camag, cluidh bhall or iomain had sent down deep, strong roots. It had travelled a hazardous, eventful road since Columba first took his pack-horses and attendants into the forbidden pagan lands of King Brude, there to terrify druids, convert royalty and possibly allow his followers to introduce to their new friends a game which was played with a small, hard ball and a curved stick called a caman. It had, nonetheless, survived.

2

Shinny, Cammock and Clackans

'All this has passed as a dream.'

The 1690s were a significant decade in the kingdom of Scotland. They had started with the apparent 'pacification' of the nerve-wracking clans of the north, who renounced their allegiance to the claim of the exiled James to the throne of England and Scotland and transferred, on paper, their oath to his son-in-law, William.

The decade saw the connivance in high places to isolate, entrap and extirpate – as an example to others – Alastair MacIan MacDonald, which reached its bloody climax on a bitter Saturday morning in February 1692, when the old man and some forty of his *clann* – his children – were slaughtered in the fastness of Glencoe on the orders of Edinburgh and London.

In the capital city and parliamentary seat, a Dumfries man named William Paterson was persuading the great and the good of Scottish society to invest half of the nation's available capital in sending an expedition to establish a Scottish colony and trading post at Darien on the Isthmus of Panama. The first ships set sail from Leith in 1698 before a buoyant breeze of national optimism and pride. Darien, a feverish wind-locked hole, was abandoned with its Scottish dead in 1700 after twenty-one months of squabbles, internal feuds, skirmishes with Spaniards, starvation and disease.

While the Commission of Inquiry was finding most people (apart from King William II) guilty of the massacre at Glencoe, but punishing nobody, and while Paterson was cheerfully noising about Edinburgh the scheme which would cause so much grief, bitterness, bankruptcy and national humiliation, on the island of Skye one Martin Martin was planning an ambitious investigation and voyage of his own.

Throughout the late 1690s and into the 1700s, Martin was to travel from his Skye home throughout the Hebrides. He recorded the fish, fowl, flora and fauna to be found in their waters and on their almost innumerable inhabited islands. He wrote down, credibly, accounts of second sight, and he discounted as imposterous the claims of a previous visitor to one small island to have been sent by St John the Baptist. On reaching the distant landfall of St Kilda – a journey which Martin understandably considered remarkable enough to merit a published volume all of its own – he found that, beneath the savage cliffs of Hirta, 'They use for their diversion short clubs and balls of wood; the sand is a fair field for this sport and exercise, in which they take great pleasure and are very nimble at it; they play for some eggs, fowls, hooks, or tobacco; and so eager are they for victory, that they strip themselves to the shirts to obtain it.'

Martin's account of a diversion on the sands of St Kilda was published in 1698, at about the same time that the poet and publisher John Dunton was first coming across the game of hurling on the outskirts of Dublin. It is remarkable not so much for the fact that one of the first written records of the playing of shinty in Scotland should have come from the country's most distant and isolated province, nor because the 'short clubs' sound more like hurling than shinty camain (wood was ever at a premium on St Kilda, and anyway, what's in national boundaries when you're on the edge of the world?). But it is strange that Martin should have chosen to record the game as a peculiarity of the small island group when it was certainly a common feature of life not only on his own island of Skye, but all across the larger, more heavily populated Hebrides which he diligently explored and on the mainland, with which he must have been familiar. Perhaps Martin's social class had kept him apart from the leisure activities of the commonry until he reached St Kilda where, there being nobody other than commonry, there was no escape.

Certainly, by the 1690s camanachd, shinty, or *iomain* – the driving game, as it would become best known all down the western seaboard – was to be found not only in St Kilda. It was all over Scotland.

It was played in Glencoe, on the afternoon before the massacre, between the unsuspecting Macdonalds and their uniformed guests who were already under orders to turn on their hosts before dawn and kill them. One of the many cryptic warnings given to the people of Glencoe by soldiers sickened in advance at the thought of what they were expected to do came during this game of camanachd. A Campbell watching the match found a small boy standing beside him. Making sure that the child was paying attention, the trooper placed his hand on a large boulder known as MacHenry's Stone and said; 'Great stone of the glen. Great is your right to be here. But if you knew what will happen this night, you would be up and away.'

The hundreds who sailed for the New Caledonia of Darien on the *Saint Andrew* and the *Caledonia* included shinty players among them, from the Lowlands and from the Highlands, as surely as they included bakers, carpenters and soldiers who had been present at Glencoe. For the game had travelled like a pilot fish alongside the great body of Christianity which transformed Scotland in the centuries following Columba. Its popularity had reached even as far as the other journey-man companion of missionary Christianity in Scotland, the Gaelic language; for shinty, or shinny, or cammock was to be found not only in Edinburgh and Glasgow but in Ayrshire and the Borders, in Galashiels and on the south-east coast.

But its heartland was then, as it was to remain, the Highlands. The defeat of the aged King Hakon's seaborne forces by the sailors, archers and cavalry of Alexander III on the Ayrshire coast in 1263 signalled the end of Norse rule in the Hebrides and on the western seaboard. The vacuum which was left was filled, not from the Maiden Castle of Edinburgh, despite the nominal claim of the occupant of that throne to be King of all the Scots, but by people who exercised an older seisin.

The Lordship of the Isles may not have been the Gaelic Avalon which romantics, aided naturally enough by the bards and *seannachaidh* (tradition bearers) of Clan Donald, like to depict. But it was an ordered society. At its head were the descendants of Somerled, the first Lord of Argyll, who had been snuffed out in his prime while fighting against a Scottish king in 1164. The foremost of these descendants bore the name of Donald, and until the end of the fifteenth century the MacDonalds led a society which was a common medieval blend of feudalism and chivalry, culture and brutality, in a paternal style that could veer, at the drop of a false word, from rule by kindly consultation to rule by the mailed fist and the broadsword. The great songs and legends of Fionn mac Cumhaill and Conall Gulban were heard and embroidered upon in the feasting halls of Clan Donald. Outdoors, when they were not raiding the lands of Ross or settling some more trivial internal dispute, their sports were horseback riding, hunting and camanachd. The clan system,

which was to be in greater and lesser forms the only effective discipline
of government in the Highlands and Islands of Scotland until after 1746,
matured in the Lordship of the Isles.

Edicts issued from Edinburgh had as little effect in these lands as if they
came from Sumatra. When James II and later James IV echoed the
obsession, popular among monarchs of the time, with their subjects
wasting precious energy on the games field and ordered that 'unprofitable
sports' be 'utterly cryed down and not to be used', they can hardly have
expected their liege subjects in Benbecula and Kintyre to rise as one man
and make bonfires of their camain. These people did not even bother to
answer charges of mass murder. (It may be incidental, but such an edict
came particularly badly from James IV, whose Lord High Treasurer
dutifully recorded that the king enjoyed, on 17 March 1507, something
which he called the 'Irish gayme'. This was not, we may be sure, chess.)

The edicts were largely ignored, of course, throughout Scotland, as
they were in England and Ireland. The game continued to be played
even on the doorstep of the seat of government. It offers us a foretaste
of the way that shinty was to give birth to a whole new international
sport two-and-a-half centuries later in Canada to learn that in
February 1607 (during the reign of James VI, who was to advise
his son, if not others, to 'avoid violent games') a game of *chamaire* was
played on the ice 'a mile within the sea-mark' on the Firth of Forth.

Long before it travelled to Canada, shinty was a fruitful tree. Just to
the north of the Firth of Forth, on the grassy coastlands of the Kingdom
of Fife, another game developed in the Middle Ages which was to
travel the world and which still regards the town of St Andrews as its
birthplace and as its home. It is known from the old manuscripts and
sagas what different habits, in different circumstances, the old game of
camanachd adopted. One of these was *cluiche- poill*, or *áin phuill*, or *cluich
dhesog.* This style of play involved as few as two players, although more
could take part, each equipped with a caman and a ball and each
attempting to drive the latter with the former into a hole dug into the
ground. When the early sports historian Joseph Strutt wrote in 1801
that he took the game of *cumbucam*, as prohibited by Edward III, to have
been 'a species of goff' (*sic*), he may not have known which sport
preceded the other, but he was surely correct.

Even in the fifteenth century the agile minds of the students at St
Andrews University were allowed some relaxation on the games field.
Sadly, we only know what they did *not* play there. Football was frowned

upon, as was cock-fighting (the latter because it was usually practised at Lenten time and therefore distracted the students during their examination period). But we know that these scholars were escorted to the fields by tutors who insisted that they conversed in Latin en route, and that after 1432 they were ordered to wear academic dress while trooping through the town and to hear Mass on their return from games, thus 'setting aside all superfluities and vanities'. It is only possible to conjecture as to what were these superfluities on the fifteenth-century playing fields at St Andrews, although by the seventeenth-century it is clear that the two main outdoor sports at Aberdeen University were shinty and golf.

Few Scottish historians have commented on the link between the two, with one notable exception. Reverend Charles Rogers came from Fife, although he spent most of his days as a minister in Edinburgh. He spent almost forty years, from 1844 onwards, researching the social life and history of Scotland. His collected findings are a treasure trove of early social history, because Rogers believed that in order to understand people and their way of life, 'we must search the cot rather than the castle'. The history of Scotland, said this radical Victorian, 'is not to be found in the chronicles of her kings, or in the narrative of her contendings with a powerful neighbour; not even in the records of her commerce'. For an historian with such principles, Rogers' single reference to shinty is disappointing in all but one powerful respect. He describes the game as 'a primitive description of golf, and not improbably its pioneer'.

If both games were to circumnavigate the world, one went Port Out, Starboard Home, and the other travelled steerage. In Scotland the relationship between the two games for the past hundred years and more is nicely encapsulated on Colonsay. There is on that island a low hill known as Cnoc nan Gall. For centuries Cnoc nan Gall was the meeting place for the traditional New Year's Day game of *iomain,* or shinty. Stories galore surround the site, from tales concerning the origins of its name (which means Hill of the Stranger), to the late arrival of seaborne whisky on a dry Hogmanay – all the stuff of latterday Hebridean folklore sits on Cnoc nan Gall. The visitor will, however, no longer hear the crack of caman on ball there: the New Year's Day game of shinty died on Colonsay during the nineteenth century. Cnoc nan Gall is now Machrins Golf Course.

As the seventeenth century gave way to the eighteenth, Scottish camanachd developed the rituals and the basic languages of play which were to characterise and to sustain the game until the last two decades of the reign of Queen Victoria.

Its diversity, in those years before organisation and nationally observed rules and standards became necessary, was glorious. There were a few consistent particulars. In the Highlands, if not throughout Scotland, the great inter-village games were usually organised on the same celebratory days of the year. The Celtic feast days of Bealtainn (the first day of summer), Samhainn (the last day of summer) and Lughnasaid (1 August, the day called after Lugh of Ireland) took longer to fade from popular memory than did the pagan druids who had once supervised their observance. But they were generally replaced by the Christian festivals of the turning of the year: the days of St John, St Stephen, All Saints, Epiphany, Nollaig (Christmas Day) and New Year's Day. Always and everywhere New Year's Day saw the dusting down of old camain and the forging of new, the gathering of whole communities to watch and to take part in the game on the machair, on the strand or on the grazings. Even after the Reformation had changed the religious inclinations of most of the Highlands, and only a few Catholic enclaves such as Strathglass, South Uist, Eigg, and Canna were left with their full complement of early Christian festivals, New Year's Day (which until

The uproarious meleé of Scottish shinty, pre-organisation, as drawn for the early Victorian *Penny Magazine.*

at least the middle of the nineteenth century was *Oichde Calluinn*, the Old New Year, observed on 12 January or 13 January) remained a day set aside for, and distinguished by, shinty.

These were the days before referees, when the order of a match was dictated by tradition rather than by a rule-book. The New Year's Day game in the eighteenth and nineteenth centuries at the Machair-Ionain in Kintyre (which probably derived its name from *iomain* and is now, mirroring Colonsay's Cnoc nan Gall, part of Machrihanish Golf Course) would begin 'early after breakfast'.

People began to assemble from all the districts round about, many coming as far as five or six miles. Before mid-day there would often be perhaps a thousand people on the ground between players and onlookers.

The players arranged themselves in teams according to age and other circumstances. Sides having been formed, the course was marked off, usually from a quarter of a mile long and upwards. At each end there was a goal, called the 'den', which was formed by placing two little heaps of stones, large enough to be seen at a distance, about nine or ten feet apart, and in such order that a line drawn between them would be right across the course.

'Lots' were then cast as to which side was to be in, and so have the right to 'put out the ball' and in accordance with the lot each party took its side of the course. These preliminaries having been all settled, which never took up much time, the game was at once commenced.

The person entrusted with 'putting out' the ball stood directly in the 'den' between the two little heaps of stones, and was allowed, according to the rules of the game, to make a 'cogy'; that was something to place the ball on a little point above the surface of the ground. It was usually made by beating a little of the earth up with the caman into a pyramidical shape, about an inch or so above the ground. He placed the ball on this point, and then struck it out with his caman.

The play was then fairly begun, the object on the one side being to carry the ball through the 'den' at the other side of the course, while the opposite side tried to send it back into the den from which the start had been made. No person was allowed to carry the ball or throw it with his hand, but *crapachs* were permissible, that is, a player might, if he could, catch the ball, throw it out from him into the air, and strike it with his caman in the direction he wished to send it.

The play was manly, and, for fit subjects, healthy exercise; it, however, afforded considerable opportunity for provocation, and the day's sport was not unfrequently brought to a close with a fight. It sometimes happened that matches of a more select kind than what I have described took place, and on these occasions parties were formed and conditions attached in advance. In such cases there was usually a wager attached, and the game played under patronage, the patrons being the wagerers.

Goals were hard to come by in the uproarious mêlée. A Kintyre man, John MacConechy, who scored a hat-trick in helping his side to victory, was approached after the match by his team's 'patron', a local landowner, who offered MacConechy the tenancy of a vacant farm in the Laggan of Kintyre 'on easy terms' to ensure his continued residence in the district and consequent involvement with the parish shinty squad. MacConechy, who had an ageing father needing help with his land at Balligrogan, declined.

It was almost unique to the Scottish game that the Kintyre men, fifteen sea-miles from the coast of Antrim, often played one-handed, using shorter, thicker, hurling camain. The brawling finale to many a contest referred to in the report is supported by legal documents of the time. In 1818 John Galbreath, a tacksman of Tayinloan, was the victim of a serious assault during the Old New Year's Day match on Dalcrennan Park. And on the same day in 1836, 12 January, a Gartvain farm servant, John MacCoag, was beaten about the head with shinty sticks on the Strath Mor of Southend. MacCoag died on the following morning. In the murder hearings which followed, a local blacksmith, James McMillan, testified that the violence had started when 'a big Irishman named Robert' interrupted the match to announce that he would 'fight any Scotch or Highland bugger who stood on the strand'. Two local men, Duncan McMillan and Duncan McDougall, were sought by sheriff's officers in connection with the fatal assault, but they were never apprehended and a month later the Campbeltown pro-curator-fiscal had to report that 'it is believed that they crossed over to Ireland and have absconded'.

The squabbles did not inevitably end in death. When James Robertson of Auchtarsin remembered his boyhood on Rannoch Moor in the 1860s, he was able to paint a vivid picture of a game which was, while not altogether lawless, often necessarily settled by rough jurisdiction and the power of one man's personality. Perched on his father's shoulders, the young Robertson recalled looking down over a dizzying sea of blue bonnets towards the turn-of-the-year game between the men from south of the river and the men from its north.

The match was played, as usual, on the Mon Mhor near Inver Chadain and, as usual, the captain of the south was the veteran David Mac-Donald or Daibhidh Las an Tulaich as he was more familiarly called. I do not now remember who the captain of the north was that day but I remember each of them standing before a crowd of his own young men from which he drew one, alternately with the other side, by touching him with a caman. The teams thus chosen, often, I believe, to the number of thirty or forty a side, ranged themselves on opposite sides and the play began. There was no referee and no rules except those sanctioned by old tradition so that the play was generally of a rough and tumble description, verging pretty often on caman-cuffs.

Fortunately in these days the ground was at that season covered with six or eight inches of hard, dry snow, which rendered the 'tumbling' part of the game slightly less abrasive. The captains took no active part in the contest, contenting themselves with shouting encouragement to their followers. When a player felt tired, he leaned on his caman and took a rest, perhaps a smoke. If his jacket, or any jacket, lay conveniently near to serve as a cushion he sometimes sat down. But the day at length drew to a close and the leaders called a parley during which it was understood that the side declared victorious was agreed upon.

On this particular day it was evidently not agreed upon for the argument between the captains waxed hot. By and by the rival players took part and finally the spectators began to range themselves on their respective sides and things looked threatening. It was then that Daibhidh Las an Tulaich pushed two or three boys off a boulder and took his stand on the top. He had a powerful voice which reached all parts of the field and I remember his words now as if they had been spoken but yesterday. 'Choisinn Bratach nam Mogan ged strac thu,' he roared at his late opponents ('The Bratach nam Mogan won although you struck well' – Bratach nam Mogan was the name applied to the people of Bim Rannoch) and taking off

his bonnet and whirling it round his head he jumped off his perch
with a final triumphal whoop of 'Bratach nam Mogan gu bràth' and
landed near the piper. 'Sei luas a Chaluim,' he ordered and the
Mogaim, marching to the martial strains of their own *caismeachd*, left
the field. That was the first and last and only time I saw Daibhidh
Las an Tulaich though I heard many a story related about him.

If the ball was placed on a 'coggy' or 'coggie' (the Lowlands word for a
golfing tee) at the start of play in Kintyre, in the islands of Lewis and
Mull and on the shores of the Dornoch Firth it was actually buried in
the moss or sand, and the two captains had to scrabble and dig with
their camain to disinter the ball and get the game underway. The
Lewismen also devised a rule for the odd man out after two sides had
been picked out of an uneven number of players. He was christened
bodach eadar da cheathairne (the old man between two troops), and was
required to play on either side alternately.

On the sands at Balnakeil in Sutherland the ball was first placed into
a trough and then tossed up into the air, in what was to become the
modern fashion, to signal the start of a game. 'Each man firmly grasps
his club, each eye is on the alert, up it ascends, and then begins the fight
of heroes,' as a Sutherlander, exiled to London, fondly remembered. It
was also usual in Sutherland for one of the two captains to toss his
caman into the air to determine first choice of players when picking
sides, or to establish who attacked which end. While the caman whirled
up and down the other captain called 'bas' or 'cas' (handle or striking
end). This manner of tossing for choice is now almost universal in
shinty, but throughout the west coast and much of the rest of Scotland
another, older, custom prevailed until recently. Two captains would
stand facing each other, a few yards apart. One threw his caman to the
other, who caught and held it, handle upwards. The thrower then
advanced and gripped the caman above his opposite's fist, which was
removed and replaced further up the shaft, and so on, in quick
succession, until one captain only was left holding the top of the
caman, and he had the right of choice. In some areas, such as Skye, if a
small part of the handle was still protruding after the final fist had been
clenched around it, the other captain could choose to take it between
thumb and forefinger, and if he could swing it unfailingly in a full
circle around and above his head he took the upper hand.

Pre-match *politesse* reached the level, at times, of dramatic verse. A

simple, chivalric 'Leag leam' ("May I?") from the captain successful in
the initial lottery, answered by his opponent with 'Leigidh mi leat'
("You may"), was extended occasionally to a wholly lyrical ritual, a
rhyming, rhythmic dialogue between the two protagonists. In Islay the
dialogue went, broadly, as follows:

Thulla gus an iomain	Come to the driving
De an iomain?	What driving?
Iomain camain	The driving with camain
De an caman?	What caman?
Caman ur	The land caman
De an ur?	What land?
Ur ar	Plough land
De an ar?	What plough?
Ar iteag	Feather plough
De an iteag?	What feather?
Iteag fhithich	Raven's feather
De an fhithich?	What raven?
Fitheach feoil	The flesh raven
De an fheoil?	What flesh?
Feoil duine	Man's flesh
De an duine?	What man?
Duine gionach	The greedy man
De an gionach?	How greedy?
Gionach eich	Greedy as a horse
De an t-each?	What horse?
Each mara	A sea-horse
De 'm mara?	What sea?
Mara iasg	A sea with fish
De 'n iasg?	What fish?
Iasg dubhan, dubhan briste bairnich. Chaidh mi leis thun a ghobha a chairadh. Cha robh a fein na chuid mhac a stigh. Peasair dhuitse, 's ponair dhomhsa. 'S coltar rap.	Hooked fish, a broken baited hook. I took it to the smith to mend. Neither himself nor any of his sons were in. Peas for you and beans for me. A ploughshare digging.

Across the Sound of Jura, on Lochaweside, the following local variation was used:

Ciod an iomain?	What driving?
Iomain camain	Driving with camain
Ciod an caman?	What caman?
Caman iubhair	Caman of yew
Ciod an t-iubhair?	What yew?
Iubhar athair	Yew of air
Coid an t-athar?	What air?
Athar eoin	Air of bird
Ciod an t-eun?	What bird?
Eun iteig	Bird of feather
Ciod an iteag?	What feather?
Iteag fithich	Feather of raven
Ciod am fitheach?	What raven?
Fitheach sleibhte	Raven of the slope
Ciod an t-sliabh?	What slope?
Sliabh mara	Slope of the sea
Ciod mhuir?	What sea?
Muir eisg	Sea of fish
Ciod an t-iasg?	What fish?
Iasg dubhain	Fish of hook
Ciod an dubhan?	What hook?
Dubhan airgeid	Silver hook
Ciod an t-airgiod?	What silver?
Airgiod briste, brute, pronnta cul ciste na ba'ri'n.	Silver, broken, bruised turned to dust in the back of the Queen's chest.

The forging of equipment took many an ingenious turn. In wooded areas, wood was used. Branches of hazel, willow, oak, elm or birch were cut and whittled into shape. Birch, willow and elm were light but easily broken. Oak was so hard that 'a sting came up through the shaft of the caman and through your hands', which some players tried to alleviate by boring a hole through the caman shaft with a thin gimlet. If the branch was not of an appropriate shape at the *bas*, or *bois*, the palm, the striking end, it would be laid gently in a smouldering peat fire, then removed, strapped up and bent while still hot in an improvised clamp. The bevel of the *bas* was an object of great pride and care. Its shape was essential in striking the ball, although some players preferred it to be round, claiming that this facilitated better ground control. Throughout the treeless islands, such as the Uists and Berneray, thick dried staves of seaweed tangle were called into use, and in South Uist at least, canvas sail-cloth was rolled tightly, twisted and strapped into the model of a workable caman.

The ball, or *cnag*, was mainly of wood in the earlier days, occasionally a hazel-root chipped and filed until smooth and boiled in water to toughen it and keep it from splitting. The district of Badenoch is credited with first adopting the Irish custom of binding horse or cattle hair into a tight, dynamic ball, which had the incidental advantage of causing less permanent injury to anybody who got in its way. In the coastal areas a cork net-float was frequently used, particularly when the game was played on a frozen loch. Small portions of hard black peat would do at a pinch, and in the district of Ballachulish and Glencoe a fungus known as *fomes fementarious*, which is to be found on birch trees and which dries into a cork-like consistency, was called into play, originally in its native state, latterly wrapped in wool, string and leather.

The lexicography of the name would fill a small dictionary. The word 'hail', meaning a score in shinty, slipped into the Scottish language. *Jamieson's Dictionary* of 1880 defines it as 'the act of reaching this place, or of driving the ball to the boundary'. It is credited elsewhere with seventeenth-century origin and with being chiefly confined (in 1880) to the county of Roxburgh – a disputable attribution. The ball could be *cnag*, or *ball gaoiseid* when made of hair, *ball leathair* when coated with leather. It was usual for two teams to change ends when one had scored, and this was known as *leth bhàir shios*, followed by *leth bhàir shuas*, if the same side scored again. A ground stroke of the ball was *deas*, an aerial one *foirnead* or *sgailleag-adhair*. Throughout all the airts, the *caman* alone retained its singular identity.

And out of the cluster of nouns, crude and dignified, used to describe the game itself from the Borders to the Butt of Lewis, out of *cluidh bhall*, *iomain*, *cammock*, *clackans* and their host of clamorous relatives, a single word emerged to bring order to Babel. The Gaelic use of 'sinteag' to describe a skip, bound or hop, long strides or a bouncing motion, was gradually adopted, corrupted and anglicised; and the old Celtic game of camanachd became known in Scotland as shinty.

If the uprising of 1745 was a folly, then it was at least a considered folly. The clans of the Highlands and Islands were neither stupid nor ignorant of the ways of the world: in many cases their hierarchy were better educated and better travelled than were their equivalents in the urban south. They understood at least as well as did their southern counterparts the meaning of a dynastical war and the consequences of losing one. In choosing to support with arms the Jacobite claim of Charles Edward Stuart to the throne of Scotland and England, it is often suggested that they flocked, blinded by emotion and deafened by bardic mythology, behind a hopelessly lame bell-wether. But they were not that innocent.

Nor was it entirely that they felt their religious commitments to be threatened by the presence of a Protestant family on the throne of Britain. While Scottish Catholics did come out in force, easily half of the Jacobite army was Protestant.

The clans had been given ample warning for many a year that in the eyes of two parliaments and of countless civil servants their days were numbered. It had become unacceptable for British commanders waging wars in Ireland and in France to find, pitted against them, trained and ruthless armed men from a part of their own kingdom. It was, if anything, even more unacceptable that a nation which was busy bringing half of the globe under colonial rule had no more control over the inner workings of the northern one-sixth of its own small land mass than it had over the social habits of the Forbidden City in Peking.

Highlanders had presented as canny a mime as possible in the diplomatic charades. When their own interests and freedoms could not conceivably be threatened, they ran willingly to the assistance of the throne. In 1678 they were called upon to police the Covenanting Presbyterians of the south of Scotland, and a 'Highland Host' of 4,500 clan levies set up camp amid the smouldering, resentful people of Ayrshire. But as they withdrew after a month, carrying pots, pans and furniture taken randomly and without much violence from southern households, it must have crossed the minds of a few that if such oppressive indignities could be imposed upon ordinarily peaceful, God-fearing Lowland Covenanters, what might happen north of the Highland line when official patience snapped?

The writing had been on the wall for quite some time. James VI, the forebear of the man they were to rally behind in 1745, exasperated by the prolonged bickering over the carcass of the Kingdom of the Isles between MacDonalds and Macleans and by the bloodsoaked soil of Strathnaver, insisted in 1597 that Highland chiefs should produce titles to their lands and promise to behave. On three occasions between 1598 and 1610 'adventurers' from Fife were despatched to the island of Lewis, the largest of the Outer Hebrides, in a doomed colonial experiment, a precursor to what was shortly to happen with rather more success in north-eastern Ireland.

The massacre at Glencoe may well have succeeded in sending a shiver through the spine of the Highlands. More importantly, it stated with brutal clarity the mistrust, disrespect and often hatred felt in the offices of power for the 'bruti' in the north, and indicated the plain fact that their word of intent was (often justifiably) not considered to be worth the paper that it was marked upon. The Highlanders had even coined a phrase to describe the inexplicable mixture of fear and contempt felt towards them by their southern countrymen: *mi-run mor nan Gall*, the great hatred of the stranger.

In 1745 they rose as much as anything else to assert their claim to their lands and to their right to live, at work, war and leisure in those lands as they saw fit. It was a final, bloody gamble which they lost. They cannot have expected, as they bivouacked beneath bridges in Derby or received word back in the glens of the taking of Carlisle Castle, that the consequences of failure in such a campaign would be slight; and their fears for the aftermath of defeat were well founded. The condition of life in many parts of the Highlands in the years after Culloden would be dignified by the word chaotic. Even in those places where the social order did not entirely collapse, where clan chiefs, their captains and their families had not fled to hilltop caves, to France or to the Carolinas, the old way of life was ended.

Social revolutions are reflected in small as well as in great things and of course there are few records of light-hearted games of shinty on the meadow or the machair in the years immediately after Culloden, of gay, pre-match ritual rhymes being exchanged while Cumberland's men were hanging suspect stragglers and houses were burning.

But if it slept at all, the game slept briefly. When Thomas Pennant, a sympathetic, curious traveller, toured Scotland in 1769 he found in the Highlands and Islands a people whose 'forebearance proves them to be superior to the meanness of retaliation', whose chiefs were 'tasting the sweets of advanced rents', and whose workaday toil was so hard and unremitting that 'they have no leisure for any amusements: no wonder then at their depression of spirits'. Pennant reported that 'most of the ancient sports of the Highlanders . . . are now disused', with a few exceptions. One of these exceptions was 'the shinty, or the striking of a ball of wood or hair; this game is played between two parties in a large plain, and furnished with clubs; which-ever side strikes it first to their own goal wins the match'. Five years later, when Pennant's *Tour of Scotland* went into its third edition, a lengthy appendix on the customs of 'the shire of Murray' (Moray) was provided by an Elgin minister, Reverend Mr Shaw. The sports of his parish, said Mr Shaw in 1774, were 'hunting, firing at marks, foot-ball, club-ball, etc . . .' Their only annual festival, he added, was at Christmas time, which was observed 'more as the Saturnalia were of old, than as Christ's birth ought to be'.

In 1773 Samuel Johnson and James Boswell followed Pennant's footprints. Boswell did hear of the Christmas contest on the island of Coll ('. . . there is a ball thrown down in the middle of a space above the house, or on a strand near it; and each party strives to beat it first to one end of the ground with crooked sticks. The club is called the shinny. It is used in the low country of Scotland. The name is from the danger that the shins run. We corrupt it to shinty.') But Johnson was not interested in ball-games – indeed, he criticised Pennant for wasting printer's ink on such frivolities. The old philosopher looked about him and saw, not idle games of shinty, but a social and spiritual vacuum waiting to be filled. Pennant and Boswell saw more, but Johnson had telescopic vision. Pennant interpreted the dismissal by chieftains of their retinue as hopeful signs of the shaking off of 'the former instruments of oppression'; Johnson observed the creation of a new and wholly disturbing moral and cultural emptiness. 'The lairds, instead of improving their country, diminished their people,' he mused aloud on the state of post-Culloden Highland Scotland. He found a nation 'dejected and humiliated'. He responded with bitter outrage to tales of racked rents and emigration. On being told that Sir Alexander MacDonald of Sleat was always frightened at sea, Johnson quipped: '*He* is frightened at sea; and his tenants are frightened when he comes to land.' Confronting the urbane MacDonald in his home at Armadale, Johnson cocked an eye and observed with matter-of-fact prescience that an unscrupulous or careless laird could make a wasteland of this place.

Samuel Johnson was right as often as he was wrong. The vacuum which he observed to be left in Highland society by the official terrorism, fallen dynasties, proscriptive laws and by the profiteering, unaccountable lairds who followed the battle of Culloden was to be filled spiritually first. It would be quite some time before things began to improve on the temporal plain.

The Reformation which had first gathered strength in the Lowlands of Scotland in the sixteenth century could only now, 200 years later, move in force north of the Highland line. The burnings of Patrick Hamilton and George Wishart, the vengeful return of John Knox from galley slavery, had lit a beacon in the south which was, however, scarcely visible over the Grampian range. The riotous events at the High Church of St Giles in July 1637 left the Highland Gael largely unmoved. At least another century was to pass before he would feel the power of the movement and experience its Sabbath, which then began at 6 p.m. on the Saturday evening and ended at 6 p.m. on the Sunday evening and forbade, for those twenty-four hours, such unseemly activities as the playing of games.

In 1709 a group of Edinburgh worthies determined that the Reformation of the Highlands was long overdue. Possibly alarmed by the recently published reports of Martin Martin, which passed on dutifully the information that even in those areas of the Highlands and Islands which now paid lip service to 'the Reform'd Religion' the festivals of Christmas, Easter, Good Friday and All Saints' were still observed, and oaths were still taken on altar crucifixes, they established The Society in Scotland for Propagating Christian Knowledge. The aims of the Society were simple. They were to start schools throughout the Highlands and Islands, and in them to teach four subjects only: the English language, the Presbyterian Calvinist religion, church music, and arthmetic. The 'Irish Language', the web which bound this ancient culture, was to be methodically and mercilessly 'rooted out'.

The first schoolmaster to be despatched by the SSPCK was one Alexander Buchan, and he was sent to St Kilda. We do not know what Buchan's first impressions were of his new office. It is unlikely, though, that they differed greatly from the conclusions formed by a Dr Kennedy of Dingwall, who wrote later: 'Papacy claimed the whole region as its own, although its dogmas were not formally known or its rites practised . . . the priesthood had been content to rule the people without attempting to teach them.' (Presbyterians were always ready to accuse their Catholic predecessors of a degenerate lack of interest in the educational advancement of their flock. Where it has been tested, the allegation has been found wanting.)

Individual teachers and ministers trod at first with varying degrees of care on this new and fertile soil. Some were relentless in their hostility to the Gaelic language and its old, associated customs, and in their strict observance of the Sabbath. Some stuck to just one or two of the principles and let the others, meantime, take care of themselves. Some were even easy-going about all three.

In the parish of Laggan in the district of Badenoch, for example, there are some strange anomalies. In 1725 one Malcolm Bain of Miltown was deleted and rebuked by the Presbytery for a 'manifest breach of the Lord's Day' – he had sold shoes on the Sabbath. In 1730, Annie MacPherson of Knockachalish was rebuked for baking 'a little bannock' for her husband to take to work on the following Monday morning. But in 1747 a new minister arrived at Laggan. Duncan MacPherson was thirty-six years old when he left Mull for Badenoch. He was a huge man, of great strength, and was quickly dubbed the *Ministeir Mor.* He was also flexible in his approach to his charges, happy to conduct business in Gaelic and, on at least one occasion when the River Spey was in spate and unfordable, to conduct a wedding ceremony from a knoll on one side of the torrent, addressing the half of the congregation which included the bride and groom who stood on the other bank. MacPherson lived at Dalchully, and would, when able, cross the Spey on horseback to reach his thatched church at the Eilean Dhu, near Blaragie. Getting there, he would find that:

> For hours before public worship began the young men of the parish met and played shinty before the arrival of the clergyman, who, *nolens volens*, was compelled to join the players, otherwise he was given clearly to understand that he would have to preach to empty benches.
>
> So, after a hail or two, shinty clubs were thrown aside, and a large congregation met to hear the new doctrine. The sermon was short but pithy, and people began to think there was something in the new doctrine after all. Immediately after services were over, shinty was resumed, and carried on at intervals till darkness put an end to their amusements, when many retired to neighbouring crofts and public houses, where high revelry was kept up till morning.

The *Ministeir Mor* was not entirely unique. Aeneas Sage, who ministered to the parish of Lochcarron between 1726 and 1774, had a fond familiarity with the game. During the Christmas holidays, his grandson noted later, 'which the Highlanders observed by assembling to play at club and shinty, he [Aeneas Sage] observed a body of young fellows approaching his dwelling. The road they took passed close by his Manse, and led to a plain east of the church.'

Nor was the game of shinty always linked with its old companion, the Gaelic language, by those who wished to 'educate' young Highlanders out of their birthright. Daniel Kerr, a Perthshire man who was headmaster at the Parish School of Urquhart during the 1790s and the 1800s, took a very personal and almost sadistic interest in the extermination of the language. But Kerr's time at Urquhart School was not without some redeeming features. He personally favoured for entertainment a cock-fight in the schoolroom, which was temporarily converted for that purpose; he also allowed that the boys 'delighted in their sports – the shinty matches between the Braes and the Strath being specially exciting'.

Shinty may have been robbed of its traditional itinerary by the scrapping of the feast days and by the spread of increasingly strict Sabbatarianism, and found its vocabulary fading as efforts to eliminate the Gaelic tongue continued, but the game flowed on, going underground at some places in some times, to resurface elsewhere. Indeed, when the Reverend Thomas Thompson came to publish the third volume of his *History of the Scottish People* in 1894 – a great year for shinty – he chose to regard the game as having been very much a recreation of those troubled years in the eighteenth century. The rural games then, wrote Thompson,

> were hand-ball, football, penny-stanes, quoits, trundling a cannon-shot along the highway, golf, and an imitation of that game called *shinty*, chiefly practised in the Highlands, where a stick crooked at the extremity, and a little piece of wood served instead of golf-club and ball. But as this was a keen and close contest in which two parties were engaged pell-mell, while the ball was to be driven by one or other party over its opponent's boundary, many random hits were bestowed on the occasion that lighted upon the rags and shins of the players by which Highland ardour and wrath often rose to a dangerous height. In the Lowlands, however, where golf predominated, the game of shinty [was] practised by school-boys, who could find the necessary instruments always at hand.

Thompson was hopelessly wrong about shinty being an imitation of golf and about it being a child's game only in the south. But he was right to identify the dangerous Highland wrath which did occasionally spill out on to the shinty pitch. Writing altogether more reliably, apart from his conclusion, from the eighteenth century in Strathdearn, Sir Eneas MacIntosh noted:

> Playing at shiney is thus performed – an equal number of men drawn up on opposite sides, having clubs in their hands; each party has a Goal, and which party drives a Wooden Ball to their adversary's Goal wins the Game, which is rewarded by a share of a cask of Whiskey, on which both parties get drunk.
>
> This game is often played upon the Ice, by one Parish against another, when they come to blows if intoxicated. The players' legs being frequently broken may give it the name of Shiney.

Perhaps it was this, the association of the game with intoxicated folly rather than with the 'Irish language' and Catholic ancestry, which led many of the new moral and spiritual leaders of the Gaidhealtachd to attempt to suppress shinty. Perhaps it was their anxiety to bind their torn and weary people into a new and lasting unity under God that led such men as the Reverend Roderick MacLeod of Skye, *Maighstir Ruaraidh*, to lump shinty together with all the other bad old weak ways and attempt to throw them all into the fire.

Maighstir Ruaraidh certainly tried, and there was no person better qualified to succeed. His evangelistic ministry in Bracadale and Snizort after the Disruption, and the massed desertion of the established Protestant church to the Free Presbyterian banner, gave him the unwelcome nickname of 'the Bishop of Skye'. He was a much-loved figure in Skye and Raasay, a wholly charismatic leader. In July 1863, he attracted no fewer than 3,000 people to Communion Sabbath at Snizort – and it was generally agreed that the congregation would have been larger if so many men and women had not been away working at the herring fisheries or on the new railway line to Strathcarron.

Maighstir Ruaraidh preached in the open air while his Snizort Free Church was denied a site. With 'the hailstones dancing on his forehead, his hearers wiping away the snow before they would sit down', he preached of the people's rights on this earth and of their vanities and weaknesses in the eyes of the Lord. Prominently among the latter he counted the smoking of tobacco, the drinking of whisky and the playing of shinty. In his lifetime, he thought that he was winning the battle. 'I have raised the standard against shinty and tobacco both,' he wrote in 1857, 'and with some measure of success.'

There is no doubt that MacLeod enjoyed a 'measure of success'. Alexander Nicolson, the historian of Skye, wrote of that time: 'All gatherings except those held for religious purposes, were viewed with disfavour, with the result that none but the wayward now joined in the dance. At the waulkings, the women no longer sang their rhythmic labour-song, as they heartily tossed the web from hand to hand; and innocent assemblies for athletic contests, and such games as shinty, were practically discontinued.'

Nicolson's words are borne out by documents of the time. The *Statistical Account* of the parish of Duirinish in 1841 tells that 'gatherings for shinty playing [have been] discontinued'. Its equivalent for Inverness says in 1835 that 'although the games of football, shinty, throwing the stone, hammer and bowls were formerly common among the lower orders, no amusements of the sort are now practised, except among boys and apprentices on Christmas and New Year's Day'. Although an Old New Year's Day game took place in Portree in the January of 1850, Patrick Cooper, the commissioner and chamberlain to Godfrey William, fourth Lord Macdonald, found himself sent to meet the participants in order to stress that the estate was 'desirous of reviving the old sports of the season'. Reporting a game of shinty in Kilmuir in 1881, a local correspondent to the *Inverness Courier* said what an unusual sight this was: shinty used to be common, but there was 'hardly any in the district now'. And when thirty men from Aird of Sleat met thirty from Ardvasar in the grounds of MacDonald's Armadale Castle in January 1887 before a large crowd of spectators, one of the promoters of the match (which Aird won 5–0), Donald Macdonald of Tormore, a JP and a local farmer, commented on how pleased he was to see the game restored. There was never much love lost between those two claimants of the loyalties of the people: the Episcopalian Lords of Armadale Castle and the ministers of the gospel of the Free Church. On the issue of the game of shinty, which appears from the comfort of a chair more than a century later to have been comparatively trivial, the arguments of *Maighstir Ruaraidh* and his fellows held the upper hand in large areas for almost fifty years.

Some thought this to be no bad thing. When J.A. MacCulloch

moved to Skye in the 1890s he was told that, forty or fifty years previously, 'On market days in Portree, the farmers all joined in the ordinary at the village inn, where they sat eating and drinking till they were quite tipsy, afterwards sallying out to play shinty. No shame was attached to these proceedings, and indeed they were quite *en règle*. Nowadays things have changed for the better . . .'. Others disagreed. Addressing the Gaelic Society of Glasgow in 1890 on the subject of 'Life in the Highlands a Hundred Years Ago', John MacKay told his listeners:

> In the olden days the pipe and song were frequently heard in every Highland clachan, and the youths of the country could enjoy themselves in a rational manner. Shinty, putting the stone, tossing the caber, and other manly exercises, were freely engaged in, the different districts and parishes vying with each other in friendly rivalry. But the Calvinistic doctrines of the Highland clergy preached all the manliness out of the people, and I don't think that even they will be bold enough to assert that they have preached anything better into them.

With a bit of investigation, MacKay might not have been so despondent. In Inverness in 1890 the game of shinty was no longer spurned by all but apprentices and young boys. Following an exciting contest which they had recently witnessed in the town, the employees at the Highland Railway Workshops determined in March 1887 to form a club of their own. They were quickly followed by fifty-two citizens of the town, who met in the Burgh Court House to establish the Inverness Town and Shinty Club. The two sides met in April 1887 and drew 0–0 before a large crowd.

And a hundred miles away on Skye the name of Reverend Roderick MacLeod was still spoken with reverence, but his strictures on the subject of shinty were being slowly, conveniently, forgotten. In the February of 1894 ten shinty players from the Portree Athletic Club (which was shortly to abandon the word 'Athletic' and replace it with the name of the game which occupied most of their time) met ten from Breakish Shinty Club. By the November of that year the Portree Club found itself facing an unexpected crisis. A field belonging to the town's Home Farm, which had been on loan to them for shinty purposes, was withdrawn from use by the farm's lessee. An angry deputation from

Portree approached the feudal superior of the land, claiming breach of faith. Over the years, they said, the Portree Club had spent more than £30 on draining and levelling the field. Some club members were of the opinion that, if all else failed, they should retake it by force. The feudal superior to whom they appealed with outrage and anger was Ronald Archibald, sixth Lord MacDonald, the second son to Godfrey William. Looking down, *Maighstir Ruaraidh* may have managed a smile.

Above all else, this was the period in Highland history when calendar years came to be popularly remembered not for heroic deeds, glorious victory on the battlefield or the invasion of wild sea-men from the north, but for the introduction of a long-legged, woollen-coated pestilence from the south. These were the years of the Cheviot sheep and the first methodical Highland clearances.

It was the time when Highlanders slowly gained evidence that their old links as a clan with their chief were severed forever; when an already traumatised people were evicted from their homelands to make room for 'agricultural improvements' by a new breed of laird whose ancestors had taken the advice of James VI and prepared written title to their lands, and who would now use that title in a once-unthinkable manner to claim the land as theirs alone. These were lairds with an expensive, foreign lifestyle to sustain, with heirs to support at Eton College. They made these years the era of burnt thatch and transportation hulks; of starvation at home for some, privation for most, and for those fit and ready enough to go, a tormented voyage across the world to Carolina, Manitoba or New South Wales.

These years would have seen, if James Loch's Sutherlandshire philosophy of estate management and 'improvement' had been carried throughout to its logical conclusion, the end not only of shinty in the Highlands and Islands, but of every form of human activity other than shepherding, shearing and slaughtering. For many they were the blackest of times, more bitterly remembered in Highland hearthside history than Glencoe, Culloden or Butcher Cumberland.

The Highlanders had few friends in high places during those stricken decades in the nineteenth century. Those that they had, they cherished, and one of them came to be known in his lifetime, and to be remembered ever since, by the sobriquet *Caraid nan Gaidheal* – Friend of the Gaels. Reverend Doctor Norman MacLeod came from crofting stock in Fuinary, in the Morvern district of Argyllshire, of Skye extraction, and he rose to become Moderator of the General Assembly of the Church of Scotland. MacLeod used his position, his handsome bearing and his compelling preacher's power to alert southern society to the enforced depopulation of the far north, and although the result of his graphic descriptions of hardship in the fading fairyland of the Scottish Gael, as delivered to the Lord Mayor of London and others, may in the end have amounted to little more than the provision of famine relief in the form of bolls of meal and the equipping of ships bound for Australia with Gaelic Bibles, psalm books, and religious tracts, *Caraid nan Gaidheal* was almost unique in his efforts and is still thought of fondly for them.

Reverend Doctor Norman MacLeod was also a prodigious writer in his native language. The quantity of his published output was in itself enough to guarantee him an influential role in the history of the Gaelic language. He covered as wide a range of subjects as any English essayist, and although he will probably be remembered for his expository articles on history, geography, the sciences and current affairs, MacLeod loved to dabble in semi-fictionalised, almost whimsical accounts of his youth and the dear, lost days of innocence. In doing so he could not avoid the game of shinty, and he chose the canvas of the Old New Year's Day game upon which to paint his best-known picture of past goodwill and harmony in the now-tortured glen. MacLeod's version of 'Finlay the Pipers' reminiscences deviates from the winsome in its brief account of the game of shinty itself, and in its stark conclusion, but it was to set a tone of writing about the old customs and way of life of the Highlands and Islands which outlived, by many years, *Caraid nan Gaidheal* himself. He describes here the end of the Hogmanay dance, at which commoners were guests of the family of the laird:

> The time of parting came. The gentry gave us the welcome of the New Year with cordiality and kindliness, and we set off to our homes.
>
> 'My lads,' says he himself, 'be valiant on the field tomorrow. The seaboard men boast that they are to met us glen men at the shinty match this year.'
>
> On this New Year's morn, the sun was late of showing his countenance, and later he came in sight his countenance was pale and drowsy. The mist was resting lazily on the hill-side; the crane

was rising slowly from the meadow; the belling of the stag was heard on the mountain; the black cock was in the birch wood, dressing his feathers, while his sonsie mate, the grey hen, was slowly walking before him.

After I had saluted my family and implored the blessing of the Highest on their heads, I prepared the Christmas sheep (*caora Nollaig*), gave a sheaf of corn to the cattle, as was customary, and was getting myself in order when in walked Pàra Mòr and my gossip, Angus Og. They gave me the welcome of the New Year. I returned it with equal heartiness. Then Pàra Mòr produced a bottle from his pocket.

'A black cock', says he, 'whose gurgling is more musical than any ràn that ever came out of the chanter of thy pipe.'

We toasted to one another, and then Mary, my wife, set before us a small drop of the genuine Ferintosh, which she had stored up long ago in the big chest for grand occasions.

It was my duty to gather the people together this morning with the sound of the pipe. So we set off, going from farm to farm up the glen, making the son of the cave of the rock (the echo) answer to my music. I played *A Mhnathan a' Glinne So* (the Women of the Glen), and if the pipe had been dry that day it had ample means of quenching its thirst!

The company continually increased in numbers until we came down by the other side to the ground- officer's house, where it was appointed for us to get our morning meal. The lady had sent a three-year-old wether to his house. We had a roe-buck from the corrie of yew trees; fish from the pool of whiting; and such quantities of cheese, butter and solid oatcake, sent by the neighbours round about, as would suffice for as many more – though we were fifty men in number, besides women and children. Grace was said by Lachlan Ceistear, the Bible-reader. We had an ample and a cheerful breakfast.

Breakfast over, I set off and played the tune of the *Glasmheur* while Red Ewen, the old soldier, was marshalling the men. We reached Guala-nam-Càrn where the gentry were to meet us; and before we knew where we were, who placed himself at our head but our own young Donald, the heir of the family! Dear heart, he was the graceful sapling!

The people of the seaboard then came into view, Alastair Roy of the Bay at their head. When the two companies observed each other, they raised a loud shot of mutual rejoicing. We reached the field, and many were the salutations between friends and acquaintances exchanged there.

The sun at length shone out brightly. On the eminences around the field were the matrons, the maidens and the children of the district, high and low, all assembled to watch the camanachd. The goal at each end of the large field was pointed out, and the two leaders began to divide and choose each his men.

'Buailidh mi ort,' says young Donald.

'Leigidh mi leat,' says Alastair Roy of the Bay.

'If so', says young Donald, 'then Donald Bàn of Culloden is mine.'

This was by far the oldest man present, and you would think that his two eyes would start from his head with delight as he stepped proudly forward, at being the first chosen.

When the men were divided into two companies – forty on each side – Alastair Roy flung his caman high up into the air.

'*Bas no Cas*, Donald of the Glen?' said he.

'Handle, which will defy your handling until nightfall!' replies Donald.

Alistair won the throw, and was about to strike the ball immediately when the other exclaimed: 'A truce! Let the rules of the game be first proclaimed, so that there may be fairness, good fellowship and friendship observed among us, as was wont among our forefathers.'

On this, Evan Bàn stepped forth and proclaimed the laws, which forbade all quarrelling, swearing, drunkenness and coarseness; all striking, tripping or unfairness of any kind; and charged them to contend in a manful but friendly spirit, without malice or grudge, as those from whom they were descended were wont to do.

Alastair Roy gave the first stroke to the ball, and the contest began in earnest; but I have no language to describe it. The seaboard men gained the first game. But it was their only game. Young Donald and his men stripped to their work, and you would think the day of *Blàr na Léine* (the Battle of the Shirt) had come again.

Broad John gave a tremendous blow, and we raised the shout of victory; but all was kindliness and good feeling among us. In the midst of our congratulations, Pàra Mor shouted out, 'Shame on ye, young men! Don't you see those nice girls shivering with cold? Where are the dancers? Play up the reel of Tullochgorum, Finlay!'

The dancing began, and the sun was bending low towards the western ocean before we parted. We returned to the house of nobleness, as on the preceeding evening. Many a torch was beaming brightly in the hall of hospitality. We passed the night amid music and enjoyment, and parted not until the breaking of the dawn guided us to our homes.

Many good results followed from this friendly mingling of gentles and commons. Our superiors were at that time acquainted with our language and our ways. There were kindness, friendship, and fosterage between us; and whilst they were apples at the topmost bough, we were all the fruit of the same tree.

. . . Now our superiors dwell not among us; they know not our language, and cannot converse with us . . . All this has passed as a dream.

3

True Gaels

'The hockey of the low country, our Scotch substitute for cricket.'

Miss Elizabeth Grant thoroughly enjoyed her annual visit to the family estate at Rothiemurchus. She took as much pleasure from their lands in Hertfordshire and from her dalliances in the society life of London and Edinburgh, but that is not pertinent to this story and would probably have been denied by Elizabeth herself, for in common with many a nineteenth-century landed lady, Elizabeth Grant preferred to regard her fashionable Highland inheritance as her true spiritual home. The Grant family was heavily invested in the wood industry and each Christmas they showed their gratitude to those men and women of the Spey valley who made their riches possible by inviting them all to a ball.

The 'floaters' of the north-eastern wood trade followed an old calling, now long gone from the Highlands, but common enough in the early nineteenth century. It was a calling which held many of them in good stead when they found themselves obliged to seek a living in the forests of North America. They were responsible for guiding felled logs down the River Spey to market. They waited for a suitable spate, or opened crude sluice gates to create one, and then they rode, chased and manoeuvred the huge trunks through gullies and over falls. Their language was Gaelic and their recreations were those of other Highlanders.

After the parlour games, whist drives, pianoforte exercises and sedate walks, Elizabeth Grant found the Floaters' Ball a rough, thrilling interruption of her Christmas routine. Of the festivities at the end of 1812 she recalled:

> The amusements began pretty early in the morning with a game at 'ba', the hockey of the low country, our Scotch substitute for cricket.

It is played on a field between two parties, who toss a small ball between them by means of crooked sticks called clubs. The Highlanders are extremely fond of this exciting game, and continue it for hours on a holiday, exhibiting during its progress many feats of agility. There were always crowds of spectators. Our people kept up the game till dark, when all the men – above a hundred – went to dinner in the barn, a beef and some sheep having been killed for them . . . two sets of fiddlers playing, punch made in the washing tubs, an illumination of tallow dips! It is surprising that the floors took the pounding that they got; the thumping noise of the many energetic feet could have been made half a mile off.

Three years later, on 4 December 1815, Walter Scott, then the Sheriff of Selkirk and, unknown to most of his companions, the anonymous author of the successful historical novel *Waverley* which had been published in the previous year, found himself on the plain of Carterhaugh, near the junction of the rivers Ettrick and Yarrow. Scott was there, with a clutch of other notables, to witness what *Ballantyne's Newspaper* (in which Scott was a partner) hailed as 'the greatest match at the ball which has taken place for many years'.

Two thousand people saw the Duke of Buccleuch and Queensberry arrive promptly at 11 a.m. with a titled and high- ranking house party, marching slowly beneath and behind the Buccleuch emblazoned banner. As the Earl of Home led a team from the Dale of Yarrow, who wore sprigs of heather, out to face the men of Selkirk, who were wearing distinguishing slips of fir and were headed by the chief magistrate, Ebenezer Clarkson, pipes skirled around the field and Scott and the Ettrick Shepherd, James Hogg, distributed sheets of commemorative verse to the crowd. Desirous at the time of concealing his identity as a writer of fiction, the 44-year-old Scott was proud of his poetic prowess. The man who had recently been offered, and had rejected, the Laureateship, wrote of this grand occasion:

> 'Then up with the banner, let forest winds fan her,
> She has blazed over Ettrick eight ages and more;
> In sport we'll arrend her, in battle defend her,
> With heart and with hand, like our fathers before.'

The game itself was, typically, a marathon. A Selkirk mason, Robert Hall, put his side ahead after ninety minutes, and the two teams

C p ꞵ o c ꞵ.

The distinguished Highlander at his recreation, portrayed for the young gentleman
of the Society of the True Gael.

changed ends. The second goal was three more hours in coming; three
hours, as *Ballantyne's Newspaper* put it, of a 'rough and animated' contest
in which the players 'though several hundreds in number' maintained
'the most perfect good humour, and showed how unnecessary it is to
discourage manly and athletic exercises among the common people,
under pretext of maintaining subordination and good order'. George
Brodie of Greatlaws, Aillwater, eventually equalised for Yarrow. The
two teams changed ends again, and 'the ball should then have been
thrown up a third time', but 'as the day began to close, it was found
impossible to bring the strife to an issue, by playing a decisive game'.
Proceedings came to a close with the nobility offering and accepting
return engagements, bets laid and taken, and the weary participants
retiring for refreshments to a booth manned by Buccleuch's domestics,
wherein no ale or spirits were available to sully the clean, fresh
atmosphere of the day.

Whether it liked it or not, the game of shinty, along with the tartan,
the sgian dubh and the clarsach, was being adopted by high society. *Mi*
run mor nan Gall had taken a strange turn. Highland was coming into
vogue and the habits and customs of the Gaidhealtachd were beginning to experience the great indignity of a defeated people: they were
being patronised.

A decent interval had, of course, to pass after the last Jacobite uprising. Pacification had to be seen to be working, memories of Killiecrankie, Prestonpans and the Highland Host to have faded. The extraordinary performance of thousands of Highland troops, fighting on the right side for once in the Peninsula wars, was beginning to sink into the national consciousness: the reputation of the Gael as an incomparable warrior in the cause of Empire was taking root. It was, for southerners, a schizophrenic experience. Donald MacKinnon, the Gaelic scholar who became the first professor of Celtic at Edinburgh University, and who remembered the essential ingredients of his schooldays on the island of Colonsay in the 1820s as being '*Gray*, Leabhar Aithghearr nan Ceist, *Bìobull Gàidhlig* air a chòmhdach le craiceann caorach, agus deagh chaman' (A copy of *Gray's Anatomy*, a short catechism, a Gaelic Bible in a sheepskin cover, and a new caman), wrote in *The Scotsman* in 1890 of that decent interval:

> Nowadays we can only imagine the feelings with which the High-land people were regarded by their southern neighbours in 1760. The storm of the '45 had burst and passed; but still the waves of prejudice ran high . . . the Highland people, loyal and disloyal alike, had alone to endure for many a day thereafter all the hatred and scorn which Saxon Philistinism could command.

The scorn and prejudice ran deeply throughout Victorian Scotland, suggested MacKinnon, and manifested in curious ways. *Jamieson's Scottish Dictionary*, for instance, defines *cammock* as a crooked stick, cites as its origin old Scots proverbs ('Airly crooks [bends] the tree, that good cammock should be'), says that it is used in Perthshire 'to denote same game elsewhere called shinty', and suggests a host of Latin and old English terms to be its forebears before offering the slightest reference to any similar Gaelic term. 'Dr Jamieson,' wrote Donald MacKinnon bitterly, 'would compass sea and land in search of an origin for a word of respectable associations rather than allow that it was borrowed from Gaelic into Scottish.'

Another folklorist and scholar, John Lorne Campbell, has written more recently:

> The humiliation which the proscription, unjust in its incident and harsh in its application, of language, dress and customs, imposed

upon a proud, spirited and reserved people, has never been ade-
quately repaired, and has perpetuated the division of Scotland into
two suspicious and hostile portions, whose dislike of each other has
only been diminished with the decline of the Highlands that has
gone on uninterrupted since the time of the Industrial Revolution.

But scorn and prejudice, tempered with tremulent curiosity, brought
about a pixillated attitude towards the Highland way of life in nineteenth-century southerners. Society men and women who would have
sooner died than spend a night in a black house or a day working the
cas chrom on runrig land, displayed upon their Edinburgh walls a caman
or a dagger or a target in the certainty that it would attract as much
chattering attention as any shrunken head from the South China Seas.
Gradually it even became modish to invoke or to invent some
evidence of Highland ancestry; to claim for a merchant banker and
his wife the blood of a barbarian warrior or a carefree maid of the Isles.
While the actual repositories of this culture and this ancestry, the
people of the Highlands and Islands, were being cleared from their
land to suffer on salt-ridden earth by the unfamiliar shore, a blinding,
mocking charade of Highland dress and music was being displayed in
Edinburgh to King George IV, to the painter Turner (who made a
messy impression of this 'Gathering Of The Clans' in 1822), to the
Grant family of Rothiemurchus and to Walter Scott.

Highland Societies sprang out of the southern ground like necro-
mancers. Many of these were harmless, and even did some good. As
early as 1778 the Highland Society of London had been formed and it
set the respectable standard for those who followed. In 1784 the
Highland Society of Scotland assembled in Edinburgh, 'a number
of gentlemen, natives of or connected with the Highlands' meeting to
see how agriculture, fisheries, roads and bridges, and other 'useful
purposes' might be advanced in the Highlands with the help of
government and 'an exertion to unite the efforts of the landlords'.
This society was able, over the following four decades, to give grants
for draining, clearing and planting, and to publish a Gaelic dictionary.
Some of the others were to be less useful. Many came to impose
themselves upon the game of shinty, for better or for worse.

More than anybody else, Walter Scott was responsible for the
romancing of the Highlands. It was certainly his work which persuaded
Victoria in the direction of her post-Albertian fetish with glens and

ghillies. Looking back on the lurid phenomenon which he helped into life, Scott decided that it was all the doing of the '45. He wrote in the *Quarterly Review*:

> It was not until after these events that the Highlanders, with the peculiarity of their government and habits, became a general object of attention and investigation. And evidently it must have been a matter of astonishment to the subjects of the complicated and combined constitution of Great Britain, to find that they were living at the next door to tribes whose government and manners were simply and purely patriarchal, and who, in the structure of their social system, much more resembled the inhabitants of the mountains of India than those of the plains of England. Indeed, when we took up the account of Cabul, lately published by the Honourable Mr Elphinstone, we were forcibly struck with the curious points of parallelism between the manners of the Afghan tribes and those of the ancient Highland clans. They resembled these Oriental mountaineers in their feuds, in the adoption of auxiliary tribes, in their laws, in their modes of conducting war, in their arms, and, in some respects, even in their dress . . .

To persuade one of these wily Pathan to attend, in full fig, a drawing-room party was to mount a major social *coup*. To hang a portrait of one on the wall was the next best thing. Highland chiefs may have become, mostly, little more than ruthless landowners, but they had inherited a sharp sense of their own value and many of them were content to go along with the game. When the artist McIan toured the Gaidhealtachd in the second and third decades of the nineteenth century to compile his illustrated guide to the *Clans of the Scottish Highlands*, he portrayed the tartan of Grant of Glenmoriston on the person of a man, possibly Grant himself, with his back to the painter's easel, flourishing a beautifully modelled caman in his right hand and holding aloft the ball in his left. James Logan, the Lowland historian who supplied the text to accompany MacIan's impressions, explained for the benefit of his readers who may not have been on the plain of Carterhaugh, or spent Christmas with the Grants at Rothiemurchus:

> He is in the attitude of throwing the ball at the commencement of the game of Camanachd or Shinnie, as it is named in the low

country. This exhilarating amusement is very popular among the Highlanders; two opposing parties endeavour by means of the caman or club to drive a ball to a certain spot on either side, and the distance is sometimes so great that a whole day's exertion is required to play out the game.

A vigorous runner, it is obvious, has a great advantage; but agility is not the only requisite; a great skill in preventing the ball being driven to the desired goal is necessary, and many awkward blows and falls take place during the contest.

Different parishes frequently turn out to try their abilities at this exciting game, and no better exercise could be enjoyed in a winter day. When there is a numerous meeting, the field has much the appearance of a battle scene; there are banners flying, bagpipes playing, and a keen melee around the ball. Young and old, rich and poor, join in this athletic sport, and though it is usually engaged *con amore*, prizes are frequently given.

Such a scene may well have been observed in the glens of Moriston and Urquhart, for the Grants of that area were unusually sparing with the eviction notice – a blessing which was, among other things, to prove of lasting benefit to the game of shinty. But Walter Scott's fancy would not be limited to just one estate. In his efforts to recreate on paper the world which the Reverend Doctor Norman MacLeod had seen passing as if in a dream, Scott went several leaps further than McIan. He took another Highland chief, one whose actual life barely required fictionalising, and turned him into the Highland hero of an era.

Alistair Ranaldson MacDonell, the fifteenth chief of Glengarry, was so bizarre a character that it should not be surprising that Scott modelled upon him the colourful figure of Fergus MacIvor in *Waverley*, or even that, fifty years after his death, Glengarry's final, strangest legacy would be to the game of shinty.

John Prebble has written of Alastair Ranaldson that he 'behaved as if the world had received an order to mark time in 1745 and had not yet taken a forward pace'. Even Walter Scott acknowledged that there was in his friend a touch of the anachronistic. 'This gentleman', the author of *Waverley* confided to his diary, 'is a kind of Quixote in our age . . . He seems to have lived a century too late, and to exist, in a state of complete law and order, like a Glengarry of old, whose will was law to his sept . . . To me he is a treasure, as being full of information as to the history of his own clan, and the manners and customs of the Highlanders in general.'

In fact, 'complete law and order' was not Glengarry's strong point. Travelling always in full Highland dress, with a small armoury strapped to his person, and accompanied by clansmen, piper and bard, he drove havoc through the Highlands. He challenged Flora MacDonald's grandson to a duel, killed him, and was acquitted of any offence. When Elizabeth Grant was just ten years old, and doubtless tucked up safely in the nursery at Rothiemurchus, her father narrowly avoided a similar extinction at the hands of Glengarry when the two fell out over a lady and only the peaceable offices of common friends prevented another duel. He roused the fury of Thomas Telford by raiding, regularly, the timber-piles and brick stocks of the Caledonian Canal which he hated as a symbol of the modern age. He mustered a regiment of Fencibles, by fair means and foul, and designed for them a bonnet which is still in use and which still bears his name. He beat, almost to death, a doctor against whom he held a grudge, in broad daylight at Fort Augustus market. And he cleared his people from their land.

Glengarry showed kindness, said Scott, 'to those of his clan who are disposed fully to admit his pretensions. To dispute them is to incur his resentment.' Scott was probably referring to Glengarry's pretension to the full title of the head of Clan Donald; to his tenants, Glengarry's pretension to the right to evict them as he chose was far more relevant. And evict them he did: former members of the Fencibles, men who had been part of the enormous tartan contingent which he paraded before George IV, the family of Elizabeth Grant and Walter Scott in Edinburgh in 1822 – none were safe as Glengarry fought debt by courting sheepfarmers. And then he fell out with the sheepfarmers.

In the course of this busy life, Alistair Ranaldson MacDonell found time to set up his own society. It was not, of course, like any other. Sobersided citizens raising money for dykes and schoolbooks were not in Glengarry's line. On 23 June 1815, he assembled ninety-seven *duine-uasal* (gentlemen) in a field at Inverlochy and announced them to be the *Comunn nam Fior Gaidheal* – the Society of the True Gael. The aims of the *Comunn*, buried beneath an ant-heap of balderdash about supporting the 'Dress, Language, Music and Characteristics of our illustrious and ancient race in the Highlands and Isles of Scotland',

McIan's portrait of the Grant of Glenmoriston 'in the attitude of throwing the ball at the commencement of the game of Camanachd'.

were simply to perpetuate the fictional world of Fergus MacIvor and *Waverley*. Glengarry was *ceannsuidhe* (chairman) and only *duine-uasal* and *bean-uasal* (gentlemen and ladies) need apply. They held three-day hunts, Gothic theatricals, balls and Highland Games at which cows were first felled with a hammer, then torn to pieces and barbecued. In this fantasy world of Celtic twilight, they were possibly not the most fantastic society to emerge. The 'Sons of Morvern', who were around at the same time, boasted 'influential' men among their number and practised a 'solemn process of initiation, and were arrayed in certain official roles' probably scoop the award for eeriness.

But the black masque of the *Comunn nam Fior Gaidheal* infected even the most level-headed laird. On Mull in 1821, it was decided to settle once and for all the old feud between the Campbells and the MacLeans in a showpiece game of shinty on Calgary Sands. The game was organised while there were still enough people left on Mull to put out two respectable teams, and it was widely publicised. The *Highland Home Journal* reported later:

> At the appointed time the shinty was tossed for sides. Then the wooden ball, as was then customary, was deposited in a hole in the sand, when a struggle took place to unearth it. Whoever was fortunate enough to get it out made off at full speed towards the goal, driving it before him, this being considered the feat of the day if well done.
>
> The playing was furious and determined. The Torluisk estate players placed their best men in reserve; they lay hid in the brushwood to the west of the Sands, whence they watched the play. From time to time a fresh man would dash out upon the Sands and enter into the fray. Ultimately they were one and all upon the field. The contest grew hot and furious. Hail after hail was scored by the MacLeans, until the Campbells were compelled to give in and leave the field, vanquished and crestfallen.

Thus did guerilla tactics on the western coast of Mull finally fell the pride of the House of Hanover.

'Giving' a game of shinty to their tenants, allowing space and time for the match to take place, and honouring it with their presence became for many lairds a talisman, a sacred link with the imagined past. This custom undoubtedly sustained the game during a difficult time, but it was to be the death of at least one of their number.

Cluny MacPherson, CB, the Chief of Clan Chattan, had, at least, a genuinely colourful Highland heritage. Cluny himself had the misfortune to be born and brought up in the heyday of Alistair Ranaldson Glengarry and the *Comunn nam Fior Gaidheal*, but his ancestors had been out in force at the Jacobite risings of 1715 and 1745. Cluny, though a Presbyterian, professed to be a staunch Jacobite. He had good reason to do so: his great-grandfather had been beheaded in the Tower of London at the age of almost eighty for his part in the cause; and Cluny's grandfather entered Highland folklore (and found a place in Robert Louis Stevenson's *Kidnapped*) by running fugitive throughout Badenoch for nine full years after the '45, hiding in caves and safe houses, sustained all along by his people before finally fleeing for the continent and dying in exile.

Like Grant at Rothiemurchus, Cluny always 'gave' his tenants a game of shinty at the turn of the year. When he reached the age of eighty in 1885, the weather on the appointed day turned out poorly, with bitter north-easterly winds carrying showers of sleet and snow. Cluny, nonetheless,

> . . . would not be dissuaded by loving counsels from attending as usual, remarking that while strength was spared to him he considered it simply his 'duty' to be present at all such happy gatherings of his people.
>
> Accompanied by the loving partner of his long and happy wedded life, he accordingly drove to the field, and they were both received with the genuine Highland enthusiasm ever evoked by the presence of the venerable pair at such gatherings. In response, Cluny made a happy little speech in Gaelic, expressive of the pleasure it always afforded him to be present with his people, particularly, as he had always endeavoured to do, in their joys as well as in their sorrows . . . Within five days an attack of bronchitis had developed itself to such an extent that the venerable chief passed calmly and peacefully to his rest.

His demise did not, fortunately, signal the end of the involvement of the clan MacPherson in organising the game of shinty.

Alistair Glengarry suffered a less timely, if no less poignant, end: he died after a serious fall on the banks of the detested Caledonian Canal in 1828. Glengarry's death was a heavy blow to the resources and morale of his True Gaels. Like many of Glengarry's tenants, they scattered to the four winds. Unlike Glengarry's tenants, they were more likely to land in the counting houses of London than in the Australian outback, and there, in the busy metropolis, they and their descendants met and regrouped around the game of shinty.

Highland exiles had been playing shinty on Blackheath and other expanses of London common land for many years. The *Comunn nam Fior Gaidheal* brought to the proceedings what they doubtless saw as a touch of class. As early as the 1820s, London's True Gaels had met at a coffee house in the Strand, taking a coach from there to Blackheath and returning in the evening to celebrate in a manner as close to the old style as could be approximated in the rattling streets of London. Songs had been composed in honour of the occasion. Given the setting and the company, Gaelic was out of the question, but David MacDonald, a native of Inverness who was working in London at the time, set words to the Gaelic air 'Ag iomain nan gamhna' in 1836:

> O! muster, my lads, for the shinnie,
>   Come, rush like the waves of the sea;
> Come, sweep as the winds from the heavens,
>   Nor these than the Gael more free.
>
> Let national fervour inspire you,
>   As bounding you march to the heath;
> O! think of your ancestors' glory,
>   Who smiled at the triumph of death.
>   O! muster, my lads, &c.
>
> The heather blooms sweet on the mountain,
>   The thistle waves proud in the vale,
> Where hover the ghosts of your fathers –
>   The brave Caledonian Gael.
>   O! muster, my lads, &c.
>
> To witness their progeny summon'd,
>   And joyously view their combine;
> With camacks to play at the shinnie,
>   The pastime and sport of langsyne.
>   O! muster, my lads, &c.

MacDonald was assembling a book of verse which he would publish in 1838 under the title *The Mountain Heath*, and the shinty players of the Society of the True Gael in London became a useful testing ground for his rhymes. Shortly afterwards, another effort echoed around the walls of the British coffee house:

'T was on June the twenty-second,
　　Eighteen hundred thirty-sax,
That the Gael met at Shinnie,
　　On Blackheath their joints to rax –
Bagpipes raving, tartans waving,
　　Phillabegs 'boon naked knees;
Banners flying, clouds converging,
　　Souls of heroes on the breeze;
Hearts inspiring, bosoms firing,
　　With the deeds of other days;
Flinging, dancing, bounding, prancing,
　　As the muse who sings their praise.

Our chief, Logan, raised the slogan,
　　Tait and Sieveweight sung encore,
Brave MacEwan and MacIain,
　　Quickly joined the gallant corps.
Warrens, Martin, and Macpherson,
　　Last of whom a bard of note,
With MacDonalds and good Reynolds,
　　Rushed to keep their vigour hot;
Scott, Mackay, and Macdonald,
　　Better pipers could not be,
Blew so loud that Scottish sailors
　　Heard it on the German Sea.

Menzies, Lossie, and MacIain,
　　Whitear, Grant, and Rouvery,
Watsons bold, and bright Glendinning,
　　Nicol, Gifford, and Macphee;
Dauntless Siccar, bold Earwacker,
　　Forbes, Watts, and Dykes and Bell;
Robertson and Murchison,
　　And Mackintosh – all mountain Gael;
Henchman Gallie, our brave gillie,
　　Brandish'd his Lochaber axe,
As if to stretch on earth the wretch
　　Who would our wives or sweethearts vex.

The activities of these latterday bearers of the banner of Fionn MacChumhail, these Whitears, Earwackers, and Giffords, came to revolve increasingly around the shinty field. The opening of a railway line to Blackheath brought hosts of more common daytrippers to those fields, making them unsuitable for the exclusive exercises of the society, and the venue was switched to Islington, to Wimbledon Common and finally to Alexandra Palace. Eventually, even the *Inverness Courier*, 600 miles away, could not ignore the Society's press releases. On 23 June 1841 it reported:

> Highlanders in London were greatly interested in a shinty match organised by the committee of a body which called itelf 'The Society of True Highlanders'. The match took place in Copenhagen Fields, an extent of rich meadow land lying on the outskirts of Islington.
>
> There was much enthusiasm and keenly contested games. It is said that before the gathering half the glens of Lochaber had been ransacked for shinty clubs. In the evening there was a dinner, at which Mr Forbes Macneil presided, and many northern gentlemen were present. The chairman was supported on the right by Commodore Sir Charles Napier, who was fresh from the laurels he had won on the Syrian Coast in the war with Mehemet Ali.

The Society's annual Camanachd Dinner became the high point of its year, attracting guests from Lowland and Highland society. And by the late 1870s it was being noised about Edinburgh and Glasgow that a Mr MacIntyre-North, of the London branch of the Society of the True Gael, was busy compiling and looking for subscriptions to a grand volume of all things Celtic; a conclusive reference work for the True Gael; a magnum opus which would 'weed out and detect the various mistakes, mis-statements, and errors which have gradually been accepted' about Gaeldom. MacIntyre-North's book would finally print the truth about such Gaelic activities as shinty.

The leather-bound, atlas-sized *Book of the Society of the True Gael* was, along with McIan's guide to the clans, a pioneer in the field of coffee-table books on the Highlands of Scotland. In its first volume it contained a history, written rules and an elementary coaching manual of the game of shinty. Camanachd, it said, must been seen as 'not only being a favourite sport of the Club of True Highlanders, but as being undoubtedly the oldest known Keltic sport or pastime.'

It formed an important part of Keltic military education. Repeated
reference is made to this game in the ancient laws. The enrichment of
the camacs with different metals is mentioned, and 'no-one was to be
fined for hurling on the green, because the green was free.' The game
must always be classed as the most valuable means for promoting
agility, speed, presence of mind, endurance, truth of eye, and sureness
of foot; no game is better calculated to bring into play all the muscles
of the body and faculties of the mind, without over- straining; and we
trust that the day is not far distant when the youth of Great Britain will
as keenly contest the hale as their forefathers did.

MacIntyre-North was obliged to fall back on an earlier historian,
Donald McPherson, for evidence of the game's antiquity in Ireland.
'It is said', he quoted, 'and no doubt with great truth, that the game of
camanachd, or club playing, was introduced into the Green Isle by the

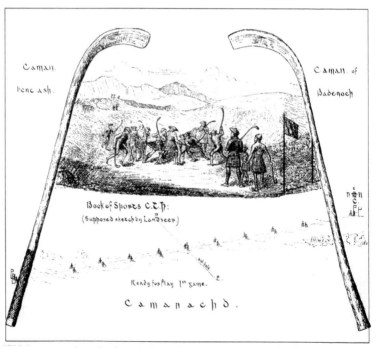

A guide to team formation from the Book of the Society of the True Gael,
*1881, apparently indicating that the society's members preferred to play eleven-a-
side, and to adopt a curiously linear information at throw-up. Note the flagged
hail-posts and the (spurious?) distinction between a Badenoch and ash caman.*

immediate descendents of Noah. On such authority we may rationally conclude that it was played by Noah himself; and if by Noah, in all probability by Adam and his sons.'

'The game is now played', continued the *Book*,

> in its utmost perfection in the districts of Strathearn, Strathnairn, Strathspey, Braidalbane, Rannoch, Lochaber, in many parts of the West Highlands; but particularly so in *Baideanach*, where the late Colonel Duncan MacPherson, the father of the present chief, greatly patronised it . . . The number – on each side – on the Prad of Cluny was never above ten, and the distance of the hales from each other was always about half a mile. This is, however, not practicable in all situations. The width of each goal was about seven feet.

The form and the rules of the game of shinty, as refined on Copenhagen Fields and Wimbledon Common, were then laid out:

> First: The players march from the place of rendezvous two by two, club over shoulders, to the field, preceded by the warder and piper.
>
> Second: When arrived in front of the marquee, the members lay aside those parts of the dress which would be cumbersome and prevent activity in the game.
>
> The arrangements of the field are under the direction of the chief, and the teams are under the direction of the two chieftains or captains who stake out the ground. The distance that the hales are placed apart varies with the extent of the ground and the number of players; each hale being formed of two flags placed ten feet apart, the mid-hale, or place from which the game is started, is also marked.
>
> Third: The chieftains then select by lot, as customary, their respective parties. The usual manner is for one of the chieftains to toss the caman towards the other, who catching it with one hand, a grip is taken hand over hand until the end is reached, and the man who can take the last grip has the first choice.
>
> The players are drawn up in two lines, as they are to be opposed to each other in order of play; the chief and chieftains will then pass between the men, and the chief will read out the following rules:
>
> 1) The club or caman to be used for no other purpose than that of propelling the ball; neither to trip the foot of an opponent nor in any way to molest him, except to turn away his club that you may gain the ball.

2) No player on any account must push the player he is in pursuit of, for that is attended with great danger; it being evident that an extra force applied to a person at full speed may easily throw him on his head. No player must voluntarily shoulder his opponent; the *fair game* being to get before him and take the ball from him, *not by force, but by dexterity.*

3) Each player must play on his own side, that is, right-handed, and no-one shall be deemed accountable for any accident that may happen to a left-handed player.

4) The ball must be driven in between the two sides of the goal (Eadar dha bhith an taoghail), either on the ground so as not to touch either side; or if it hails by a raised blow, the course of the ball must be fairly over the space between the sides of the goal.

5) If any dispute arise it must be left to the chief, whose decision shall be final.

6) The side that hails plays the next game in the opposite direction, and must be allowed to drive the ball *from the goal* into the middle space as far as he can in one blow, and he who hails has the right to give the first blow to the ball in the next game, or he can transfer his privilege to any one of his own side.

The rules proclaimed, the next duty of the chieftains is to decide in which direction each side is to play the first game; one sends a caman spinning in the air, crying 'bas na cas'; the other chieftain cries to one or the other, and his side plays to the hale to which the selected end points; they then see that their men are placed in the best position. At this stage of the proceedings great care should be exercised as to the manner in which they are placed; one or two steady, cool hands should be placed to guard the hale, and the younger and more active members should be placed towards mid-hale, or forward towards the opponents' hale. The men should be cautioned to play into each other's hands, as many a good game has been lost by an over- eager player driving the ball anywhere, regardless of consequence, so long as he could get a good lick at it. Each player should also be careful to play the ball so that it can be taken up by his comrades, and not by his opponents.

When the chieftains reach the mid-hale and are face to face, the warning given by one chieftain, 'Buail 'm ort' (I'll strike), is answered by 'leagadh me leat' (I'll allow you); the chieftain then exclaims, 'Suas e', throws up the ball, and the game commences. The hush of expectancy gives place to the excitement and animation of the camanachd; the ball is driven hither and thither, from caman to caman; sometimes a smart blow sends it flying in the air, at others it is kept bounding along by the skilful play of a fleet runner, and it is bandied about with varying fortune until it comes dangerously near one of the hales; the hale-keepers and the rear backs are anxiously on the alert; the players draw together, darting backwards and forwards like a swarm of midges, until a well-directed blow either sends the ball flying between (or over) the hale-posts or towards the centre of the field; and so the struggle is kept up until the buail- choilleag (or stroke that gains the hale) has been given. The next game is then *started from the hale which has been just gained* by one of the winning side's driving the ball from the centre of the field towards the middle of the field.

If during the progress of the game the ball should be driven past the hales, the party defending the same has the right to one hit to drive the ball as far towards the middle as he can.

And so, with a brief note explaining why they chose not to have a dead-ball line down the side, with a throw-up six yards into play when the ball crossed it (it gave, thought the society, too great a reward to the side who 'by bad play or an exhibition of mere animal force' had put the ball out in the first place), and a commendation for shinty on ice ('one of the most exciting games it is possible to conceive'), the book concludes 'This manner of playing the game ... carefully handed down in the records of the Club of True Highlanders'.

Throughout the western world the last three decades of the nineteenth century were the years of constitutionalised sports, of committees scrubbing down crude village games and ironing out their rules. MacIntyre-North and his colleagues must have thought that they were performing this duty, for the first time, for shinty. In the early days of their book's preparation they were justified in such an assumption. But the *Book of the Society of the True Gael* was kept away from the public gaze by printing delays and late subscriptions; it was not published until August 1881. In the meantime other minds had been at work, far to the north of Watford Gap. MacIntyre-North's rules remain today as easily the most expensively prepared guide to playing the game of shinty to be published, but it was not the first. The True Gaels may or may not have been pleased to learn that those who beat them into print had, however, considerable experience of the game of shinty in London.

4

Foreign Soil

'The Sassenach paused in his passage across the familiar heath to
gaze upon the scene, which might well have suggested some wild
and lawless pursuit.'

The True Gaels, lately of Inverlochy, were not the only Highland
expatriates who, once established upon foreign soil, fashioned a caman
and a ball and arranged to meet on common ground. They were not
even alone in the capital of the Empire.

The Highland Camanachd Club of London surfaced in a less
ornamental social pool. They organised Boxing Day matches on
Wimbledon Common from the early 1870s onwards, picking roughly
even sides of Cattanachs, Munros and Frasers and throwing themselves
into a lengthy, often goalless, fray. Their organisation in the early days
was basic and efficient. It took care of the essentials. On 26 December
1873, in front of 'several Enerys and Arries looking on and gazing with
bewilderment', they broke for half-time to enjoy oatmeal bannocks,
Highland cheese and 'a liberal allowance of the real dew of Ben Nevis'
thoughtfully laid on by treasurer J.C. MacKenzie. A Chisholm and a
Guy scored both goals in the second half, during which many
spectators – one of them a Mr James Watson, who was recognised
by other participants as 'an ex-member of one of the Scottish clubs' –
joined in; and at half past three in the afternoon the goal-posts which
had been planted at noon were lifted and the party retreated, 'gualainn
ri gualainn', to the Fox and Hounds in Putney.

In January 1878 they decided to constitute themselves into a club,
booked a room in the Caledonian Hotel on the Strand and formed a
willing and energetic committee. By the time of its third meeting, just a
month later, the Highland Camanachd Club of London was occupying

itself with matters more weighty than the procedure of shinty matches on Wimbledon Common.

Back home in the far north, *The Highlander*, an Inverness-based weekly newspaper which had been founded and was edited by a committed, articulate radical called John Murdoch – who had, as a boy in Islay, played shinty with John Francis Campbell – was locked in mortal battle with the Scottish landowning fraternity. When a flash-flood had torn away the earth from a Kilmuir graveyard and washed skeletons and skulls up against the home of one of Skye's most disreputable lairds, Captain Fraser of Kilmuir, Murdoch had been unable to resist a couple of powerful lines about the dead even rising in protest. Fraser, aware of the impecunious state of *The Highlander* and of the garlands which would be bestowed by the Highland establishment upon the man who brought down Murdoch, sued for libel.

Down on the Strand in that February of 1878, the Highland Camanachd Club of London frowned upon Fraser. Upon the close of ordinary business they passed a couple of resolutions regretting his libel action and expressing sympathy with *The Highlander*. The shinty players then formed another large committee with a simple brief: to raise funds not only to support the newspaper in its legal affray with Fraser, but also 'for placing that organ of Highland interests and opinion on a better financial basis than ever'. Fourteen men sat upon that sub-committee. One of them was a tall, bearded former Army officer with twinkling eyes and a ready smile who had spent many years in the colonial service and who was temporarily in residence in Old Broad Street in the City of London before retiring to his native Strathglass. His name was Archibald MacRa Chisholm, and if he could not ultimately prevent *The Highlander* from folding under financial pressure he was, over the next two decades, to be the principal author of the most important chapter in the history of shinty.

In the short term Archibald MacRa Chisholm was more concerned with his responsibility, as official club-bearer, for finding sufficient camain to equip the thirty playing members of the Highland Cama-nachd Club of London. He finally resolved the problem by ordering fifty to be sent down by train from Scotland, and on 23 March 1878 the club's captain and vice-captain picked sides on Wimbledon Common. The first match of the properly constituted club was watched by wives, girlfriends and daughters perched demurely upon a row of carriages, cabs and dogcarts drawn up along the boundary line, and by inquisitive cockneys arguing as to whether the action represented hockey or a Highland game. It resulted in a spirited and satisfactory 3–3 draw, and had nothing to do with the rites and rituals of the Society of the True Gael – a draft set of rules which recently had been drawn up in Glasgow were rushed down along with the camain and these, along with a team formation suggested from north of the border, were adopted.

The Highland Camanachd Club, with its cheerful democratic set-up and its invariable post-match adjournment to the Fox and Hounds, was the midwife for popular, organised shinty in London. It had a short life but an interesting one. Within a year it had attracted the patronage of Lord Lovat, the presidency of Lord Colin Campbell and the honorary captaincy of John Murdoch's friend, the radical Inverness MP Charles Fraser-Macintosh. Its meetings and its functions were as gay and varied as its matches, but when it folded in 1881 the Highland Camanachd Club of London, isolated in its southern fastness from all but the young gentlemen of the Society of the True Gael, had never met another shinty team in open competition.

The sudden quiet on Wimbledon Common did not last for long. Over the next thirty years no fewer than eight shinty clubs were formed in London. The strange sound of Gaelic at full tilt was heard not only in the leafy outlying village of Wimbledon – where it certainly preceded gentlemanly intonations of 'forty-love' – but in the grounds of Lambeth Palace, on Irish Acre in Muswell Hill, on the council cricket grounds at Parliament Hill, in Hampstead and at the Stamford Bridge grounds which are now home to Chelsea Football Club.

The London Northern Countries Camanachd Club was followed by the London Scots Shinty Club, the London Highland Athletic Club Shinty Team (1897), the London Inverness-shire Association Camanachd Club (1883), the London Ross-shire Association Camanachd Club (1884), the London Clans Shinty Club (1900), the Wimbledon and District Scots Association 1910 Shinty Team and the London Camanachd Club (1894). Only the last-named was to survive the first World War. London Camanachd lasted through until 1939, when it went into suspension and was not revived again until 1982.

Trophies were played for. In 1882 a silver cup, valued at £5 5s. 0d, was presented to London Northern Counties by Mr J.R. MacLeod. A six-a-side competition was started in 1901, administered jointly by

London Inverness-shire and London Camanachd. In 1906 Harry Lauder offered a gold medal to the winners of a 'Highlanders versus Lowlanders' clash. The first Dewar Shield, presented by Sir Thomas Dewar in 1908 for 'annual competition between Scottish Societies in London', was won by London Camanachd after a 9–1 trouncing of London Scots. Even as far into the century as 1922, London Camanachd was presented with its own trophy, for internal competition at an annual tournament, by Sir John Young.

By 1922, however, the level of interest had dropped considerably from its peak in the 1890s. On Good Friday 1893 the pitch at Wimbledon Common was lined from corner-flag to corner-flag with more than 2,000 spectators, jostling for a view of the London Scots challenging Northern Counties for a silver cup presented by Lieutenant Neil MacKay, a prominent figure in London Highland affairs of the time. Fifteen players on each side competed under one referee and two umpires, and Northern Counties, whose weekly training sessions were another innovation in the London shinty world, ran out easy winners by 4–0. The London Scots optimistically called for a rematch in May, when they were trounced 7–0.

Most of the time the clubs just played among themselves. Boxing Day came to replace New Year's Day as the annual shinty festival for young men so many miles and so many long years away from home, whose metropolitan employers often did not respect the old Scottish holiday. On 26 December 1892 both the Northern Counties and the London Scots enjoyed a game of shinty several miles apart; the former at Lambeth Palace Grounds (and later in the neighbouring Horse Shoe Hotel), and the latter on Wimbledon Common.

They attempted sporadically to attract one or another of the teams which were springing up in Scotland to take the long journey south. On a couple of occasions they succeeded. London Northern Counties, flushed with their MacKay Cup success against London Scots, issued a challenge to Glasgow Cowal after their AGM in October 1893 (an AGM which, incidentally, attracted a 'large and enthusiastic' attendance, reported a healthy bank account, and attracted fourteen new members). Cowal, who had gradually been slipping into a missionary's cloak on the Scottish shinty scene, accepted and the two sides met on Wimbledon Common on Boxing Day.

The visitors found the weather a trifle warm for their liking, but soon shook off the inconvenience and established a 7–0 lead by half-

time. The Cowal men found the exiles to be equally 'stalwart in body
and fleet of foot', but simply unwilling or unable to play a passing
game. After the tenth goal had gone in, the posts had been lifted and
the company had retired to the Horse Shoe Hotel for refreshments,
speeches and songs, the Scottish masters assured their southern
colleagues that 'the introduction of a little science' would do their
game no harm at all. The London Northern Counties, said their guests,
were certainly not lacking in pluck.

It was the last time that Cowal were invited to London. The
following Boxing Day Northern Counties satisfied themselves with
picking two sides from within their own ranks, pitting those whose
surname bore the prefix 'Mac' against those whose surname did not.
Two goals from Smith were equalised by one apiece from MacLean
and MacGillivray, but another couple in the second half from Da-
vidson brought the non-Macs through to a comfortable, but happily
narrow, victory.

A little science was undoubtedly introduced into the London game
over the years. London Camanachd picked up the standard dropped by
Northern Counties in 1897, when they persuaded the newly crowned
Scottish champions Beauly to come and beat them in London. And in
1899 the Camanachd recorded the first and only victory of a late-
Victorian London shinty team over Scottish-based opponents, when
Edinburgh Camanachd went down by 7–5 on Muswell Hill. After that,
London Camanachd had to travel north for their scientific education, a
task which they undertook with some pride and no little amount of
success. In 1907 and 1909 they lost by just 3–2 and 5–3 to Newtonmore
in Badenoch. On the former occasion Newtonmore were Camanachd
Cup losing finalists. On the latter, the Badenoch men were in the
middle of their first astonishing cycle of primacy, when they dominated the Scottish scene and the Camanachd Cup for four successive
years. London did well to come away with a cheerful, relieved smile.

The men behind shinty in London at this time would not have made
the ranks of Glengarry's Gaels. They were a different, increasingly
common, variety of Highland export. The captain of London Scots
during their games for the MacKay Cup with Northern Counties was a
thick-set, impressively moustachioed New Scotland Yard police in-
spector called Duncan MacIntyre, who had been born in Bunessan,
Mull, and raised in Bowmore, Islay. He divided his leisure time
between the shinty, the Gaelic Society of London and the London

*Duncan MacIntyre, the islander who became captain of the
London Scots Shinty Club.*

Argyllshire Association. The club's secretary was Alec Fraser, a
Helmsdale man who had travelled from Sutherland to find work
as a draper in Glasgow, Middlesbrough and Manchester before
establishing a successful merchant tailoring business in Fleet Street.
Fraser was a keen Highland dancer, a member of the committee of
the Highland Ball of London and a volunteer in the London Scottish
rifle brigade.

Alec Fraser, the Helmsdale tailor, secretary of London Scots.

The captain of Northern Counties, William MacGregor Stoddart, was of a Renfrew and Perthshire family, currently enjoying employment as headmaster at St Stephen's School in Paddington. He was fond of explaining his descent on his mother's side from Rob Roy Mac-Gregor. One of his team-mates, William Martin, was a Stornoway man, a product of the Free Church School and the Nicolson Institute who had graduated at Kings College London, before enlisting on the trading routes of the Empire with the British India Steam Navigation Company and later the New Zealand Shipping Company.

They were, in short, the exiled professional classes of the Scottish Gaidhealtachd. What they were no longer able to organise at home, they organised abroad: a state of affairs which brought at least as much benefit to the game of shinty as it brought to the Metropolitan Police or to the British India Steam Navigation Company.

In 1905 the London *Morning Post* had its attention drawn to the Boxing Day festivities on Wimbledon Common. A journalist was sent to the scene, and he filed his report in the following morning's newspaper. 'There was a skirl of the bagpipes', he wrote, with the Victorian froth that survived in the pens of writers on Hielan' affairs well into the twentieth century,

> . . . with a 'Hooch!' and 'Hooray!' and a rushing to and fro of big, brawny men armed with formidable sticks. The Sassenach paused in his passage across the familiar heath to gaze on the scene, which might well have suggested some wild and lawless pursuit. In reality it was only the game of shinty as it has been displayed every Boxing Day on Wimbledon Common for more than a quarter of a century by Scotsmen in London.

The froth subsiding and an earnest attempt to explain the origins of the game dispensed ('It was played . . . by the primeval Celts in the Stone Age with sticks cut from the nearest oak and smooth stones that made musical rattle against the virgin timber . . . It has been suggested that the name shinty derives its origin from shins. It would probably be equally near to the mark to suggest that it springs from Shintoism.'), our correspondent got down to an account of what the London Camanachd Club was up to on Wimbledon Common.

They had been brought together by a genial 62-year-old, who stood out on the field of play by virtue of his ample beard, unruly shock of snow-white hair, Glengarry bonnet and an artful, experienced use of the caman. This was James Watson, the man who thirty-two years earlier had joined with the lads of the Highland Camanachd Club of London in one of their early matches on the common, and whose ability with the caman had led them to identify him as a player with Scottish experience.

William MacGregor Stoddart, descendant of Rob Roy and captain of the London Northern Counties team which Glasgow Cowal advised to introduce 'a little science to their game'.

Watson was not the only survivor to be there that day. Ewen Cattanach, the first vice-captain of the Highland Club, who had served with Archibald MacRa Chisholm on the committee formed to help *The Highlander* in 1878, brought along his caman to Wimbledon Common on the Boxing Day of 1905. Cattanach had left for South America in 1895 but had recently returned to Britain where, with others, he helped establish the Crofters' Association.

Watson picked one side and William Grant, lately of Glenurquhart and now president of the London Camanachd, picked the other. Hundreds of spectators watched under a wintry sun, frequently crowding over onto the field of play, as the *Morning Post* reporter noted that 'the centre scrummages were wonderfully exciting, and whenever the opponents met in these strenuous encounters there was a clashing and clatter and rattle of sticks which might well have made a nervous man apprehensive of results . . . but the casualties were few and trivial, and the only medicine administered to the players in a perspiring interval was just a "wee drappie" . . .'.

William Grant's select defeated James Watson's by 7–1. At the close, Watson raised three cheers for Grant and his victorious team, commenting ruefully that it was the first time he'd suffered defeat on Wimbledon Common for thirty years. Grant laughed, and praised Watson as the author and mainspring of the meeting. The players on both sides, he added, were of Watson's own choosing. Whisky was passed around, the pipes played and reels danced.

In 1913, when he was seventy years old, James Watson was still gracing Wimbledon Common. On Easter Friday he organised a team of veterans, the 'Old Comrades', to take on the 'All-Comers'. After an hour's play a storm caused the game to be abandoned while Watson's comrades were leading 2–1 and forcing a series of corner hits. The teams and their friends adjourned to the Railway Hotel, where Watson congratulated the All-Comers on their enthusiasm before revealing that one of his own side was an octogenarian. That Boxing Day, Watson's team was defeated 7–6, and the post-match gathering at the Fox and Hounds was told by Graham Horton-Smith, chief of the London Clans' Association, of the old man's energy and zeal in 'keeping the shinty flag flying for many years in the Metropolis'.

The weather was splendid over Wimbledon Common at Easter 1914, as it seemed always to be in the spring before a war. A record crowd saw James Watson celebrate his fortieth year of wielding a

caman on the common grounds of London by helping his fifteen to
beat a select captained by Roderick MacLeod. The teams were
accompanied to the Fox and Hounds on this occasion by more than
a hundred friends. An evening of Gaelic song was concluded by 'For
He's A Jolly Good Fellow', and James Watson responded by remind-
ing the company of the Dewar Shield match to be played on Whit
Monday.

London Camanachd won the Shield that year, beating the Wimbledon and District Scots Association (1910) by 2–0. Two months later
the heir to the Hapsburg thrones was assassinated in Sarajevo. Fledgling shinty clubs the length of Britain were disbanded and dispersed.
Many of them never re-formed. James Watson had played his last
match on Wimbledon Common: the golden age of London shinty,
which he had seen through its youth and its maturity, was at an end.
From Putney to Poolewe, younger men than Watson laid aside their
camain in order to be taught an altogether deadlier range of skills, and
too many of them never returned to hit a ball in anger again.

In the winter of 1847 a battalion of the Royal Canadian Rifles, an
Imperial unit which contained – as most did – a good proportion of
Highland Scots, was stationed at Kingston in Canada, where the St
Lawrence River flows past a thousand islands into Lake Ontario. In the
frozen landscape, the outdoor pursuits of these bored troops were
inevitably connected with the ice.

When, one day in that winter, a group of about a hundred soldiers
strapped crude metal runners on to a wooden base which they attached
to their boots, placed two sets of boulders several hundred yards apart
on the thick inshore ice of the St Lawrence, took up long curved sticks,
divided into two teams of fifty, and began to knock a piece of solid
rubber about between themselves on the ice, they were doing no more
than enjoying a game which their predecessors in the Kingston
garrison had been playing since at least 1783. They were playing
shinty on ice.

In Scotland, this activity was nothing new, as a literate observer
standing by the Firth of Forth in 1607 had noted. Nor did the practice
die quickly in this country, even when the game on land flourished and
became organised. In January 1879 the ice on Loch Fyne between the
New Bridge and Inveraray Pier was so thick – between three and four
inches – that a New Year's game took place upon it. But in Scotland, it

William Martin, the Stornoway-born servant of the shipping companies of the Empire, and star of London Northern Counties Chinty Club.

did not develop into an international sport, and a national obsession, called ice-hockey. In Canada, it did. Those hundred soldiers innocently disporting themselves on the frozen St Lawrence River in 1847 were observed by an assiduous diarist named Horsey. 'Most of the soldier boys', observed Horsey, 'were quite at home on skates. They could cut the figure eight and other fancy figures, but shinny was their first delight. Groups would be placed at the Shoal Tower and Point Frederick, and fifty or more players on each side would be in the game.'

The regional bickering over which area, or town, in the country was responsible for introducing ice-hockey to Canada (and, therefore, to the world) had grown so clamorous by 1941 that the Amateur Hockey Association of Canada appointed a committee to determine its origin and settle the argument. The committee found itself able to start work with just one shared view: 'that the rules of ice-hockey had evolved from those used in a similar game known as "shinny", "shanty", "hurling", or "hurtling" '. Eventually Horsey's diary, along with other subsidiary and circumstantial evidence, was accepted by the committee as conclusive, the committee's opinion was favoured by the Association and a Hockey Hall of Fame was built at Kingston, in acknowledgement of its position as the *alma mater* of ice hockey.

But the argument did not die and there is no good reason why it should. Scottish emigrants had settled in other parts of Canada well before 1847. A Londoner who visited the Highlands in the 1780s, John Knox, reported that between 1763 and 1775 some 20,000 Highlanders left for the colonies in what have become known as the 'voluntary' emigrations, as opposed to the forced clearances – as if opting to leave a homeland which was spiritually, morally and fiscally impoverished in favour of a fresh start in what was advertised to be a brave and luxuriant New World could be distinguished by being called a 'voluntary' action.

The 200 people of Ross who left Ullapool for Nova Scotia in July 1773 on board a rotten hulk named the *Hector* were typical of this first wave of Highland emigration. When those that survived the voyage arrived in Nova Scotia in October they found, of course, no promised land, but an unbroken hostile wilderness in the early stages of a winter far longer and infinitely more severe than that of the western seaboard of the Highlands of Scotland.

Some news of their plight, of the fact that by the following spring only 78 of the original 200 were still alive, trickled home; but it was not enough to dissuade those left behind. It has been estimated that between 1801 and 1804, 10,000 Highlanders sailed for Canada. In 1801 alone, eleven ships left Fort William for Nova Scotia, with a cargo of 3,300 emigrants.

Canada was settled by Highlanders. Their influence on the country was immense. The first two prime ministers of the new nation were Gaelic speakers. The settlers took with them their language, their customs, their music and, naturally, their games.

Shinty was played in Canada in the more usual fashion – on dry land – from the earliest years. In Antigonish, which was heavily settled by Chisholms from Strathglass, Christmas and New Year was celebrated in the usual manner. Down in Kingston a 'Camac Club' was formed in 1840, following a New Year's Day game the previous year. The *Kingston Chronicle and Gazette* reported at the time that in January 1843, 'a shinty match took place between Scots men born in the counties of Argyle [*sic*] and Ross, which lasted three hours'. On the shores of Lake Erie, just across the border from Detroit, the *Chatham Gleaner* reported in 1848 that the sons of 'Old Scotia' played several games of shinty on Christmas Day 'with great gusto'.

And the game, more or less in its traditional form, survived well into the twentieth century. In July 1893, the sobriquet 'Sgian Dubh' wrote from Toronto to the *Celtic Monthly* in Glasgow that 'the warmth of summer sunshine is not sufficient to keep the Canadian Highlander off the field of sport . . . The arena is changed from the platform and hall to the green sward, where the bagpipes are heard cheering on the shinty players . . .'. Among the other, more celebrated, activities, wrote 'Sgian Dubh', such as putting the stone, tossing the caber, sprinting, vaulting, jumping and the tug-of-war, 'a game of shinty is always popular'.

As the generations passed, the practitioners of the game naturally lost touch with the changes in style and rules of play, even of names, which shinty developed on the other side of the Atlantic. A Cape Bretoner by the name of Archie MacKenzie, who grew up before and during the First World War in the Christmas Island district, was asked in December 1988 by Professor Norman MacDonald, then of the University College of Cape Breton, if he remembered anything of the game of shinty in his youth. 'He protested strongly', writes Professor MacDonald, 'that no such game was played in rural Cape Breton but that, as children, he and his friends played "camag". The "camag" was the crooked branch of a tree which was then used to play with a stirk's dung (it being the appropriate size and shape) on the ice.'

To this day the names, the unconscious references to source, still apply to what Canadians will think of as *ad hoc* games of ice-hockey. Dr

Richard MacKinnon, who teaches folklore at the Cape Breton college, recalls:

> When growing up in New Waterford in the 1960s we didn't have indoor rinks, we played on outdoor parks where it was very common to go as individuals, and what was played was known as "shinny-hockey". It wasn't organised beforehand, but usually eight or ten people would turn up. The goals would be boots or lumps of snow, but most would have an old hockey stick and we'd find a hockey puck.

Shinny-hockey was, nevertheless, distinguishable from ice-hockey, says Dr MacKinnon:

> Ice-hockey was something different, it was more organised. People would travel to Sydney or Glace Bay to play ice-hockey because there were links there. And shinny did not require gear, no shin pads, although some guys would put a catalogue in their pants!, no helmets, and the distance between the two goals depended upon how many were playing.
>
> It was not always called shinny-hockey, sometimes shinny, some-times shinty. My father told me that they played shinny with frozen dung instead of a puck. I'm not sure if they do it so much now, as the place is full of organised ice-hockey leagues. But shinny, you'll still find it on Lingan Bay, when the bay freezes over, and most still refer to it as shinny.

A large number of Canadians would suffer severely if they were no longer able to argue the origins or the birthplace of ice-hockey. The debate is a national forum and there is certainly no good reason for an advocate of Scottish shinty to enter it, particularly as shinty is already acknowledged by most historians of ice-hockey, albeit cursorily, as the mother of their game – with hurling as an occasional stepfather.

The facts appear to be that 'Sgian Dubh', when telling of the game of shinty on the lush fields of a Canadian summer, was describing the exception rather than the rule. Shinty in Scotland was a traditional winter game, invariably played at the turn of the year. It was simply impractical during this season in North America to play any sport on the snow-laden open ground and so the immigrants turned, as they had often done in Scotland, to the plentiful frozen lakes and bays.

They did not immediately turn into amply-padded speed-skaters. 'Shinny was, at first, a kind of field hockey played on the ice, but without skates,' wrote Sandy Young, a Nova Scotian sports historian, in 1988:

> In early shinny games some participants would be skating and some not. The truth is that since hockey sticks really did grow on trees, anyone who took the time to tear down a branch would feel free to swat at the ball any time it was within striking distance.
>
> At times, hundreds of participants would be involved and more often than not, few knew or cared which goal they were aiming for. Before the invention of rubber, the puck could be the knot of a tree, or a knucklebone from a large animal.
>
> The goal was simply rocks, usually about the size of curling stones, placed about four to six feet apart. To score, the puck had to be down on the ice and go between the two markers from in front. The goals were sometimes one hundred yards apart. A ball eventually replaced the other 'puck' items and did not itself evolve until someone discovered that it worked better if it was cut in half. Then someone else cut off two opposite ends of a ball which left the flat round puck now in use.

It is also possible that the 'flat round puck now in use' owes its origin to the flat round cork net float which was often used in Scottish village games of shinty.

In colonial Canada shinty on ice had to share its name with the stick sports of other nations. Although 'ricket', or 'wicket' as the game was known in some areas, seems to be stretching the point, hurling, bandy and the eventually paramount 'hoquet' or hockey were understandable and reasonable enough. One of the first ice games with a real claim to being properly organised and played according to rules took place in Montreal in February 1837 between two sides of eight. The surnames of the 'Uptown' team were tellingly Caledonian: Mitchell, Bannerman, McCulloch, Fairbairn, Campbell, Melson, Ross and MacDonald. An Irishman, Michael Knox, had arranged the fixture and drawn up the basic rules in the company of a few Gleasons, Stapletons and Glennons, and they christened the game 'ice hurley'.

'Ice hurley' stuck for a while. When the *Arcadian Recorder* of Halifax – that most Scottish of settlements – printed a complaint about Sabbath desecration in January, 1853, it reported:

The streets of Halifax on Sundays at the usual hours for worship are generally thronged with old and young, on their way to their respective Churches and Chapels, thus giving the appearance to all events of reverence for the day of God.

Not so was it in the vicinity of the Town on Sunday last. The Lake above Mr Hosterman's was literally covered with skaters, with their hurlies, and the small spots of ice available on the N.W. Arm were similarly occupied, to the great peril of those upon it . . .

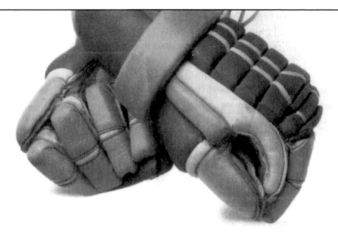

The equipment and the playing surface may have changed, but the old name lingers on . . . this advertisement appeared in the Canadian Hockey News *in December 1988.*

A later article in the *Arcadian Recorder* suggested that the dangers of fast ball games on the ice extended beyond Sabbath-breaking. They were 'not only annoying but dangerous' and 'ought to be sternly forbidden'. By 1869 the youth of Halifax had to contend with a man who they nicknamed 'The Dragon', whose paid function was to keep them and their camain off Griffin's Pond.

But boys will be boys, and if the *Arcadian Recorder* disapproved, they found a friend in the other Halifax journal, *The British Colonist,* which applauded their 'energy, skill and daring . . . when, skates strapped on and hurly in hand, the ball is followed over the glassy surface of the lakes, which ring to the skaters' heel'. The same newspaper offered, in November 1859, a detailed description of shinty on ice – or 'ricket' – in Nova Scotia in the middle of the nineteenth century. Two rickets, or goals, were 'formed at about the same distance, one from the other, that cricketers place their wickets'.

If there are many players the rickets are further apart. A ricket consists of two stones – about as large as the cobble stones with which some of our streets have been lately paved – placed about three or four feet apart and frozen to the ice.

Sides are then formed by two persons – one opposed to the other – tossing or drawing lots for first choice of partners. The one who obtains the first choice selects one from the crowd, the other party then chooses another, and so on alternately, until a sufficient number is obtained on each side. Any number can play the game, and generally, the 'more the merrier'.

Each ricketer is provided with a hurley and all being ready, a ball is thrown in the air, which is the signal to commence play . . . The game may be 10, 15, or 20, or any number agreed upon, the side counting the number first being winners. The counting consists in putting the ball through your adversary's ricket, each time counting one. From the moment the ball touches the ice, at the commencement of the game; it must not be taken in the hand until the conclusion, but must be carried or struck about the ice with the hurlies.

A good player . . . will take the ball at the point of his hurley and carry it around the pond and through the crowd which surrounds him trying to take it from him; until he works it near his opponents' ricket, and then comes the tug of war, both sides striving for the

mastery. Whenever the ball is put through the ricket a shout 'game
ho!' resounds from shore to shore and dies away in hundreds of
echoes through the hills. Ricket is the most exciting game that is
played on the ice . . .

In the 1930s, when the argument over the origins and birthplace of ice-
hockey in Canada was reaching new heights of stridency, a man named
W.L. 'Chick' Murray entered the ring and lodged an impressive claim
to have drawn up the first-ever rules of the game himself, while a
student at McGill University, Montreal, in the winter of 1879.
Murray's claim was, and is, given much credence: he was acknowledged as ice-hockey's first legislator by Frank Mencke, the editor of
the *All Sports Record Book*, a definitive North American work of
reference. But when he drew up his rules on 10 November 1879 –
'with very few changes, the rules which are used today' – Chick
Murray did not call the new sport ice-hockey. He called it 'Shinny on
your Own Side'. He explained later:

> As a small boy I played 'shinny' on the ice opposite the city of
> Montreal from November to early January. After that time the
> snows made it impossible to skate on the river.
>   To play 'shinny' one had to have a good stick – no umbrella
> handle, or any stick that was cross- grained, would do. So, early in
> the Fall, the boys who contemplated playing later on, would go to
> the mountains and hunt for small maple trees which had roots which,
> when trimmed and dried, made ideal sticks with which to play the
> game.
>   'Shinny' at the time was a boys' game, the players ranging in age
> from eleven to sixteen years. There was one infallible rule in shinny
> – only one. It was never to hit the puck left-handed, the puck being a
> small block of wood, or a battered tin can, or any similar object that
> could be batted along the ice. If you did so, the rule was for the
> person nearest you, unless he was a close personal friend, to say
> 'shinny on your own side', and then to give you a sharp crack on the
> shins with his stick.

That is how close the game of ice-hockey came to bearing another
name, more familiar to the Gaels who created it. Murray's claim went
unrecognised by the sub-committee of the Amateur Hockey Associa-

tion of Canada, which had been established to identify the origins of their game. They came down in favour of the colonial troops stationed at Kingston. Nobody was present to put forward a claim on behalf of the ice between the New Bridge and Inveraray Pier on Loch Fyne.

It does not matter to shinty. Its place is secure, not least as the root of the North American terms 'shindig' and 'shindy' – which signify a 'noisy quarrel, row, brawl, or disturbance'. The Irish can claim 'hurly-burly'. As Frank Mencke himself pointed out in 1948: 'If "shinny" is the parent game, then Kingston has no claim to originating either "shinny" or hockey, for the reason that "shinny" was played in Scotland many generations before Kingston was a trading post.'

Or as a Professor Orlick put it, in a bitter criticism of the Amateur Hockey Association's finding which was published in the *Montreal Gazette* in September 1943: 'The question is not when the games of field hockey, hoquet, hurley or shinny started, but rather, when and where did hurley or shinny develop into the game of Ice Hockey as we know it today?'

5

On Common Ground

'He must be sturdy, steady, temperate, and cool.'

If by the late 1870s and early 1880s, the game had accidentally gone into a lopsided formation flight, with different rules and legislation being drawn up for its different codes around the western world, it was important for shinty that the pilots in London, Dublin and Montreal remained outriders. Hurling and ice-hockey could take care of themselves, and London was no place from which to lead a Scottish sport. Fortunately, by that time there were people in Scotland ready to assume responsibility for their game.

Shinty may never have been stronger before than it was in the last three decades of the nineteenth century. In the Highlands and in the Lowlands, old teams consolidated and new sides were born by the month. The Lowlands had their own shinty tradition, which extended to the Borders and even into the north of England. The game was played in Cumberland up until the First World War under the names of shinny, scabskew, cabsha and catty. Cumbrians even devoted to shinty one of the pithy, rhyming folk-*haikus* of which they were enormously fond and which were usually reserved for their chief object of philosophical concern: the weather. According to A.C. Gibson's *The Folk Speech of Cumberland*, a common truism on the hills overlooking the Irish Sea was: 'Shinny's weel aneuf if shins were safe.'

In Galashiels, the game of shinty had been known before the oval ball and the rugby union code were thought of. When Robert Chalmers visited Roxburghshire in the 1820s, as part of his under-taking to present a comprehensive *Picture Of Scotland* to his hero, Sir Walter Scott, he was told that 'the Golden Age of the Barony' had gone. Within living memory, the people of Galashiels assured Chalmers, 'every man lived by his mailen, or by his individual exertions as a weaver, laid in his meat and his meal at Martinmas, and then had nothing to do but look forward to a long winter of festive amusement':

> When the stores had all been secured, a bell rung on a particular day, and 'the haill town' assembled in front of their bailie's door. Headed by that important personage, and joined by the minister (thus having both law and religion upon their side), they adjourned to a field in the neighbourhood, and spent the greater part of that day in a social match at that most spirit-stirring and delightful of all games – the shintie.
>
> Their mode of choosing, or rather forming *sides*, was very singular. Hab and Jock, Tom and Andrew, Adam and Dan, played against all the other names in the town. On this account, the festival was usually called 'the day o' the Hab-and-Jock Ba'. When frost or snow prevented a game at shintie, the bailie's bell as regularly sounded the happy villagers to assemble on the Pond of 'the Place', to enjoy the sport of curling. On these occasions, as at the shintie, there prevailed the most obstreperous mirth and the utmost harmony; and always, at twelve o'clock, a mess of nowt's feet brose was brought out from the Manse, sufficient to feast and enliven the whole 'Rink'. Alas! those gala days of Galashiels are gone, never to return.

So was the sport of shinty gone, not just from Galashiels, but from most of the other provincial burghs of Lowland Scotland. Only in Glasgow and Edinburgh, with their constant incoming stream of expatriate Highlanders ready and willing to boost the morale and the numbers of the cities' shinty players, did the game not just survive, but blossom.

Edinburgh Camanachd laid claim to being the oldest constitutionalised shinty club in the world. They were not. If any club can make that claim it is, as we shall see, Aberdeen University. Even if Edinburgh were to skip a point and suggest that they were the first *independently* organised club side, that would not, in the full context of the history of the game, mean that they originated organised shinty in Scotland. Kingussie had met a team from Banchory on the first Monday of the Old New Year in 1823, in a field at Ballchroan. (The game, which took place between two sides of equal numbers, was refereed by Captain MacDonald, RVB, and ended in a draw. Captain Gillies MacPherson provided a post-match repast, and his health, as 'the descendant of the celebrated translator of Ossian', was drunk.)

William Murray of Latheron, Caithness, who became a wine merchant in Stockbridge and a founder member of the oldest Lowland shinty club, Edinburgh Camanachd.

Teams from Inveraray, under the captaincy of Lord Archibald Campbell, had been meeting such local opposition as the Land of Ardkinglass Shinty Team since at least 1865. As surely as there were boys in Inverness getting up the noses of the town's authorities by playing shinty in the streets, there were identifiable shinty teams in Scotland before the winter of 1869–70, when Edinburgh Camanachd was formed.

But when 150 ladies and gentlemen gathered in Grindlay Street Hall on Friday, 22 April 1895 to celebrate the 25th birthday of Edinburgh Camanachd, they were honouring the crucial watershed when native shinty players and their peers began to organise their game for themselves, to shape its direction with their own hands through democratically elected, popularly accountable committees and appointees. From those days onwards, patronage existed in word alone, as a nominal, honorary term of office.

When Patrick Cameron of Corriechoille, the chieftain of Edinburgh Camanachd, rose on that Friday night in 1895 to celebrate the first quarter-century of his club by paying due tribute to the days of yore, he spoke of shinty's quite recent past as if it were the stuff of legend and fairytale. He asked the assembly to marvel that in 1603 a feud between two opposing septs of an Appin clan had been resolved through a game of camanachd. He told of David, Earl of Orkney, vying for supremacy with the caman with the Earl of Sutherland in 1604. He remembered the roguish Ronald Roy of Nigg, and the Provost of Inveraray who in 1793 captained a shinty team in his 101st year – and won the game. Patrick Cameron spoke of days which had gone, as Norman MacLeod might have put it, as if in a dream. He was standing securely in the modern world and gently wondering at the past. The movement of the Lowland teams away from the form and the traditions of the patronised game of the last quarter of the eighteenth century and the first three-quarters of the nineteenth was stealthy and not too apparent to those participating, let alone to the casual spectator. But it was real enough.

In January 1874, eleven years before his death from a bronchitic attack brought on by that touchingly ill-advised visit to his tenants' annual game, Cluny MacPherson watched benevolently over the New Year's Day contest on his Inverness-shire estate. His was already a dying breed: the Gaelic-speaking Highland laird of antique pedigree and a military reputation which – even as he stood that day in 1874 on the park below Cluny Castle watching two sides captained by John

'Garbh' MacDonald and Charles Og MacPherson, both of Crathy, fight out a scoreless draw – his son, a Major in the 42nd Highlanders, was preparing to perpetuate by being shot through the leg while leading a charge against Ashantees on the Gold Coast of Africa. These were the Victorian lairds. Their offspring distinguished themselves not in cattle raids or in bloodcurling rampage down the steep cliff walls of Killiecrankie, but in the service of Queen and Empire on tropical shores; while they, surrounded by their remaining family and with their pipers in the van, strode religiously forth on the day of the Old New Year to bless the people at play.

That year, further south, Edinburgh Camanachd held its New Year's game on 1 January, twelve days earlier than at Cluny Castle. They met in Queen's Park before a large and boisterous crowd on a blustery, inauspicious day. Two senior members grasped the caman, hand over hand, until one was left holding it and made first choice of players. He picked the young Pat Cameron of Corriechoille. The opposing captain opted for Cameron's brother, George, and then the selection proceeded briskly – Sandy MacDonald from Skye, a Cattanach from Badenoch, big Sandy Cameron from Dochanassie in Sutherland, a MacNicol, a MacLeod . . . until two sets of kilted men stood divided by the wearing of blue or red rosettes. George Cameron, wearing a blue rosette, scored the first and only goal of a lengthy contest against his brother's team, the efforts of the 'Reds' to snatch an equaliser before the death being frequently obstructed by excited spectators spilling on to the pitch and even occasionally helping the ball in a favoured direction with walking sticks or umbrella handles. At Cluny Castle, the game ended with whisky, bread and cheese being served by the old laird's domestics. In the Queen's Park, the treasurer of Edinburgh Camanachd supplied the post-match nourishment out of club funds. In both places it was the same game of camanachd – but only just.

During its first few years of existence Edinburgh Camanachd found similarly well-organised opposition hard to come by. In 1872 they met with a scratch team from the 93rd Sutherland Highlanders on New Year's Day, but not until 1876 did worthy opponents present themselves, from the city on the Clyde.

Glasgow Cowal shinty club grew on fertile ground. Far more than Edinburgh, Glasgow was the city of the Gael. Exiles from the northwest Highlands and Islands flocked there during the nineteenth century, fleeing to a metropolis which might not have offered as clean a break as did the tempting shores of Nova Scotia, but at least suggested freedom from the threat of eviction and hunger.

Shinty was a common sight in the public parks of Glasgow. In 1876, the year of Glasgow Cowal's inauguration, the Skye poet Mary MacPherson, Màiri Mhór nan Oran, herself exiled temporarily to the city, wrote in prose and verse of a New Year's game held in Glasgow's Queen's Park. On the eve of the match she wrote to a friend in Bernisdale, Skye:

> . . . were I as wealthy as I am poor I would give a pound sterling to have you where I am tonight, in the Highlanders Great Hall in Glasgow; my sleeves rolled up to my shoulders, blinded with perspiration as I prepare and bake bannocks for the Hogmanay lads; the President of the place is seated surrounded by three score shinty sticks, getting them ready for tomorrow.
>
> I'll tell you about the shinty when its over. It will remind you of the days of our youth, when the people of Skeabost and Carbost used to be on the great green by the stream, with a bottle at each end of the field, with plenty bannocks and cheese. We go tomorrow to Queen's Park – three score strong Highland lads; thirty in the kilt, and thirty in knickerbockers, with their sticks on their shoulders, pipers before and after them, and I with a horse and cart full of creels of bannocks, kebbocks of cheese as big as the moon, and a drop of Ferintosh to put spirit in the lads.

Màiri Mhór kept her word to tell of the shinty when it was over, in a Gaelic poem entitled *Camanachd Ghlaschu.*

While the exiled Highland songstress was up to her elbows in flour, preparing sustenance for the boys in the following day's fray, moves were already under way to establish a constitutionalised shinty team in Glasgow. It is retrospectively unsurprising that one of the new club's brightest early lights was a young man from the village of Tighnab-ruaich on the Kyles of Bute.

Alexander MacKellar was a shrewd, imposing figure. As a young man he achieved remarkable all-round athletic success. In 1893 it was estimated that the value of silver plate in his personal trophy cabinet amounted to £100. But Mackellar's great love was the game of shinty. In 1876, when the Cowal club was formed, MacKellar's careful sporting intelligence was given free rein: he was made its first captain.

He refused to regard the position as being merely honorary. In hard, regular training sessions he induced his players to abandon – or at least to moderate – their natural, traditional, headstrong style of direct running play in favour of a low, fast passing game. He taught them not to be afraid of releasing the ball early, even of releasing it immediately. He told them to play it sideways, or, unthinkably, backwards into defence, if this would buy time, space and possession. MacKellar's tactics became feared, admired and known by opponents as the 'scientific principles' which in 1894 were still new and baffling to the hitherto untested players of London Northern Counties Camanachd Club. Teams in Scotland had begun to catch on before 1894 – they had to. Alex MacKellar's Glasgow Cowal side was unbeaten for four full years after its inauguration. MacKellar must be regarded as the modern game's first serious tactician and coach. As well as team-play, the use of space and the quick interpassing game, he is credited with introducing the more controllable, less deadly, leather ball to replace the old one of hard, seasoned wood – the leather ball was, of course, considerably better suited to the style of play employed by Alexander MacKellar and the Glasgow Cowal shinty team.

After Cowal and Edinburgh, other teams were not slow to meet, formalise a constitution, elect office-bearers and issue challenges on the common playing grounds of the south of Scotland. Some, such as Cowal, Glasgow Inveraray and Glasgow Skye, selected their club's name as well as their players from a shared bond of birthplace or parentage. Others, such as Ossian and the Fingalians, were inspired by bardic fancy. Some teams were born out of a fascinating mongrel mix. The first decade of organised association football in Scotland was dominated by Vale of Leven, who lifted the Scottish Cup at Hampden Park for three successive years between 1877 and 1879, in the face of Rangers (twice) and Third Lanark, and who were beaten finalists in the three years between 1883 and 1885. The team of Renton were almost as feared in the emerging soccer world, going down 3–0 in the 1875 final, but lifting the Scottish Cup ten years later. Throughout this period both Vale of Leven and Renton doubled as shinty and soccer teams; their players divided their time equally and, with almost equal measures of success, between the two sports.

In the wake of so much committee-forming, a governing body and a competition open to all became essential to shinty in the south. Inevitably, a Highland society had a hand in bringing these things to pass. The Glasgow Celtic Society had been formed in 1856 with the expressed purpose, common to such associations, of 'preserving and promoting the language, literature, music, poetry, antiquities and athletic games of the Highlanders'. Throughout the rest of the nineteenth century the Celtic Society rose diligently and effectively to its task. Poverty relief money was distributed in the Highlands, Gaels were given the wherewithal to return from the disappointing city to their family crofts, bursaries were offered to Gaelic-speaking students and to teachers of Gaelic, and capital was invested in the foundation of the Chair of Celtic at Edinburgh University. It is not surprising that when shinty came to be organised in their adopted town, the members of the Glasgow Celtic Society should have cocked an ear and expressed an interest.

The shinty association in the south was given first breath by the newly organised clubs themselves. In the late summer of 1877 George Cameron, who had progressed from scoring goals against his brother's select in New Year's Day matches to become the chieftain of Edinburgh Camanachd, travelled to Glasgow to chair a meeting of representatives from southern clubs. Vale of Leven were there, as were Fingal, Ossian, Glasgow Inveraray, Glasgow Camanachd and Cowal. Rules of play and the constitution of a proposed association were discussed at such length that late into the night the meeting had to be suspended and reconvened a month later.

At this second gathering, in September 1877, agreement was reached. A draft set of proposed rules was drawn up and forwarded to each shinty club in the south of Scotland, along with an invitation to send along two authorised representatives to a final meeting in Whyte's Temperance Hotel, Candleriggs, on 13 October 1877. Here, the first shinty association in Scotland was formed. Captain James Menzies, a colleague of Alex MacKellar in the Glasgow Highland Regiment, was elected president; a Mr M. Leitch of Glasgow Inveraray became secretary; and MacKellar himself was appointed treasurer. The first item of their constitution decreed that they should be called 'the Shinty Association'. Their committee consisted of two representatives from each club, and the clubs, who were asked to pay a ten shilling subscription, were entitled to three votes each at the Annual General Meeting.

Their rules of play were not the first to be agreed upon by a committee and written down in Scotland. That accolade, again, must

Alexander MacKellar, the Tighnabruaich man who became captain of the all-conquering Glasgow Cowal team, and modern shinty's first great tactician.

go if anywhere to Aberdeen University. But they were the first to be widely circulated, anywhere. They were written down before the Gaelic Athletic Association standardised the game of hurling in Ireland, before 'Chick' Murray laid the ground-plan for shinny, or ice-hockey, in Montreal and long before hockey in England had any distinct identity.

They were ten in number – George Cameron had pleaded at some length for simplicity of legislation. They read:

  I)   Two goal posts five yards apart shall be erected at each end of the field.
 II)   At the commencement of play and after each goal the ball shall be thrown up in midfield by the umpire. Sides to be changed after each goal.
III)   When the ball passes the touch line it shall be taken ten yards inside and thrown up between the player in possession and his opponent, opposite where it crossed the line.
 IV)   No one shall be allowed to lift, throw or kick the ball during play.
  V)   The ball to be used shall consist of cork, covered with worsted and then with or without a covering of leather.
 VI)   When the ball passes the goalposts, by whomsoever it is struck, the ball shall be taken ten yards inside and thrown up by the umpire opposite where it passed through.
VII)   That in the event of a player getting disabled his opponent at commencement of play retires.
VIII) No one shall be allowed to push, trip, catch or charge.
 IX)   Should no goal be taken before half-time, sides shall be changed and the ball thrown up in midfield by the umpire.
  X)   Profane language strictly prohibited.

These modest rulings represented, after so much debate, a nice compromise between tradition and the urge to bring the game into modern conformity. It was assumed that the numbers on each side would be agreed beforehand – although most southern teams had by 1877 adopted the rugby union code of fifteen players per team. MacKellar's arguments for a softer, leather-bound ball were only accepted in part. The gentlemanly notion of a player voluntarily leaving the field with his disabled opponent – an interesting early variation of the substitute principle – was enshrined in print.

Hugh MacCorquodale from Furnace, Argyllshire, was for more than a decade in the 1880s and '90s a formidable, high-scoring forward in Alex Mackellar's Glasgow Cowal side.

The rules of play were carefully designed to confuse and annoy as few people as possible. They could not, of course, annoy *nobody*. Complaints were voiced about the size of the annual subscription. The tenth rule, forbidding swearing, was, claimed some, quite uncalled for. A gentleman 'who has played shinty in Inverness-shire and other counties for 25 years and upwards' protested to the press that rule four should never have been passed, that 'lifting' was occasionally indispensable and that kicking was 'unavoidable when there is little room to work your club'.

But the teams which had helped to form the Shinty Association and its rules took a fresh impetus from their new organisation. Annual general meetings abounded. Fundraising Gaelic concerts and dances filled the halls of Glasgow and Edinburgh. Some acquired a playing field of their own, such as Glasgow Camanachd, who established themselves at Vermont Park in Kinning Park and then promptly offered their ground to the other sides, such as Glasgow Inveraray who, with Alex MacKellar guesting, overcame Fingal by 8–0 during a properly ordered contest in that winter of 1877.

Within twelve months the Glasgow Celtic Society had offered to the southern clubs a new trophy for which they could all compete, under the rules of the Shinty Association. The oldest 'open' shinty competition in Scotland was won for the first time by Alexander MacKellar's Glasgow Cowal on 26 April 1879, when they put Renton to the sword by 6–0 to take home the Celtic Society Challenge Cup. Renton never did get revenge on the shinty field – they were knocked out of the following year's competition on their home ground by Cowal. They had to wait until the 1885 Scottish soccer Cup Final when they beat Vale of Leven 3–1 at Hampden Park, for a taste of success. That taste must have been doubly sweet: Vale of Leven had overcome Cowal to win the Celtic Society Cup in 1880, its second year.

Captain Archibald MacRa Chisholm finally retired home to Glassburn House, Strathglass, in 1879 after a lifetime of distinguished military service to the Empire. Born in Strathglass fifty-four years previously to an artillery surgeon and the daughter of a colonel of the Cameron Highlanders, Chisholm was destined for the army from birth. But before he joined the Black Watch at the age of sixteen, was shipped to Malta and began a globe-trotting services career that introduced him to Bermuda, Greece, Sicily, Canada and the Crimea, Archie Chisholm was lucky enough to spend his formative years in one of the great shinty centres of nineteenth-century Scotland.

Shinty thrived during those troubled decades in the Catholic townships of Strathglass and in its Protestant neighbourhood, Glen Urquhart. Writing fifty years later of shinty in the area at the time of

Archibald Chisholm's boyhood, another much-travelled Strathglass man, the scholarly Colin Chisholm of Glencannich, remembered the winters of the 1820s and 1830s in the strath as being a feast of camanachd:

> As the winter set the practice at the ball and club commenced at the different farms and hamlets. This early attention to their favourite sports and pastimes was considered a healthy winter exercise as well as the best possible preparation for their great shinty matches.
>
> There were four of these matches every winter. The first was played on St Stephen's Day, the second on St John's Day, the third on the feast of the Circumcision of our Lord, or New Year's Day, and the fourth on the Epiphany of our Lord. Directly after mass was over about noon, people and priest repaired to the broad fields of Balanahaun and Baile-na-Bruach without loss of time and without the least attention as to equal numbers on each side.
>
> The Brae and Glencannich men united against the more numerous inhabitants of the whole Strath. Thus the contest was invariably a very determined affair. Each man imagined that the honour of the district to which he belonged rested on his own shoulders. With this feeling animating the breast of every shinty player on the field, the ball used to be thrown up midway between Alt-a-bhodaich on the west, or Brae side, and Beath'og on the east, or Strath side.
>
> In less than one minute afterwards hundreds of men were usually engaged. Each party running hot haste to the brunt of the contest. The rallying cry of the Brae men was 'Suas am ball' [West with the ball]; and that of the Strath men, 'Sios am ball' [East with the ball]. These simple short cries called forth tremendous exertions. Every nerve was strained . . .
>
> Now comes the tug of war. Each party is equally determined to conquer. The result is that all, or the most of the players close round the ball and press against each other so hard that they form one compact mass of human beings, heaving and surging to and fro in the best possible humour. This little divergence was called in the phraseology of the district *caiginn*. Very few minutes were quite enough of this squeezing process, and splendid playing was soon resumed and continued until dusk, or until the priest came and 'air ghaol Dias air eagal conais' took up the ball.

This was shinty in Strathglass in the youth of Colin Chisholm and in the boyhood of his clansman, Archibald. Colin Chisholm also had experience of shinty in London, where he had become a super-intendent in the Metropolitan Police, and in Lancashire where 'in an inland part of that county they played it much the same way as in the Highlands. The whole male population of a district *bho fhear liath gu leanabh* seem to engage in this exciting game . . . it is known by the name of hockey'. For a man of learning, he wore with unusual pride a most unacademic scarred eyebrow and broken nose – a shinty stick had transformed the latter, Colin Chisholm would laugh, from a Grecian cast to a Roman one. He told stories of the Lochaber drover, Iain Mor Mac Choinnich, who walked eighteen miles before dawn to take part in a game and went home missing an eye, tales of broken kneecaps on the plains of Strathglass, stressing all along that no good player ever inflicted an injury. Colin Chisholm told stories of a game in an uncommon state of rude and robust health.

These epic contests in Strathglass attracted even the attention of the local press – an unusual thing to happen at this time, when a game of shinty was more often judged to be too common a sight or too super-fluous to the pressing issues of the day (which included, in that winter of 1825–26, the opening of the Stockton to Darlington railway, the crowning of Nicolas I as Czar of Russia and the granting of indepen-dence by Spain to her mainland American colonies) to merit precious editorial space. But in 1826 the *Inverness Courier*, startled no doubt by the scale of the event, reported that on 18 January 'upwards of 150 Chisholms and other natives of Strathglass had their usual match at shinty. The match was betwixt the Braes and the Strath. The Braes men supported the character for superior activity and expertness which they are said to possess, and, although less numerous, carried the day.'

The genesis of the organised teams which came to call themselves Beauly and Lovat was reported by the same newspaper in 1850, when the men of Strathglass took on the men of the low ground of the Aird, the districts of Kirkhill, Kiltarlity and Beauly, in a river basin near Beaufort Castle. On this occasion no priest led his flock to their secular pleasures. Instead, the young Master of Lovat brought forth his forty picked Aird men, wearing scarlet ribbons in their buttonholes, to be defeated by the fit and accomplished hill men of Strathglass, who had blue ribbons fluttering from their shirts and the Master of Lovat's even younger brother at their head.

*The magisterial Captain Archibald MacRa Chisholm, 1825–97, founder of the
Strathglass Shinty Club, author of the first constitution of a Highland club, compiler
of the first set of printed rules in the Highlands, and the first chieftain of the
Camanachd Association (Courtesy 'Glen Urquhart', by Peter English)*

Throughout the nineteenth century the parishes of Glencannich, Glenstrathfarrar, Eskadale, Glen Affric, Buntait, Knockfin, Glen Guisachan and Breacachy held the flag of shinty steady in the Highlands of Scotland. The winter games were observed as religiously as the chapel services which preceded them. Even as the Chisholms began to leave the strath in their hundreds to find land in Antigonish County and Port Hawkesbury, the games continued: with diminished numbers perhaps, but with no less enthusiasm and with never a thought of letting the winter saints' days pass without the caman being taken from its place of summer storage and exercised in the clear, sharp air.

It must have been odd indeed for the likes of Archibald MacRa and Colin Chisholm to return from the fields of Wimbledon Common and Alexandra Palace, where the participants compensated for their naivety on the pitch with a burgeoning, enthusiastic democratic organisation off it, to the hills and glens of their home, where unparalleled skills held sway but effectively no organisation existed apart from the ministrations of the priest and the blue and red ribbons and India rubber balls distributed by the house of Lovat.

In the event of his final return to Strathglass, Archibald MacRa Chisholm wasted little time in making good the deficiency. Captain Archie was a formidable figure. He stood at six feet two inches tall in his stockinged feet, he was a committed, practising Roman Catholic and a Gaelic speaker whose love for his native language and for the culture of his people had been crystallised, as so often, by too many years spent away. He disliked tobacco and strong drink, warning the shinty players of Strathglass on at least one occasion that 'Ach chan ionan fear air mhisg is fear an uisg' (The drunken man and the drinker of water are not alike), and he succeeded eventually in persuading most of them to spurn whisky immediately before, during and after a match. Although he was reputed to be a serious character, even a martinet when he deemed it necessary, the photographs of Archibald Chisholm present a relaxed, authoritative figure with smiling eyes. His sympathies with the Highland radicals and land reformers of the day may be judged by the assistance which he freely offered to *The Highlander* when it was in mortal danger and he was far away in London, and by his lasting friendship with the newspaper's editor, John Murdoch. Murdoch was not accustomed to being honoured guest at Highland Gala Days, this position being more usually filled by his sworn enemies; it must have been a pleasant experience for the political firebrand to be invited by Archibald Chisholm in July 1881 to dignify the Strathglass gathering with his presence and to hand out six-month subscriptions to *The Highlander* as prizes.

Archibald Chisholm was a shinty visionary. His tactical awareness may not have matched that of Alex MacKellar of Tighnabruaich and Glasgow Cowal, but Chisholm was a good selector of teams. He was not afraid to dispense with traditional formations in an attempt to deploy his players more effectively. He recognised at a very early stage that if shinty was to grow as an organised sport it must attract spectators; that this in turn meant that more goals must be scored, and that the smothering scrimmage of 100-a-side, enjoyable as it may have been for the players, was at best inaccessible to most of those watching and had to go, in favour of smaller teams and more open, free-scoring games.

But most of all, Archibald MacRa Chisholm, lately a captain in the 42nd Royal Highlanders, was an organiser of men. When he set his steady gaze upon introducing the Highlands of Scotland to the constitutions, committees and written rules which he knew of in Glasgow and had experienced in London, that gaze would not be easily deflected.

On 27 January 1880, he took the chair of a meeting in the Glen Affric Hotel and asked representatives of all of the districts of Strathglass if they wished to constitute a shinty club. They keenly affirmed this, and wasted no further time in electing Archibald Chisholm as the chief and president of *Comunn Camanachd Straghlais.* Duncan Chisholm of Raonabhraid was then elected secretary, and it was agreed to form a committee with representatives of every district, whose job it would be to elect a management committee at every Annual General Meeting.

Wasting no time, Captain Archie urged that the inaugural general meeting of the club should take place in a few days, at the Cannich Hotel on 10 February, and that the assembly should proceed from there to their first trial match under drafted new rules on the field belonging to Mr Robertson at Comar.

When that meeting had taken place and the 'large and enthusiastic turn-out of players, friends and supporters' had drifted out of the Cannich Hotel into the cold February afternoon, Chisholm mounted his waiting carriage and addressed the crowd, like a church-less Presbyterian minister, from this impromptu stage. With his long white beard and unruly hair streaming in the wind he spoke of his pride 'to see so great and gay a gathering'.

The Strathglass club was in its infancy, he said, and would require kind nursing for a time. But the sport was truly venerable. To laughter and cheers he asked: 'Did not some of the antedeluvian historians – though I fear their works perished in the flood – mention the game as having been played for hundreds of years by the sons of Adam and Eve? But we leave it to the learned to solve that problem.' Highlanders had taken their game around the world, said Captain Chisholm. 'I have played it with our cousins and relations in Canada during the winter on skates, with a splendid field of ice ten feet thick.'

At Strathglass, however, the game would be played on dry land according to 'scientific principles':

A good shinty player must be active in all his faculties; he must be active in his mind to prepare for every advantage, he must be active in his eye and limb to avail himself of these advantages. He must be sturdy, temperate, and cool; but to acquire these good qualities he must, like the best rifle shots, avoid as much as possible the use of tobacco, whisky and other stimulants.'

Eighty young men carrying camain, corner-flags and goal-posts flexed their muscles outside the Cannich Hotel that day, counting the minutes before they could be off to the field at Comar, as Archibald Chisholm looked directly at them and said, to wild cheers, that every playing member of the *Comunn Camanachd Straghlais* must be 'a true and real Highlander'. Chisholm's horses were flicked into movement and his carriage driven round to the front of the procession, while the great man rummaged in his belongings and produced a set of pipes. Blowing a stirring march, Captain Archibald MacRa Chisholm – who, among his other accomplishments, was judged to be one of the best amateur pipers of his time – then led the people of the Highlands of Scotland away down the road to organised shinty.

It took a spring and a summer of dedicated activity to produce the first printed constitution and rules of a Highland shinty club. While the enthusiasm generated that winter spilled over into the summer months, and on showery July afternoons teams of twenty-two under William Chisholm, Erchless, were keeping their reflexes sharp against the pick of William Macdonald's Easter Croicheal, Archibald

Chisholm, his secretary and his committee of ten elders met in gas-lit –
if not, it must be assumed, smoke filled – rooms to debate counter-
proposals and amendments, subscription fees and qualifications of
membership, size of playing area and method of scoring.

The constitution which was finally agreed upon and printed in July
1880 was a model of efficiency and purpose. It defined the geographical constituency of the club and decreed its objects as being 'the
maintenance and improvement of the old and national game of Shinty,
the encouragement of manly out-door amusements, Highland Sports,
Games and Customs and the promotion of friendly intercourse among
the members'. It established an elegant system of staggered re-election
to various positions, guaranteeing some continuity of management.
The Chisholm of Erchless Castle was drafted in as Honorary President
for life, but the club's figurehead, its Chief, the position held by
Archibald Chisholm, was to be voted on every five years, and that great
intangible, The Club, was paramount: its interests, its property, its
purpose on earth were merely lent on trust to the temporal members of
the committee. These men were to guard its good name jealously and
punish without mercy any member found guilty of 'unbecoming
conduct, improper language, insobriety, and such like'.

The rules of the game, as suggested by the Strathglass committee,
would not all survive the test of time. The registering of a score was
particularly unwieldy and unsuitable: it was proposed, in accordance
with Archibald Chisholm's belief that more goalmouth action was
necessary to attract spectators, to award single points for every ball
driven past the goal-line outside the goals and over the crossbar, and
twenty-five points for a goal. But the rules also echoed Chisholm's
anxiety to open up the field of play by reducing the number of players.
A diagram which accompanied the written legislation described the
formation at throw-up of two teams of fifteen men, although this
limitation was never prescribed in the written, numbered rules.

Whatever their faults, they were printed rules, they were rooted
firmly in the birthplace of the Scottish game and they were in the
hands of committed, accountable, local men. The Strathglass Shinty
Club was justly proud of itself. In 1881 the proprietor of the Glen
Affric Hotel, a Mr Kerr, offered a cash prize and a bound book to the
author of the best poem written in praise of the *comunn* which had spent
so many hours deliberating in the rooms of his establishment. The
secretary of the Gaelic Society of Inverness, William MacKenzie, was

called in to act as judge, and shortly before the New Year of 1882 he announced that the winner was William MacDonald, a committee member from Easter Croicheal.

For the shinty players of the glens of Affric and Cannich and the banks of the River Glass something was still missing. They could not yet be completely content. At the other side of the brae, south of the parish of Cannich, a long and fertile glen rolled down to Drumnadrochit and the banks of Loch Ness. Shinty had been played in Glen Urquhart for as long as it had been played in Strathglass. One area was as fervent in its enthusiasm about the game as the other. But as shinty was discussed in those excited days of the early 1880s, at hearth-sides, on open fields and in hotel taprooms throughout the area, a surprising, tantalising fact came to light. In living memory, the men of Glen Urquhart had never met the men of Strathglass on the shinty field.

As Strathglass had occasionally looked north and east to Beauly and Kiltarlity for opposition, and had at least once taken advantage of an old connection of Archibald Chisholm's to meet Lochcarron, so the players of Glen Urquhart had turned their faces south and west, down the Great Glen to Corrienmony, Fort Augustus and Glenmoriston. When Glen Urquhart followed the example set by their neighbours and formally established their own shinty club in the reading room at Blairbeg in November 1884, the great divide between Cannich and Loch Meiklie had yet to be crossed.

It was obvious that the two teams had to meet. Upon their inauguration the Glen Urquhart club was presented by its new president, Mr Alastair Douglas Campbell of Kilmartin, with a new trophy, the Kilmartin Challenge Cup. It was being contested between Glen Urquhart players within weeks. Seven hundred people watched two selected sides from the glen play out a draw at Delshangie on New Year's Day 1885. The replay twelve days later did not take place on a public holiday, and the crowd was down to 150. Milling among that crowd, however, were some highly interested young men from the district of Strathglass. After the match it was reported that a side of twenty Glen Urquhart men were preparing themselves to take up a challenge thrown down by their northern neighbours. Archibald Chisholm and his committee were quick to stifle such unconstitutional behaviour: letters were sent to the *Inverness Courier* denying that an official Strathglass delegation had been present at Delshangie and that any authorised challenge had been made.

But the stopper was out. The genie had slipped from the bottle when the first *bodach* mentioned in public that he could never remember Strathglass playing Glen Urquhart, and it was now running riot in the imaginations of people throughout the Highlands. A Great Game was going to take place, a demonstration of Highland shinty's new-found organisation and self-confidence was destined to be mounted and nothing was going to stop it.

The winter of 1886–87 came around, the players of Strathlgass turned out on Epiphany and New Year's Day, and by now even the *Inverness Courier* could not resist noting that a group of youths from Glen Urquhart were to be seen on the sidelines clutching pencils and paper, brazenly taking notes and baiting their rivals on their own hallowed turf. There was only one thing to do. On 22 January 1887 officials of the Strathglass and Glen Urquhart shinty clubs met in Drumnadrochit and agreed that twenty-two players from each club would play at shinty at the Bught Park, Inverness, in three weeks' time, on Saturday, 12 February 1887. These diligent legislators were then faced with the problem of drawing up a compromise set of rules for the Great Contest. Luckily the meeting between level-headed parish elders was an amicable one and they were able to reach agreement over an enormous package of no fewer than forty rules – easily the most substantial shinty legislation thus far put on to paper. Archibald Chisholm's 'point-scoring' system was dropped; goals alone would count. Specific fouls, such as charging from the back, tripping and jumping at a player, were to be punished by 'expulsion from the field of play'. Regardless of the tension and fierce rivalry which had developed around the fixture, and which by now had spread as far south as Glasgow and London, the two sets of club officials agreed: 'It is confidently hoped that the members of both teams will observe the greatest civility and cordiality towards each other. To lose temper is to part with reason, which would be a pity. Cuimhnich air na daoine bho'n d'thainig sibh (Remember the men from whom you have come).' The Glen Urquhart committee then offered their Strathglass counterparts refreshments, after which the two parties shook hands, mounted dog-carts and carriages and carried back to their townships the news that the game was on.

People travelled from all over the north of Scotland to be at the Bught Park on 12 February 1887. Those who could not get to Inverness, who had to spend that Saturday afternoon in Edinburgh,

Glasgow, London, or even, like the ten- year-old Andrew Fraser and his friends, on the hills above Loch Ness, made arrangements with friends or relatives to be telegraphed the result at the first opportunity. Archibald MacRa Chisholm, alive to the prospect of Inverness hosting the largest sporting crowd in its history, requested the commanding officer of the 79th Queen's Own Cameron Highlanders to provide a sergeant and twenty-one men to police the field of play. It was as well that he did so: the Inverness constabulary was unused to such occasions and could only spare twelve men on the day when 3,000 shinty enthusiasts entered the Highland capital from all points of the compass, anxious for a touchline position at the Great Game.

Chisholm's team left Strathglass in three brakes for Beauly in the early morning, catching the train to Inverness and breakfasting in the Caledonian Hotel. The Glen Urquhart contingent ate heartily on board the steamer *Loch Ness* between Temple Pier and Muirtown Wharf.

Shortly before noon the thousands lining the Bught hushed their voices in respectful anticipation. The skirl of pipes preceded Alastair Campbell of Kilmartin and his twenty-two players, wearing blue jerseys, white duck knickerbockers and blue socks, on to the field. They were followed by the favourites, the hitherto undefeated men of Strathglass, carrying flags and hailed by their own pipers. No dwarf himself, Archibald Chisholm stood inches below several of his players. In white shirts, knickerbockers in the tartan of Chisholm's old regiment, the 42nd Highlanders, and Glengarry bonnets, the Strathglass men looked formidable and experienced opponents. They were certainly experienced – one of their number, a young man named James MacDonald said later that two-thirds of the Strathglass team were between thirty and fifty years old.

The two sides posed for photographs; the young Glen Urquhart squad casually, leaning nonchalently on their camain, some looking curiously over at the humming crowd and at their waiting opponents. Archibald Chisholm arranged his players, pipers and club officials into a kind of order, had them all look directly into the lens, and sat himself, kilted and erect, in the midst of his people, his brow furrowed and a wary smile upon his face.

The neutral referee, Mr Gillespie of Tulloch, threw the ball up at about 12.15 p.m., and from the moment it was struck into open play it became apparent that Strathglass had a battle on their hands to retain their proud unbeaten record. The younger men of Glen Urquhart were fast, fit, determined and well organised. At a signal from their captain, John Fraser, they would rally en masse behind the ball, leaving just one or two defenders behind, and harry the scattered Strathglass players into error and desperate defence. After fifteen minutes they had their reward. A Strathglass break by Thomas MacGillivray was closed down, the ball swiftly returned upfield, and in the resultant goalmouth mêlée the Strathglass 'keeper, Alex Chisholm, scored into his own goal.

A spectator ran to the post office and telegraphed the news to Drumnadrochit, where a large crowd whooped and a cannon was fired by Mr Burgess, the local banker. The ten-year-old daughter of a Glen Urquhart man who was farming at Tomnahurich, adjacent to the Bught, ran home to pant out the news to her family's houseful of visiting relatives. Back on the field, Strathglass prepared for a second period of intense pressure. Glen Urquhart, spirits high, ran riot and the older Strathglass legs began to falter. During this period, recalled James MacDonald later, 'only a few of us who were in the early twenties devolved the issue of preventing the score from being that of cricket'. Some Strathglass players removed their boots and played on in stockinged feet, in a vain attempt to match the speed and agility of their younger opponents. A Glen Urquhart 'goal' was disallowed after the referee's attention was drawn to the fact that a member of the public standing behind the goal had helped the ball on its way, but with half an hour to go some unrecorded hero from Lewiston, Balbeg or Bearnock got in a decisive touch a foot or two from the Strathglass goal-line. When Mr Gillespie called time, Glen Urquhart had won the Great Game by two goals to nil.

The twenty-two Cameron Highlanders accompanied Archibald Chisholm and his crestfallen squad back to the Caledonian Hotel, where Maria Frances Chisholm, the captain's wife, had arranged a celebratory meal. Mrs Chisholm had however been possessed of sufficient good sense to inform the club's secretary, Duncan Chisholm, that the food was to be consumed whether his team won or lost, and as her health was drunk good spirits returned. All things considered, it was a cheerful Strathglass team which caught the four o'clock train from Inverness to Beauly.

In Glen Urquhart, the youths of the district were busy building bonfires. Young Andrew Fraser had been sent by the adults of Balbeg down to Drumnadrochit to hear the final telegram read out: 'we got the news that Glen Urquhart had won and came up to Balbeg like deer'. Telephone calls and telegraphed messages swamped the small post office at Drumnadrochit, as exiles from Glasgow and elsewhere wired in for the news or, having heard it, flooded the place with their congratulations.

The team was piped and cheered into Inverness town centre, before making its way to Muirtown Wharf and taking the afternoon steamer back down Loch Ness, the air around the smiling players singing with jubilation. A cheering crowd met the boat at Temple Pier and followed the victors up the glen. As night fell, bonfires blazed on the hills above Milton, Delshangie and Balnain.

The Strathglass team, flanked by their pipers and with Archibald Chisholm at their heart, before the Great Game of 1887.

Back (left to right): *Thomas MacGillivray, Cosac; Donald Cameron, Struy; James Fraser, Knocknashalauaig; Sandy Bain, Glen Affric; Alexander Forbes, Leanassie; Donald Chisholm, Imir; Kenneth Chisholm, Carnich; James MacDonald, Tomich; Wallach MacDonald, Tomich; Ralph Mackinnon, Struy; Hugh Forbes, Farley; George Tait.*
Second row (left to right): *Alexander Ross, John Chisholm, Imir; Donald MacKenzie, Wester Crochail; Theodore Campbell, Hughton; Pipe-major Lachlan Collie, James Fraser, Mauld (captain); William MacKenzie, Wester Crochail; Duncan Scott, Cannich; Finlay Macrae, Eilean Aigas; Mr Collie, Angus Fraser, Inshully; Roderick MacLennan, Fasna-Kyle.*
Third row (left to right): *William Forbes, Struy; Donald Chisholm; Archibald Chisholm, Cannich; Captain Archibald MacRa Chisholm, James MacDonald, Cannich; Mr MacPherson, Glen Affric Hotel; Donald MacDonald, Carnoch; Ewen MacDonald, Melness.*
Front row (left to right): *Kenneth Moss, Tomich; Donald Macmillan, Kerrow; Alexander Chisholm, Craskaig; Alexander Chisholm, John Matheson; Duncan Chisholm, Runavraid; Donald Chisholm, Alexander Chisholm.*
The late Archie Scott pointed out that his father Duncan Scott (second row) was 6 feet in height. This gives some idea of the massive stature of those standing to the left of Duncan in the photograph – William Mackenzie from Wester Crochail and James Fraser of Mauld.
(Courtesy 'Glen Urquhart', by Peter English)

When he finally sank into an armchair in the peace of Glassburn House that evening, Captain Archibald MacRa Chisholm could reflect that the defeat before 3,000 people of his beloved Strathglass may have been the price demanded by fate and the Almighty for the elevation of shinty into a spectator sport so popular that it was literally threatening to set the Highlands alight.

As inevitably as there had been a first Great Game, there had to be a second; a chance for Strathglass to repair their wounded pride, or for Alastair Campbell's men to put their superiority beyond question. It took place on 3 March 1888, and once again a crowd of up to 3,000 people, controlled by a detachment of Cameron Highlanders, waited at the Bught Park with bated breath for the teams to arrive from the Loch Ness steamer and from breakfast at the Caledonian Hotel.

In blue jerseys and white duck knickerbockers, the men of Glen Urquhart prepare to face the hitherto undefeated pride of Strathglass.

Back row (left to right): *Angus MacDonald, Lewiston; Peter John MacDonald, Balbeg; Donald MacLean, Bearnock; Finlay MacLean, Upperton; Donald McPhee, Milton; Alexander Cumming, Drumnadrochit; Alex Fraser, Achmonie; Ewan MacDonald, Upper Lenie; John Campbell, Achtuie; John Macmillan, Balnaglaic.*
Second row (left to right): *John MacDonald, Lewiston; Hugh Mackenzie, Achtemarack; Finlay Fanning, Lochletter; John MacDonald Jun., John Ross, Lewiston; John MacDonald Sen., Balbeg; Goalkeeper – unknown.*
Kneeling (left to right): *Ian MacDonald, Balbeg; Charles MacDonell, Kilmartin House; Alexander MacDonald, Bearknock.*
Front (left to right): *James MacDonald, Lewiston; Peter MacDonald, Balbeg; Donald MacDonald Jun., Balbeg; Donald MacDonald sen., Balbeg; Andrew MacDonald, Balbeg.*
(Courtesy 'Glen Urquhart', by Peter English)

Strathglass had issued the return invitation three weeks earlier and this time they came prepared. Glen Urquhart made just five changes to the previous year's line up, mostly necessitated by players having left the area. Only half of the 1887 Strathglass squad of twenty-two kept their places in 1888. Chisholm's selection committee had opted to fight youth with youth.

In the event, it was a more even contest, although some spectators left arguing as to whether it was the finest, most competitive game of shinty seen yet in the Highlands, or simply the worst-tempered. 'No man spared himself, and unusual risks were taken in the tackles and scrimmages with the result that few, if any, escaped without some mark of the fray,' remembered Ewen MacDonald, a Glen Urquhart man, fifty years after watching the game as a youth of eighteen. 'It was probably the most bitterly contested match ever witnessed at Inverness or elsewhere.'

Whether or not the memory of their forebears urged upon them by their village elders was translated by the forty-six shinty players – the 1888 game was played with twenty-three players per side – into a bitter vindication of clan and regional pride, there can be little doubt that the crowd was entertained. From the outset Strathglass turned the tables on Glen Urquhart, applying persistent pressure and nearly taking the lead in the opening minutes when a through ball slipped past the Glen defence and only speedy footwork on the part of the Glen Urquhart goalkeeper stopped it from rolling into the temporarily unguarded goal. There was little light relief in the torrid contest during the goal-less first period, apart from the occasion when a high clearance landed in the branches of a tree on the field. Glen Urquhart's Alex MacDonald caught the ball on his caman, as it bounced down the trunk, and took advantage of confusion in the Strathglass ranks to embark on a searching run.

With ten minutes to go Strathglass, despite the injection of younger legs, were patently tiring. They set themselves to play out the draw, defending in a solid wall. It was their undoing. With just two minutes left, the same Alex 'Ally Ban' MacDonald who had received a pass from a tree slipped through the formidable line of white shirts and scored. The guesting referee, Sir Harry MacAndrew, threw up the ball, watched a few seconds' desperate counter-attack from Strathglass, and called time. A huge roar went up and, a telegraph's distance away in Glen Urquhart, young boys began once more to build bonfires.

Highlanders are aware that Highland memories are long and it would not have surprised Archibald MacRa Chisholm of Glassburn or Alastair Campbell of Kilmartin to learn that the Great Games which they organised at the Bught Park, Inverness, in the early months of 1887 and 1888 would still be the subject of debate, controversy and treasured second- hand reminiscence a century later. Some events are blown out of proportion by such persistent attention. Their true significance is exaggerated as the decades pass and stories gain colour in their endless retelling, like fishermen's tales of the escaped Atlantic salmon. But the significance of the games between Strathglass and Glen Urquhart is almost beyond exaggeration. In the history of shinty in the Highlands they marked the watershed where the game flowed off in the direction of spectator sports. They showed that shinty could entertain and excite neutral spectators, even people with no previous experience of the sport and no roots in the homelands of the competing teams. Ordinary Highlanders, buoyant after their successful wringing of crofting legislation from a previously impervious government, had now proven themselves easily capable of and willing to transform their ancient, traditional outdoor game into an ordered, accessible modern entertainment without reshaping it beyond recognition and while keeping its enormous strength: the roots which it had sent down for centuries into the separate scattered communities of the Gaidhealtachd.

At the end of the penultimate decade of the nineteenth century, while its Celtic cousins were dying in other parts of Britain, shinty was given a new lease of life in the Highlands. The two clubs which made this possible were not to meet again until two world wars and more than sixty years had come and gone. Strathglass took their revenge on that occasion in November 1948, beating by 5–2 a Glen Urquhart side which had just been re-formed after the Second World War. Ewen MacDonald, the eighteen-year-old who came away from the Bught in 1888 commenting on the bitterness of the contest, served as a goal judge during the third, distant encounter.

But other local rivalries would flourish in the years following 1888; other neighbourhoods separated by a brae or a strip of water, or by a boundary invisible to the stranger, came to capture the imagination of the Highlands. Village sides which had been getting together for centuries to take on the pick of their neighbouring parishes took the hint, underwrote themselves with constitutions and issued glamorous challenges the length of the land. For one thing, in this way they attracted the serious attention of the press.

Victorian newspapers before the 1880s had been as fickle in their acknowledgement of the game's existence as had Victorian travelogues, and neither can really be blamed. Few local sheets in those days employed a sports reporter and no Victorian traveller considered it as his or her main brief to record the curious activities of people upon playing fields. The indexes of the best stocked Scottish libraries are quite devoid of entry between 'Caithness' and 'Cambuslang', 'Shetland' and 'Shipping'. The game attracted little attention from Highland, or even Lowland, Scottish writers, to whom it was commonplace; and less from visiting scribes, who wrongly if understandably considered that more could be learned about people from their eating habits, dwelling places and agricultural implements than from their outdoor sports. Whether or not a newspaper devoted space to a certain sport was almost entirely dependent upon its proprietor or its staff members being involved in that sport. Thus, while shinty was almost ignored for long years in the *Ross-shire Journal* of the 1870s and 1880s, the game of cricket in Dingwall and Fortrose was given almost as many column inches as the election campaigns of Cameron of Lochiel. The papers could not, of course, ignore an organised sport, or a game which attracted 3,000 spectators to within a few hundred yards of their offices, which is partly why the *Inverness Courier* devoted an enormous amount of ink to the Great Games of 1887 and 1888, thereby launching a thorough coverage of competitive shinty which it has maintained to the present day. (The *Ross-shire Journal* gave one sentence – the score – to the 1887 match, and ignored the return fixture.)

But it was left to the editors of two other publications, both impecunious and less well advantaged to cover the game than any of the established Highland weeklies, to give shinty the serious journalistic coverage which it merited and which, if it was not to be swamped by the national publicity given to other sports and the heroics attributed to other sportsmen, shinty needed for survival. Both of these editors had played shinty themselves, both were from the Highland dispossessed, and both saw the game as a crucial element in the conservation and rebirth of the Gaidhealtachd. One has already introduced himself.

John Murdoch was born in 1818. Between the ages of nine and twenty, when his father was the tenant of a small farm at Claggan, Murdoch lived in Islay. In his autobiography he remembered the shinty matches of his boyhood, which were mostly organised by the laird's son, the fledgling folklorist John Francis Campbell, with the bittersweet clarity that distinguished Murdoch as a journalist:

Coming home from school on Saturdays, we had a field day at Traigh an Luig at shinty playing. This was one of the best fields possible for the game and the players were good. My great delight was to play at this game; and soon I became not only a good player but came to be recognised as such.

Shortly before I got home there was a New Year gathering for a shinty match. The 'chiefs' were John Francis Campbell and Colin Campbell, Balnaby, who was very often with the young laird. I remember I was the first person called by John Francis. Whether this had anything to do with what I am going to notice or not, I do not know. But there were famous players on the ground, among them David Crawford. David and I were on opposite sides and, even in a scramble with him, I justified the selection made by my chief. This did not go down well with David whose temper had not been improved by the drams which were going in the morning. So he made at me and when nothing else would do he raised his club to strike me. I, however, kept my temper, seized him by the wrists, and held him. And trying to pacify him, I said, 'Of course you are better than I am.' But Finlay MacArthur, hearing my protestations of inferiority, came forward and protested in his turn that I had proved in the play that I was better than my assailant. The story of the scuffle got abroad and it put a feather in my cap.

These reminiscences are in striking contrast with the present state of things along that part of the country. Traigh an Luig is silent under the feet of cattle. And the small farms from which the keen shinty players of these days came are consolidated into the large farms.

Murdoch came to identify the forces which had emptied Traigh an Luig of young men playing shinty and replaced them with the profitable cattle of a large estate as the same forces which were causing desolation and misery throughout the Highlands and Islands, and he came to hate them for it. He launched *The Highlander* in Inverness in 1874 not because there was a paucity of local newspapers in the area, but because there was in the pages of the established press a glaring absence of criticism of the smug cabal of Highland landowners who dominated the affairs of the area, and a concomitant lack of sympathy for the distinctive cultural traditions of the Gaels: their language, their attachment to the land, and their sports.

The good health of the game of shinty was, to John Murdoch, as

important a Highland issue as any other. At times news of the game
and the activities of those involved in it comprised the only good
tidings to be found in the pages of *The Highlander*. Murdoch was
delighted to be able to report in January 1880 that a packed meeting in
Glasgow's Standard Hall which had been organised by the Glasgow
Skye Shinty Club heard calls for those present to 'use every effort in
their power to make the Government recognise the teaching of Gaelic
as a special subject to be paid for out of the rates'. He was moved
beyond measure when, in 1878, Archibald Chisholm and his colleagues on the committee of the Highland Camanachd Club of London
voted to defend *The Highlander* in its lawsuit and support it out of their
own pockets. This showed, wrote Murdoch, 'that notwithstanding the
misrule of nearly two centuries the spirit of the Gael is far from being
extinguished; that although it may be dormant amidst the beautiful
glens and hills of our beloved Alban, it lives in the Metropolis, and will
show that the highest freedom of all – the liberty to do the right even if
we suffer for the doing of it – is beginning to be understood and acted
upon by the expatriated sons of the mountains'.

His friendship with Archibald Chisholm was important to Murdoch.
Chisholm, although no landowner, was a man of substance and
standing. He had been for a time the factor of the Duchess of Leeds
at Applecross and had become a Justice of the Peace who was not in the
least concerned about upsetting his social peers in the smoking rooms
of Inverness by associating with the maverick Murdoch and refusing to
conceal his fondness of the man's scandalous newspaper. Chisholm,
said Murdoch, was a 'prince of Highlanders'.

So in the short life – less than a decade – of *The Highlander*, its pages
contained as much writing on the subject of shinty as might be found in
half a century of any other northern newspaper. *The Highlander* did not
survive to see the Great Games or the concerted flurry of organisation
which followed them, but it faithfully reported the minutes of meetings of the early clubs in London, Edinburgh, Glasgow and Strathglass,
it featured histories of the game, praised the budding legislators and
gave details of matches which were of the smallest account. And in the
course of this catch-all approach, Murdoch attracted to the correspondence columns of his newspaper one of the great sporting
controversies of all time; the kilt *v.* knickerbocker debate of 1878.

It all started harmlessly enough when a Mr A.G. Cameron wrote
from the Waverley Hotel in Bradford on 21 April to protest against

emergent shinty clubs using the word 'camanachd'. As 'camanachd' meant 'clubbing', Mr Cameron suggested, surely a better noun would be the traditional 'cluich-iomain' or 'cluichbhall'. As an afterthought, he added that it was a little silly that the Highland Camanachd Club of London, whose members could dance in the kilt, fight in the kilt, 'and perform all feats of manliness that any other nationality dare or can do in kilts', should not play shinty in the kilt.

The secretary of Highland Camanachd, Alastair MacLennan, responded huffily from London within a fortnight. 'Players are very liable to tumbles and falls – rough ones too,' he argued, 'and a wearer of the kilt, when put *hors de combat,* is anything but graceful, nay, he is *barely decent.*' As far as his club was concerned, concluded Mr MacLennan, the matter was closed.

This was not good enough for H. Whyte of Glasgow, 'a member of the Glasgow Shinty Club whose dress is in knickerbockers'. It was all very well for Alastair MacLennan to protest against the kilt, said Mr Whyte, but he should not attempt to perpetrate 'a weak and vulgar pun at the expense of the national garb . . . I have a great admiration for the Highland dress, and must protest against the mock modesty of the writer who cannot touch the subject without being immodest and who take upon them, *ex-cathedra* to put an end to discussion'.

The secretary of the Glasgow Ossian Shinty Club entered the fray by protesting that he had never heard of a caman getting entangled in a kilt. If, however, decency was the issue at stake, then, suggested J.G. MacKay, 'Let each player wear a pair of thin drawers, and should he be placed *hors de combat* I would like to know wherein the indecency exists. I wonder what these squeamish folk think of the ladies at a fashionable ball . . .'.

By the middle of May, Alastair MacLennan had apparently been gagged by the London club. His colleague, vice-captain Archibald MacTavish, wrote instead, with a choice suggestion for bringing the matter to a head. Mr MacTavish was prepared to put ten pounds sterling on three knickbockered shinty teams in Scotland beating any other three in kilts – 'this I think will be a proper test,' he explained, adding that it was a little difficult to go trotting around London in kilts before and after training sessions.

'Cannot this discussion be carried on without betting?' protested 'Lonach' the following week, adding that if three teams in knickerbockers did beat three teams in kilts it might have at least as much to do with their playing ability as with their apparel.

J.G. MacKay of the Ossian Club chose this moment to inform the discussion with some historical detail. This same matter had, he said, been debated in Glasgow some time ago, 'and I am sorry to say was the means of creating a little ill-feeling among several good Highlanders, so much so that a split in the club was the result'. Shortly after their formation the Glasgwegians had taken on Vale of Leven and had undertaken to do so wearing kilts. Unfortunately, many of them were uncomfortable in the garment – 'the greater part of them did not wear it since they were boys till that day' – and they chose to blame the kilts for their subsequent 3–0 defeat at the hands of the crack Vale squad. One of those who vowed never to play in the kilt again, revealed Mr MacKay with a fine sense of timing, was none other than Archibald MacTavish, the present vice-captain of the Highland Camanachd Club of London and latterday scourge of the kilt!

Archibald MacTavish replied from London within the week. It was true, he said, that he preferred to play his shinty in knickerbockers and had preferred to do so since his experience with the Glasgow team against Vale of Leven. He was not alone in this. He reminded J.G. MacKay that at the subsequent AGM of the Glasgow club, twenty-three players voted for knickerbockers and only nine for kilts. Mac-Tavish added incidentally that he had not intended to place a bet in his first letter. He did not know where that line had come from, but it was assumed to be the result of 'some hocus-pocus' in *The Highlander*'s office. 'Lonach' should therefore, he concluded, be satisfied, and stop writing letters under assumed names.

Donald MacPherson, the secretary of one of the 'kilted' clubs, Glasgow Fingal, pleaded that he 'would not change uniform with any other that could be worn' and suggested a friendly match between a select from knickerbockered clubs and a kilted select. William Bogle, the captain of Glasgow Ossian, supported MacPherson's call to arms. 'I crave that a day be fixed and the parties be ordained to meet and fight it out *à l'outrance*,' he declared, wondering in passing what had happened to Alastair MacLennan, the instigator of the row.

Ronald Walker of Glasgow Camanachd wrote in to deplore the animosity which had been generated 'for the mere gratification of rival correspondents'. As for a kilts *v.* knickerbockers game, he said: 'Playing matches till doomsday won't decide which is the most suitable dress . . . a Highlander is a Highlander though he should play shinty in pantaloons.' Mr Walker admitted, nonetheless, to a definite preference for knickerbockers: they were light and they held their place when the player was upside down.

Archibald MacTavish wrote from London to take up the challenge thrown down by the Ossian and Fingal clubs, but asked that the Shinty Association formed a year previously in Glasgow should organise the game, 'as I am rather out of the way here'. It apparently never did: there are no records of the debate ever being brought to a head on the shinty field.

Alastair MacLennan finally broke his silence, however. He wrote to *The Highlander* in June, just as John Murdoch was closing the correspondence. 'Mr MacLennan has written a letter which so strongly and so clearly condemns the controversy,' Murdoch explained to his readers, 'that we have to give in so far to his reasoning that we must deny ourselves the pleasure of publishing his own letter.'

John MacKay was of the generation which followed Murdoch's. He was born in Glasgow in 1865, to a Sutherland father and a Kintyre mother, and bred a Gaelic speaker. Although he spent his working life, from leaving school until his premature death at the age of forty-four, in the employment of a Glasgow flour merchant, MacKay's absorbing interest was in the lands to the north of the Highland line. He became secretary and president of the Clan MacKay Society, worked enthusiastically in the early years of An Comunn Gaidhealach, was elected president of the Glasgow Gaelic Society, occupied the chair of the Glasgow Cowal Shinty Club, was a worshipper at St Columba Parish Church, and – his most memorable achievement – was able to advertise all of these interests through the successful establishment of 'a magazine for Highlanders': *The Celtic Monthly.*

A 27-year-old clerk with no striking academic or business distinction, MacKay was a doughty founding editor of this magazine. From the date of its launch in October 1892, he established the views, the range and the campaigning grounds of *The Celtic Monthly.* Its first issues were able to include a lengthy report on the inaugural National Mod, held by An Comunn Gaidhealach in Oban, a history of Celtic Christianity, stories of Clan MacKay and a lengthy, explicit commitment to coverage of the game of camanachd. The magazine deplored the disappearance of the game from southern rural districts of Scotland ('where it was usually called knotty or hummy') in the first four decades of the nineteenth century, but pointed out that although its fosterage may consequently lie in the hands of the people of the northern

John MacKay, founder-editor of the Celtic Monthly, fervent supporter
of Glasgow Cowal Shinty Club, and the man who brought photo-feature
journalism to shinty in the last decade of the nineteenth century.

counties, even there it was under threat. 'At one time Durness was
famous for its great Shinty Gatherings,' deplored *The Celtic Monthly*.
'Have Caithness men forgotten the good old times on Dunnett Sands,
when they waged earnest warfare at "knotty", headed by their lairds –
Traill of Ratter and Sinclair of Freswick? Why is this grand old national
game allowed to die out in such places as Helmsdale, Brora, Golspie,
Dornoch, Lairg, Bonar, not to speak of Tongue, Farr, Assynt, etc?'

The first shinty action photographs? With characteristic ambition, flair and partiality, John MacKay devoted a page of The Celtic Monthly *to these experimental shots of an 1896 match between Glasgow Cowal Reserves and Edinburgh Sutherland.*

Like John Murdoch, and like many who were to follow, MacKay saw in the game of shinty a precious embodiment of Scottish Gaelic culture and identity, a link with the vital past which, if it were to be severed, would leave a vacuum as cavernous as if the language of his cradle were to succumb to the aggressive market forces of the south and disappear from the face of the earth. Like Murdoch, MacKay set himself to avert the sorry day.

Unlike Murdoch, MacKay planned his shinty coverage. He featured commissioned articles and photographs of the game, profiles and pen-portraits of its eminent figures, pieces of whimsical fiction and items of genuine folklore connected with the sport; as well as always finding space for reports of the least significant match, fund-raising event and annual general meeting. In a real way John MacKay pioneered the modern journalist coverage of shinty. Indeed, in the 1890s many of the imaginative publishing devices which he employed to draw attention to his favoured game were unknown to all but one or two other codes of team sport. MacKay elevated shinty players and organisers to a previously unknown level: they could now expect to see their photographs, biographies and heroic deeds on the field set down in blocks of type beside profiles of the Provosts of Campbeltown and the Marquesses of Bute and accounts of the exploits of Scottish regiments.

If MacKay's coverage of the game had a weakness, the reader was forewarned of it in the very first issue of *The Celtic Monthly*, when it was written of Glasgow Cowal that 'there is probably not a club in existence today that can put a better team on the field'. John MacKay was intensely loyal to his family background. We can only guess at why his father came to leave Sutherland, but MacKay, a romantic and no sworn enemy of the Highland aristocracy, could not write of Dunrobin Castle, the home of the Dukes and Duchesses of Sutherland and the spawning ground of the brutal clearances which preceded his own birth in Glasgow, except in words of unsuppressed and unchar-acteristic bitterness. With the exception of the occasional foray on to the Queen's Park of the 93rd Highlanders, there was no shinty team of expressed Sutherland origin in the Lowlands, so MacKay turned to the Argyllshire birthright of his mother and adopted Glasgow Cowal. This was one of the great teams of its time and MacKay, who was quickly elected its president, polished the club until it shone. The publicity which *The Celtic Monthly* gave to Glasgow Cowal turned the team from being a merely successful band of players and fund-raisers into a by-word for sporting achievement. Edinburgh Camanachd's 25th anni-versary meet had attracted 150 people; one year later an entirely respectable attendance of 120 passed through the doors of the Queen Street Rooms to enjoy Edinburgh's 26th annual assembly. But two weeks after that, on 25 March 1896, more than 1,000 turned up at the

Grand Hall in Glasgow's Waterloo rooms for the annual concert of 'this famous shinty club' – Glasgow Cowal. By 1894 Cowal were putting two and sometimes three sides, a first team, a second team, and a junior team, into regular competition; over fifty players turned up for their regular Saturday afternoon training sessions at Strathbungo.

MacKay's reporting of the club's results and performances undoubtedly gilded the lily. After an internal six- a-side tournament in October 1893 spectators were freely quoted as declaring 'that they never saw a better exposition of shinty on any field'. Second-team victories over such footballing shinty illiterates as Airdrie were hailed with exuberance. When Cowal did meet their Waterloo at Inveraray on New Year's Day 1895, being thrashed 8–2 by the recently re-constituted home side, who 'scored seven goals before the Cowal men had a chance', their victors had to be hailed as the new demigods of the Scottish shinty world. Inveraray did, in fact, meet and get beaten by other northern sides in the 1890s, but they remained in the eyes of John MacKay and his *Celtic Monthly* an Argyllshire legend as potent, virile and unconquerable as Fionn MacCumhail, because they had once hammered the famous Glasgow Cowal. MacKay sometimes used his shinty space like the adolescent producer of an insignificant fanzine being given unlimited use of the sports pages of the *Glasgow Herald*. When, in January 1897, the Cowal club presented him with a gold scarf ring set with diamonds and sapphires, it was no more than his due.

But John MacKay tired of shinty. As the years went by and in adulthood his energetic mind developed other interests, so coverage of shinty faded from the pages of *The Celtic Monthly*. It never entirely disappeared. Whenever secretaries could be bothered to send in reports, scorelines, even photographs, space would be found for them, particularly if they concerned his old club. But the momentous zeal which had given shinty a taste of photo-feature journalism in the early 1890s had been gone for some years when, in November 1909, the pastor of St Columba's, Dr John MacLean, told the mourners at John MacKay's funeral of a man 'who was always ready to help in furthering any cause that commended itself to his judgement and heart'.

The Celtic Monthly followed him shortly afterwards and, with it and *The Highlander* gone, shinty was obliged to wait until the later decades of the twentieth century to regain a consistent measure of imaginative, entertaining coverage in the pages of the public press.

6

Association

'The attendance was larger than it had been at any previous time, the utmost interest being displayed in the champion shinty club of Scotland.'

As John MacKay diligently prepared the third issue of *The Celtic Monthly* for his printers in November 1892, James, Alex and Kenny MacKenzie were meeting in Kinlochewe to discuss the borrowing of a suitable field for the practice sessions of Ben Slioch Rovers Shinty Club. On the island of Lewis the Stornoway Shinty Club, which had recently been formed under the captaincy of William MacKenzie, had arranged access to the drill park used by the Royal Naval Reserve and looked forward to their first official New Year's Day game. In the Pavilion, Strathpeffer, the audience at a fundraising concert for the Union Shinty Club were amused by Fred and Billy Walters of Dingwall and moved by Mrs Munro's sweet rendering of 'Standard on the Braes o' Mar'. The long-established Aberdeen University club was completing the first of a series of victories over Edinburgh University, whose team was just a year old, by beating their student rivals 5–3 after an impressive second half performance.

In the following spring of 1893 a shinty club was formed at Ballachulish and one re-formed in neighbouring Glencoe. Ordered New Year's Day games had gone ahead not just in Stornoway, Glasgow and Edinburgh, but also in Furnace, Colintraive, Mull and Ardgay. Lochaber had beaten Newtonmore by 4–1 and had then been defeated themselves 5–0 by Kingussie at Keppoch. Kingussie had also travelled to Laggan Bridge where, before the experienced, interested eyes of Cluny MacPherson (returned from the Gold Coast to inherit his father's estate), they dismantled their southern neighbours by 4–0.

The distinctive person of Donald Campbell, honorary captain of Kingussie Camanachd at the time of the club's Highlands versus Lowlands clash with Glasgow Cowal.

On their way back from victory celebrations at the Drumgask Hotel the two borrowed brakes carrying the Kingussie players were pelted with missiles as they passed through Newtonmore.

The game of shinty was in high spirits and expanding apace. The list of twenty-six organised clubs which had been printed in the first issue of *The Celtic Monthly* in October 1892 was hopelessly out of date within six months. And most importantly, the men from the northern counties were beginning to meet the men from the south.

Inevitably the missionaries from Glasgow Cowal were involved. The Southern Shinty Association which had come into being in Whyte's Temperance Hotel in 1877, had proved to have a weaker constitution than most of its member clubs: it had met with increasing irregularity before spluttering out within a decade. Even its standard, the Glasgow Celtic Society Cup, had not been competed for in 1883 and 1884 and nobody had sought to lift it from its resting place in Oban since 1889. Cowal had begun to look elsewhere for opposition. Feeling themselves sated by games in Edinburgh and Glasgow, and fed fresh inspiration from the pages of their president's magazine, they turned their faces south, to London, and north, to the newly ordered opposition in the Highlands. Early in 1893 they decided to travel on Glasgow's spring holiday to Kingussie.

This game was not only the first great contest between north and south; it was a meeting of two Campbells, one of whom was in charge of an unbeaten record. Donald Campbell was fifty-six years old. Although he had been a strictly non- playing honorary captain of Kingussie since the club's inception and through its undefeated early years, his thinning brow and enormous black beard were a regular sight on the practice field. His father had been a shepherd at Glengynack and a Gaelic songwriter of renown; Donald set up a general store at Kingussie in 1867, became the local police commissioner in 1874 and thereafter a junior magistrate, vice-president of the Liberal Association and a member of the School Board. On the shinty field he had relinquished immediate responsibility to his playing captain, the local hotelier James Pullar who lent the Kingussie club his shooting brakes to travel to away matches.

In the tradition of Alexander MacKellar, who was now the club's honorary president, Archibald Campbell of Glasgow Cowal was a playing captain. The son of a doctor from Furnace, the Loch Fyne-side village just south of Inveraray, Campbell had arrived in Glasgow as a

Archibald Campbell, successor to Alex MacKellar as captain in the seminal year of 1893.

seventeen-year-old medical student in 1888. His brother, John, had been captain of the distinguished Furnace team, but Archibald Campbell had not trailed clouds of glory on the shinty field until he joined Glasgow Cowal. At the time of the visit to Kingussie he was twenty-three years old and in his first year of captaincy.

Some compromised rules had been arranged before the Cowal men disembarked from the train in Kingussie at 9.05 a.m. on 3 April 1893, looking unruffled and unconcerned by their journey. A small southern-style ball was to be used and the teams were to be fifteen-a-side. Kicking the ball was not to be allowed. The Kingussie players and officials who met their smartly dressed, coolly mannered visitors at the station examined with envy and admiration their opponents' lightly crafted camain.

The two sides, Kingussie in scarlet jerseys and white knickerbockers and Cowal in grey and white hoops and black knee-breeches, were piped on to the field at one o'clock before a huge crowd. All shops and businesses in Kingussie had closed for the afternoon and many had travelled to the game from Perth, Glasgow and Inverness. The ball was thrown up at 1.15 p.m. and the first 45-minute half ended goalless, with honours more or less even between the hard-tackling Kingussie players and their slighter, speedier opponents. In the second period the exponents of Alex MacKellar's 'scientific' play relaxed enough to display their craft; sharp, first-time passing tore at the Kingussie defence. But as the home side continued to hold out, those watching, enthralled by what they were to agree later had been the most equally contested shinty match witnessed in Badenoch and one of the best expositions of the game yet seen in Scotland, could do nothing other than predict a goalless draw. With five minutes remaining, however, Cowal broke out of midfield. The ball was whisked through the Kingussie defence before it had time to turn, and the slim, modest figure of the Glasgow Cowal captain, Archibald Campbell, appeared from behind his forwards to hit it cleanly and fiercely past the Kingussie 'keeper.

Kingussie were still stunned and dispirited when the final whistle was blown. Afterwards and at dinner in Pullar's Hotel, while Provost MacPherson of Kingussie and MacPherson of Corriemony were making speeches and congratulating both sides on such a fine display, the northern players lamented their unuse of the no-kicking rule and the advantage of their opponents' lighter camain. But by the time the 5.05 p.m. mail train arrived to collect the Cowal boys, who were cheered back to Glasgow by a large crowd at Kingussie station, the talk had turned to how valuable such meetings were and how sad it was that no fixed rules obtained to standardise the game of shinty throughout Scotland.

What with one thing and another, it was clearly time for a national, permanent shinty association.

MacPherson of Corriemony, who had travelled from England to be in Kingussie on that Glasgow spring holiday, John MacDonald of

Keppoch, the captain of the Lochaber Shinty Club, and the officials of the Kingussie club did not let the matter drop after the train had been waved away and the last drams drunk at Pullar's Hotel. They met and communicated by post throughout the summer of 1893, and with every month that passed their task at hand, the formation of a nationally respected association, became more pressing and the need for it more apparent. In the Highlands and the Lowlands new teams were mooted on the flimsiest of common ground. From Arthur and Company's Warehouse in Glasgow to the Locomotive Workers in Inverness, from estate employees at Castle Leod to the Govan Highlanders Association, shinty was engaging fresh minds. Teams were travelling from Oban to Ballachulish, from Glencoe to Fort William to satisfy a new appetite for the game. Glasgow Cowal had issued a return invitation to Kingussie and were talking of going to London. The association was a dream waiting to be fulfilled.

At the end of September 1893, Kingussie Shinty Club agreed at a meeting chaired by their chieftain, Provost MacPherson, to call a conference of thirty-three recognised shinty clubs in their village for Tuesday, 10 October. The Kingussie secretary, John Campbell, prepared a circular which invited each of these clubs to send two representatives.

When the fortnight had passed, fourteen of those thirty-three clubs were represented in person at Kingussie. Another nine had written to indicate their support for the objective of the meeting. It had a quorum and a mandate. C.J.B. MacPherson of Belleville was elected to the chair, John Campbell as secretary. John MacDonald of Keppoch proposed that a shinty association should be formed, and that it be called 'The Camanachd Association'. Donald MacDonald of Drumnadrochit, representing Glen Urquhart Shinty Club, seconded his proposal, and it was unanimously passed.

For five hours the delegates then debated the draft rules which the Kingussie club had prepared for their consideration. The item which caused most discussion had suggested that the playing area should be 'not less than 250 yards long by 150 years broad; not more than 300 yards long by 200 yards broad'. It was pointed out that many clubs, even in the vast expanse of the Highlands, had difficulty in obtaining so large an area of suitable ground and the suggestion was amended to 200 yards long by 150 broad.

And so twenty-one rules, the first of the Camanachd Association, the first legislation to be written down for the game of shinty in Scotland as the result of a national mandate and a representative conference, were adopted. They fixed the teams at sixteen per side and the playing time to ninety minutes (with the sides turning round after a goalless first forty-five minutes, or when the first goal was scored). They abolished the 'points' system which had been used infrequently by many teams, and had been formally adopted by the Strathglass club. They amended the 'pairing' rule, whereby a fit player left the field if his opposite number was disabled, judging that this should not happen if 'the referee declare the man so disabled to be in fault'. They allowed the ball to be stopped by hand, if it was then immediately dropped. Throwing or carrying the ball was outlawed. The ball itself was to be of cork, lined with leather, to a circumference of seven-and-a-half to eight inches. Spiked running shoes were forbidden, as were clubs reinforced by metal. The result of an attacker putting the ball out of play beyond the goals was to be a goalkeeper's hit; if a defender did so the ball was thrown up again, fifteen yards into play from the point where it went over the line. If the ball went out over the sidelines, the first player to reach it could bring it back for a free-hit or, if challenged, drop it in play between himself an an opponent. All players, other than the two waiting with crossed sticks, should be five yards away from the spot of a throw-up.

At the close of the lengthy meeting, the delegates elected office-bearers. Simon, Lord Lovat, of the Kiltarlity Club which was shortly to adopt his family name, became president. Three MacPhersons – of Belleville, of Corriemony, and Cluny MacPherson – were appointed vice-presidents. The scrupulous and diligent John Campbell was made secretary/treasurer. All delegates present became the executive committee. A sub-committee was appointed to draft a constitution. And with a fine and fitting regard for the men that came before them, the Camanachd Association agreed that their first chieftain should be a man of sixty-eight years who had been unable to attend their inaugural meeting: Captain Archibald MacRa Chisholm of Glassburn House, Strathglass.

The early years of the association were not without controversy and dispute. From the start, some of the southern and western clubs objected to the apparent centralising of organisation in the north. They pleaded that Kingussie and Inverness were not a geographical focus-point of the shinty world, that Perth would be a better venue for future meetings. John MacKay argued in *The Celtic Monthly* that there might be difficulty in getting many clubs to adopt wholesale the new rules, which 'differ materially from those adhered to by many of the clubs in the west and south'. If some compromise was not put on the table, threatened MacKay, 'the probability is that an association will be started to represent the west and south of Scotland and England'.

MacKay was speaking for his constituents, for his friends and colleagues in the shinty protectorate of the Celtic Society Cup, and it is certain that he was giving voice to many of their genuine concerns. But shinty was tired of schism and separation. Too many people, players, officials and spectators, had tasted the fruits of national competition and national cooperation to allow the fledgling association to be splintered.

The association, at its first annual general meeting in October 1894, was anxious to spread healing balm. They made some alterations to the rules, 'which we have no doubt will conduce to a more explicit and better interpretation of what is meant', and they opened their arms wide to all shinty clubs in Scotland, asking them all to affiliate 'and so support a body which has the magnanimous purpose of furthering shinty'. The idea of a trophy, to be competed for by all affiliated members, was discussed with broad approval and a sub-committee was set up to decide how such competitions could be organised. The close of the meeting saw a *divertissement* which was to become familiar to shinty clubs and associations the length of Scotland over the following century. John Campbell of Kingussie, their invaluable secretary/ treasurer, made his first bolt for freedom. At the first suggestion of his intended resignation MacPherson of Belleville, who was in the chair in the absence of Lord Lovat, started with alarm. The meeting promptly agreed, with one voice, that nobody so suitable or energetic as Mr Campbell could possibly be found and he was persuaded to stay on for the next year. With a sigh of relief at Campbell's acceptance which echoes down the years, the committee of the Camanachd Association thanked their chairman and adjourned.

The notion of a national trophy to be played for under the auspices of the national association was irresistible. The giving of rewards, in the shape of silver cups and plates, for success on the field of play had not been a feature of shinty in the Highlands, however much it may have caught on in Glasgow, Edinburgh and London. Glen Urquhart and Strathglass had not needed the inspiration of a glittering salver in 1887 and 1888 any more than had their forefathers of the Braes and the Strath in the previous centuries. As a correspondent wrote to the *Inverness Courier* after the 1894 AGM, 'the setting up of trophies for competition has spoiled many good pastimes'. But this time, all were agreed, things were different. The opportunity now existed to cement the unity of the Scottish game and establish beyond doubt the hegemony of the new association by offering to the shinty world a grail, a totem of achievement upon which all players, from Govan to Gairloch, could set their sights at the start of every playing year. 'Nothing better,' the *Courier's* correspondent concluded, having pre-empted the opposing arguments, 'could be introduced, and the impetus it would give to the game could not be overestimated . . . I believe that the shinty competitions would be every bit as interesting as our football events.'

By the January of 1895 the *Inverness Courier*, editorialising on the 'no little service' which had been rendered to the game by the new association, took up the call. 'If we remember rightly', the *Courier* reflected, 'it was mooted at the Association's last meeting that a cup should be got up for competition, and a committee was formed to bring the matter to a head. So far, we do not know what has been done, but we believe the introduction of a trophy for competition would still further bring the game into popularity.'

The next AGM of the Camanachd Association, in September 1895, attracted its broadest representation to date. Lord Lovat sat down in the chair of a meeting which included, as well as the usual Badenoch and Inverness stalwarts, men from Portree, Glengarry, Beauly and Grantown-on-Spey. He wasted little time in moving that a trophy be raised, to be competed for during the following season by affiliated clubs, and he found no objecting voices. It was agreed with happy unanimity that the early rounds of the competition should be divided into four geographical districts – northern, central, western and southern – to save travelling expenses until the semi-final stages.

The unanimity was not to last for long. Two months later the Association met again to formalise entries and rules for the Camanachd Cup. John Campbell reported that he had received letters of complaint from affiliated clubs, objecting to an Association ruling that they could not play against unaffiliated clubs. It was hastily agreed that this ruling was not intended to apply to 'practice' matches. At this stage the meeting was joined by Simon, Lord Lovat, who rose to express his apologies for being late and to suggest that it was a bit much to expect mainland teams to travel to Skye. A match with Portree, he affirmed to general laughter, 'meant a three days' job'. He doubted that 'a good many clubs would find it impossible to devote that time to a match'. No representative from Skye was present, and it was agreed without further ado that the island side should play all of their matches on the mainland, on a field provided by the Association.

The response from Portree was swift and scathing. Kenneth MacRae, who had attended the September meeting which first approved the Camanachd Cup competition, wrote to rebuke Lord Lovat. The Association's president had, he said, 'evidently forgot that a match on the mainland, either at Bruaich or Dingwall, means a "three days' job" for the Portree team also.' The Portree Camanachd Club were well aware when they entered in competition for the trophy offered by the Association, that considerable time and expense would be spent in the competition, and were prepared to take their chance of the ballot. 'But why was the Portree Club selected and one law made for it and another for the other clubs? The absurdity of the position is apparent. Take the following case – to go to London from Glasgow would take three days at least, to go to Rogart would take two days from Inverness.' The Portree Club, said Mr MacRae, was being 'sacrificed on the altar of the others . . . there is neither law nor equity to justify the decision of the Association . . . a veritable grievance exists, and the sooner it is removed the better in the interests of good feeling and fair play.'

Not for the first time, a narrow stretch of water was presenting a formidable obstacle to the collective development of the old game of camanachd. And, not for the last time, a compromise provided a temporary bridge. When the names were drawn for the first round of the Northern District of the first Camanachd Cup competition, Portree came out with a bye. In the second round they were drawn away to Beauly, but it was agreed to play the game at Strathcarron. By 1898 good sense and the persuasive arguments of Kenneth MacRae prevailed: the Portree Club was 'placed on the same footing as the other clubs in the Association'. It was a concession which was revoked a few years later and which Beauly, of all clubs, may have found themselves regretting.

The names of nineteen clubs went into the draw for the first round of the first Camanachd Cup competition in December 1895. The south and the south-west were represented only by Glasgow Cowal, who found themselves sharing the whole of the southern district with London Camanachd. There was no team from Edinburgh, no Furnace, no Inveraray, no Oban, no Aberdeen, and, to the north and west of Glengarry, there was only the dogged Portree Club. But the competition was off and running. To those that chose to compete, the New Year's Day games, the dances, concerts and annual general meetings of that winter of 1895–96 had a special edge of meaning and excitement. The other clubs would come later.

Enthusiasm as never before . . . Caberfeidh actually took the unprecedented step of advertising their first round tie in the first-ever Camanachd Cup competition on the front page of the Ross-shire Journal, *January 10, 1896.*

Lord Lovat and his executive must occasionally have despaired of uniting the game of shinty behind one banner in the first four seasons of the Camanachd Cup. No sooner had the first-round matches been completed than John Campbell's letterbox was clattering with indignant appeals. Grantown protested that Newtonmore, in knocking them out of the first round on Boxing Day, had fielded two players who had turned out for Edinburgh Camanachd, and had failed to put up goal nets. It was agreed that the possibility of 'two good clubs joining and sending a strong team to compete for the cup' should be frowned upon and Newtonmore were obliged to replay Grantown using only players unsullied by connections with other, non-affiliated clubs. (This they did and duly won again. We do not know whether or not goal nets were provided on the second occasion.)

Brae Lochaber complained bitterly about the time-wasting tactics of Ballachulish in their first-round tie. While holding a narrow lead in the second half, Ballachulish had, according to the Brae Lochaber captain, 'wilfully wasted time . . . they hit the ball out of the field of play, and when it was out of play they ran and hit it further out'. After some discussion and an appeal from Ballachulish that there was insufficient evidence to sustain the Brae Lochaber protest, that game also was ordered to be replayed. Ballachulish won through on the second occasion without finding it necessary to steer the match ball in the direction of Rannoch Moor.

But elsewhere, the good, the positive and the sportsmanlike triumphed. London Camanachd, who had been drawn at home against Cowal, heard that their old friends might find difficulty in raising the money and a team to send south on the appointed date – so they duly scratched, thereby giving to Cowal a guaranteed place in the semi-finals. And in Strathpeffer and Beauly two dynamic encounters lit up the district. The first round game at Castle Leod between Caberfeidh and Beauly resulted in a 1–1 draw. The replay on 25 January attracted a large crowd to Mr Birnie's field at Wellhouse. The shops closed in Beauly and the population flocked to see their side gradually gain the ascendency over the favoured visitors from Strathpeffer. A Tom Fraser goal, scored from the right wing thirty minutes into the game, proved enough to send the Beauly support cheerfully home. Out of the competition, Caberfeidh proceeded to console themselves by beating Tain in a friendly.

Cowal found themselves drawn away in the semi-finals to the winners of the western district, Spean Bridge. The Glasgow men made a workmanlike job of dismissing their hosts, establishing a 2–0 lead shortly into the second half through the clinical finishing of the brothers Hugh and John MacCorquodale and the judicious marshalling of Lowrie and Ferguson. Ewan Cameron pulled one back for Spean Bridge with fifteen minutes to go, but John MacCorquodale settled the issue with three minutes left. Glasgow Cowal left the field and the Highlands and shortly afterwards found themselves considering with no little satisfaction the prospect of a place in the first final of the Camanachd Cup against a team which had taken a rather more arduous route through the densely stocked central and northern districts: Cowal were to face, on Saturday, 25 April 1896, Kingussie Shinty Club. It should not have been otherwise.

The two teams had met once since their seminal clash in Kingussie in April 1893: exactly a year later, on the Glasgow spring holiday of 1894, Cowal again emerged victorious by 2–1. But nobody approaching the Needlefield in Inverness on the afternoon of Saturday, 25 April 1896 could have believed for long that past form would have any bearing on

Simon, Lord Lovat, the first president of the Camanachd Association, and its chieftain between 1898 and 1933.

the result of this game. The Highland Railway Company had laid on extra trains from Badenoch, carrying as many as 600 excited kilted and knickerbockered supporters into Inverness. In all, one thousand people paid a shilling each to line the ground. Cowal, whose name preceded them to the north, gave the game, as ever, their greatest respect, arriving on the Friday evening in order to relax by the swollen Ness, to plan and to prepare themselves.

But Kingussie were not, this time, about to let down the district of Badenoch and the pride of northern shinty. Cowal began well, Tom Scott stretching John Campbell to a fine save, and for a while in the first half it seemed that the Glasgow trademark, their unerringly accurate, lightning passing game might once again overcome Kingussie. But seventeen minutes into the game Kingussie broke and their captain, Ross, to the deafening jubilation of the crowd, put his team into the lead over Cowal for the first time ever. Cowal pressed on grimly, but inspired defence from MacPherson and Campbell frustrated what appeared to be irresistible pressure from the Glasgow team and before half-time Alex Campbell took advantage of a rare break to drive a scorching shot past Robinson in the Cowal goal. Cowal never recovered. Scott and John MacCorquodale plugged away through the second period, but Kingussie were on the point of writing history and that realisation is a formidable motivator of powerful defenders. There was, reported local newspapers, 'intense excitement' on the Needlefield when Mr MacGillivray of Tomatin blew the final whistle shortly after 4.30 p.m. Provost MacPherson led his team back to Kingussie on a train whose engine was decorated with ribbons in the MacPherson tartan, and whose engine driver and fireman had donned Kingussie jerseys. Cowal returned to Glasgow in happy ignorance of the fact that they would never appear in another Camanachd Cup Final.

There was now, it appeared, very little standing in the way of the game of shinty. Newspaper correspondence columns reflected the sport's new-found attraction to 'Interested Spectators' who took every opportunity to advise the Camanachd Association on the management of their game. The flurry of controversy over the rules of the game had settled down, after a fileful of amendments, into reasonably widespread acceptance, although some quibbles, such as about the size of the ball and of the goals, would never die. Some clubs shared the anxieties of the official from Tain, who regretted that 'shinty practice is now a rare thing . . . I cannot understand how it is that people who seemed enthusiastic at the beginning of the season have now grown cool and apparently indifferent', but the teams as a whole were in a buoyant state. When James Campbell reported to his Association's AGM in September 1896 that it possessed the remarkably healthy bank balance of £64 10s. 7d, as against only £5 4s. 8d a year previously, the game appeared so healthy that the executive committee finally agreed to release him from the job which he had done for such a crucial three years.

The quarrymen of Ballachulish, who twice thwarted Kingussie's Camanachd Cup ambitions at the turn of the century.

Back row (left to right): *John MacKenzie, Aleck Cameron, Donald MacKenzie, Dugald MacMillan (captain), Dr Grant (honorary vice-captain), John Gemmell, John Robertson, John MacDonald, Aleck Rankine.*
Middle Row: *Hugh MacInnes, Robert Carmichael.*
Front row: *Donald Maclachlan, John MacDonald.*

Fortunately, the broad strength of the game was quickly reflected in the competition for the Camanachd Cup. Entirely to their surprise, the first finalists, Kingussie and Cowal, who could have been forgiven for believing that they would dominate the arena for some years to come, were knocked out of the semi-finals in March 1897 by Brae Lochaber and Beauly respectively. The final, which was held at the Haugh Park, Inverness, shortly before it was developed as a building site, was an even greater event than its predecessor. More than 3,000 people turned up, two-thirds of them having travelled from outside Inverness by train, brake and steamer up Loch Ness from Lochaber, to see a fit and well-drilled Beauly side crush their cumbersome opponents 6–0. If the scoreline might have been unsatisfactory to anybody whose home did not overlook the Beauly Firth, the performance of the new champions was not. That precious asset of Glasgow Cowal, the 'scientific shinty' which they had exported to the darkest corners of south London and Speyside, was now in the hands of Highlanders. The Beauly players were slim, quick, agile and alert. Their style of play was, said one observer after the rout at the Haugh, so different – scientific, I would say – compared with the old style, that the game is no longer one for giants, but for the swift and wiry. It has become a pastime in which fleetness of foot, mobility of body, dodging, feinting, and general trickiness, combined, of course, with accurate hitting and unselfish passing of the ball, are the winning factors . . . Viewing the play as a whole, it must be conceded that Beauly gave a splendid exposition of the most modern style of shinty.'

For reasons other than the fact that their six goals against the luckless men from Roy Bridge could easily have been sixteen, Beauly were truly worthy champions. No sooner had they taken the precious trophy than they were off on tour, going as guests of honour to the London Highland Athletic Club's annual gathering, which was held on 5 June 1897 at the Stamford Bridge grounds which are now the premises of Chelsea Football Club. They were awaited there by an enormous expectant crowd – no exact numbers are available, but contemporary reports refer to 'an immense concourse of people', and 'by far the largest attendance of spectators that ever patronised these interesting exhibitions'. The Duke of Argyle, Archbishop Sinclair, the MacKintosh of MacKintosh, the Count of Serra Largo (who established his Highland credentials so convincingly with an initially dubious audience that he was, later that year, elected as an honorary vice-president of the Camanachd Association) all strolled from their carriages down the Fulham Road and into the brightly sunlit arena. Early arrivals heard a young man from Badenoch called Angus MacPherson finish second in the piobaireachd competition and joint third in the Strathspey and Reel, before going on to pick up other medals in the dancing. Prizes to the value of £150 were distributed by the Marquis of Tullibardine. The Gaelic Athletic Association had sent over the Ireland United Hurling Club (who played out a 4–4 draw with London Camanachd, each side performing according to their own codes of play) and an Irish tug o' war team who triumphed over the London Scots.

But the top item on the bill and the last event of a long day was the visit of Beauly Shinty Club to play a select from the Highland Athletic Club. The Beauly men had travelled south in style, booking an East Coast Company saloon carriage, and they were greeted at Stamford Bridge with more awe and respect than any aristocrat. They stood before the humming crowd in jerseys of green and black, captain Roderick MacLean at their head, to hear themselves introduced as the champions of Scotland, and then proceeded to demolish their un-tutored opposition, scoring six times in quick succession before relaxing and paying due respect to their exiled hosts by allowing the London Highlanders to retrieve one goal. 'This was the last event of the meeting,' said the correspondents,

> but by far the most exciting . . . the attendance was larger than it had been at any previous time, the utmost interest being displayed in the champion shinty club of Scotland . . . towards the close it seemed as though they [Beauly] could have scored twenty if they had cared to try. The London Club were encouraged by winning one hail, and, considering that the Beauly team have played 45 hails in the course of the season and have lost only three, including this one, it was perhaps natural that the London men should feel elated . . .'

Back in Scotland, Beauly found themselves with bigger fish to fry. *The Celtic Monthly* had ungraciously opined that Beauly could not properly consider themselves to be champions of Scotland. Noting that Inveraray, who were yet to affiliate with the Association and enter the competition, had just beaten Kingussie 5–2 in a friendly, MacKay's magazine said, 'there is no team in Britain can defeat Inveraray . . . A match between Beauly and the Lochfyne men would decide the championship.' Any thoughts that the large Beauly committee might have entertained about inviting the Argyllshire team to take part in a grudge 'friendly' were dispelled when, in September, the Camanachd Association's new secretary, Mr MacGillivray of the Bank of Scotland in Inverness, told his AGM that he had received a subscription and a request for entry from the Inveraray club. MacGillivray nodded in the direction of two new faces at the meeting and the large attendance broke into gleeful applause as he welcomed the legendary Argyllshire team into the fold. John MacKay and Roderick MacLeod of Glasgow Cowal were also present in the Burgh Court House, Inverness, that Friday, applauding as loudly as any. Their joy lasted for less than six months.

It was nicely ironic that Cowal should meet Inveraray in the Camanachd Cup before Beauly had a chance to make MacKay eat his words. But the manner of Cowal's departure from the fourth round of the competition in favour of the Loch Fyne men was deeply disturbing to shinty and presented the young Association with its gravest crisis. Drawn away, Cowal did well to get a 3–3 draw at Inveraray. Two further draws took place, and when the fourth match was rescheduled by an Association secretary desperate to see the fixture completed for a Wednesday night at Dalmally, Cowal could not make the game and Inveraray were announced the winners by default. Cowal conducted a bitter correspondence with the Camanachd Association and finally withdrew their membership. They tried, unsuccessfully, to take their friends from Kingussie out with them. 'The business of the Association', wrote John MacKay, 'is conducted in a most unfair and exasperating manner, and unless some alterations for the better is made, next year's competitions will certainly be of the most uninteresting character, confined to the second rate teams.' Lord Lovat, who described Cowal's attitude as 'most insulting', and suggested that their predicament could not be helped, nonetheless perceived the withdrawal of these distinguished, testy ambassadors of the game from the Association as a 'disaster'. He and secretary MacGillivray spent a long winter in 1898, persuading the aggrieved Glaswegians to rejoin.

The truth is that by 1898 if Cowal had not been members of the Camanachd Association, they, not the office bearers in the north, would have been out in the cold. Inveraray was not the only resonant new name to take up membership that year: they were joined by Oban, Furnace, Foyers, Kyles, Lairg, Strathdearn and Perth. Edinburgh Camanachd had been members for twelve months. The Camanachd Cup was at last truly representative. To reach its final was no longer a matter of drawing a bye and winning a semi-final. The two sides which got to Inverness in March had to overcome en route the best of the rest in the country. Beauly did so narrowly in the semis, a Tommy Fraser goal just before half-time seeing off a bright and determined Kingussie side (and, it was claimed, leaving a host of confidently built bonfires unlit in Badenoch. While putting this story about, the Beauly support gleefully reported that the useless wood was distributed among the poor of the district after Kingussie's defeat, thus proving the adage that 'it's an ill wind that doesn't blow somebody good'. Officials of Kingussie Shinty Club angrily denied the truth of the story.). When it became clear that Beauly were to be joined in the final by Inveraray, John MacKay might have allowed himself a knowledgeable smile.

Once again the Camanachd Cup Final broke all attendance records for shinty games and for sporting occasions in the north of Scotland. More than 4,000 people turned up in Inverness on that spring day in 1898 to see Beauly play Inveraray. They were policed by a detachment of sixty Cameron Highlanders, the regiment having cheerfully adopted responsibility for the game since they had first been approached by Archibald Chisholm ten years before. Most knowledgeable witnesses agreed that when the ninety minutes were up this had not been a vintage Beauly performance. The northerners struggled from the start against an Inveraray squad which had a point to prove and which took the lead after just ten minutes when Eric Smith cut in from the right wing to score. It was time for the champions to display some resilence and character against the contenders who had arrived at Inverness behind a proud boast of having been undefeated for fully twenty years, and Beauly did just that. D.J. MacRae threw his teammates a lifeline by equalising before half-time, and despite fierce Inveraray pressure, Tom Forbes kept his defence calm and well-marshalled throughout a torrid second forty-five minutes. With only a minute or two remaining MacRae broke again to rifle the ball past Sinclair in the Inveraray goal and send the Beauly men home, for the second successive year, as Scottish champions. Before returning to the bonfires and the jubilant crowds Tom Forbes, the Beauly captain, told reporters that he considered Inveraray to have been the better team and that his side's winning goal had been 'a stroke of good luck'. This was not enough for John MacKay in Glasgow. 'The Beauly men can hardly,' he announced, 'claim the championship until they meet the Glasgow Cowal, who are still an undefeated team . . .'

Lord Lovat officially presented Beauly with the Camanachd Cup one month later, at a sparkling occasion in the Lovat Arms Hotel. While President MacKinley was formally declaring the United States to be at war with Spain and the Chancellor of the Exchequer announced to the House of Commons that the Jubilee celebrations had added more than a million pounds to Britain's national revenue, the president of the Camanachd Association was raising his glass to 'twelve of the best fellows' he knew. Beauly had introduced the passing game to northern shinty, he said, and had added to that 'their wonderful staying power'. In reply, Tom Forbes agreed that the club's progress since its inauguration three years before had been, indeed, remarkable. Since two early reverses at the hands of Lovat and

Kingussie, they had remained undefeated. He hoped that when defeat came, 'as it must to the best of teams', Beauly would take it as well as they had received success. Under the cruellest of circumstances, Tom Forbes was to prove true to his word.

Two bright lights went out in the closing years of the nineteenth century. On 19 October 1897, Captain Archibald MacRa Chisholm died at Glassburn House at the age of seventy-two. He had never been able to attend a meeting of the Camanachd Association which had honoured him with its first chieftainship, but had kept an approving eye on its activities, sending letters of support and encouragement and expressing regret at the occasional resignation. The *Inverness Courier* obituarised of Archibald Chisholm: 'He founded the Strathglass Shinty Club in 1880 by which he revived interest in the game generally in the Highlands . . . [he] was a courteous gentleman of humour and great integrity with the spirit of his race.' At its 1898 annual general meeting the Camanachd Association considered and rejected a proposal to do away with the office of chief, electing instead to offer to Simon, Lord Lovat, the position which he was to hold for the following thirty-five years. John Macdonald of Keppoch, who had first proposed the national shinty association, became its second president.

On a Saturday at the end of December 1898 Beauly travelled to Skye in the second round of their defence of the Camanachd Cup. They were reluctant sailors. Earlier in the month the Beauly committee had written to Portree attempting to get the game played on the mainland, but the Skye man had refused to relinquish the right to home advantage which they had so recently re-established and Beauly were forced to undertake the three-day journey without some first-team players. Before setting off they agreed at a meeting to urge the Association to once more oblige Skye teams to fulfil their commitments east of the Kyles of Lochalsh. But Beauly undertook the journey with some confidence. Their previous record against the Skye team was unblemished since the day in 1895 when they had provided the newly established Portree club with its first mainland opposition and handed out a 'friendly' lesson at Wellhouse, beating the islanders 5–0. More recently Tom Fraser and D.J. MacRae had run riot against Lovat at Kiltarlity in the first round, helping to establish a 4–0 lead before Lovat pulled back two late consolation goals.

Beauly showed no signs of losing momentum in Portree. With just twenty-three minutes to go they were leading by 5–2 when the violent wind which had swept the pitch all afternoon worsened, the goalposts blew down and the referee ordered the players off the field. Shortly afterwards, when the goalposts had been re-erected, he ordered them back on again. In the confusion that followed, the Beauly team refused to recommence play, claiming that the game had been suspended and that the weather conditions were 'such as to endanger life'. On receipt of the referee's report, the Camanachd Association awarded Portree the tie. Beauly took some consolation from the season when they won the MacTavish Cup, a trophy newly put on offer to northern sides, taking it from Skye, who had won it in its inaugural year of 1898 by beating Inverness 7–3 in the final.

But Scottish shinty's first great champions had gone out of the Camanachd Cup, which they had dominated and dignified for two of its first three years, undefeated. There were no histrionics or resignations from Tom Fraser's Beauly. Kingussie, who had put the mollified Glasgow Cowal out of the first round by 3–1, proceeded to the first of five successive finals, where they were surprisingly and controversially defeated 2–1 by the quarrymen of Ballachulish in the first final to be played outside Inverness, at the North Inch of Perth. Angus Mac-Pherson, the young piper who had made such an impression at Stamford Bridge on the occasion of Beauly's triumphal visit to London, played for Kingussie in that final, and more than seventy years later he could 'never concede that we Kingussie men were truly beaten, for the match was decided by what would be today an infringement of shinty rules'. But the name of Ballachulish, accompanied not for the last time by controversy, went on to the Camanachd Cup. The post-match dinner at the Salutation Hotel heard Mr John MacKay, president of the Glasgow Cowal Shinty Club and editor of *The Celtic Monthly*, propose the toast to the Camanachd Association.

With a healthy continuity of bloodline, of fraction and reconciliation, shinty slipped into the twentieth century.

7

Troubled Water

'That was what the young ones wanted.'

Many of the remoter islands and glens of Scotland lay beyond the reach of the helping hand of the Camanachd Association. In large parts of those sections of the Highlands and Islands which were, ironically, to become the last redoubt of the language and traditional culture of the Scottish Gael, the game of shinty ceased to be played during the first four decades of the twentieth century. It was an inexorable decline.

A warning about the survival of the game in islands separated by lengthy sea crossings from the heady progress being made on the mainland was posted as early as March 1894, when the Strathpeffer – soon to become Caberfeidh – club reluctantly announced that it had been obliged to 'postpone indefinitely' a tour to Lewis and Skye to play the Stornoway and Portree clubs, 'owing to the unsatisfactory state of the steamship communication'. They went instead to Invergordon. Within two years the Camanachd Cup had become the focus of each mainland club's season and distractions such as a visit to unaffiliated teams in the islands were even less likely to be considered. The only way to stay within the mainstream of shinty was to join the Camanachd Association and enter its competitions. This was clearly unthinkable in Stornoway, but even the Portree club, which had no intention of withdrawing, fought a running battle with the Association over its right to play a home tie on Skye for twenty years after Lord Lovat's notorious 'three-day job' remarks. In 1901, when the Sgiathanaichs must have assumed that the issue was dead and buried, having been settled in their favour in the conciliatory days of 1898, a motion from Beauly, prompted by black memories of that gale-torn exit from the Camanachd Cup in Portree in the winter of 1898–99, and which, to do the former champions justice, had been agreed upon before the mainland club set off to play the fateful tie, asked the Association to rule that Skye teams must play all of their matches on the mainland. It was passed by eleven votes to four. Skye worked hard over the years to get the ruling reversed once more, notably in 1912, but failed every time. Not until after the First World War did the islanders regain the right to home advantage.

In other places, where there had never been any possibility of entry to the Camanachd Association's competitions on any terms, the game simply withered and died. In the islands of North and South Uist and Benbecula, *iomain* had been a constant feature of winter life for centuries. It had been as common and traditional an outdoor pursuit as horse-riding on the sweeping strand and *carachd*, or wrestling, on the machair.

Alexander Morrison wrote of his native Uists as late as 1908:

> . . . shinty is a favourite game. Equal sides are picked, the object of the game being to score as many goals as possible. Stones are used for goals – the ball may be of wood, hard wound worsted, or of hair, peat, or other available material, while the caman is a bent stick of wood or a large tangle. In these islands people have to be ingenious and to make the best of the materials they have. As Uist is barren of trees a tangle caman is nearly as common as a wooden one. Another ingenious caman is made of a large piece of canvas bent with both ends caught in the hand. It is very effective. The Uist boys used to be, and in some places still are, very proficient at the game, the main qualities necessary for an ideal 'iomain' player being speed and dexterity.

Reverend Angus John MacVicar, who was at school in Kingussie when the local side won the first Camanachd Cup in 1896, and who went on to help form the Glasgow University Shinty Club in 1901, came from Claddach Kirkibost in North Uist and remembered into old age the winter games of his childhood: carving camain out of driftwood, the bruised knees and the lacerated hands. Lachlan MacQuien of Tigharry in North Uist recalled on his hundredth birthday in 1982 taking part in the last shinty cup final to be played in the Uists. That was in 1907. The North Uist Challenge Cup, which had been presented by the landowner Sir John Campbell-Orde in 1895, was contested for the last time by Sollas and West Side. Sollas protested that West Side were equipped with manufactured camain, brought home for the occasion by a team member who was working in Portree, but eventually allowed the game to get under way. West Side won by 4–0.

In South Uist, the game was sewn into the vivid tapestry of folklore which distinguishes that island still. In 1893 A.B. MacLennan of Lochboisdale published what he called *A Spectre Arbiter: A New Year Shinty Story*. In South Uist, wrote MacLennan of the early years of the nineteenth century,

> Every township sent its contingent (from the beardless youth to the grey-haired sage) to the several machairs on Christmas and New Year's Day. The machairs of Benbecula, Iochdar, Howmore, Milton, Dalibrog, Kilpheder, and Smerclate, were peculiarly adapted for this famous recreation . . .
>
> At one of these *camanachds*, on the machair of Dalibrog, on a New Year's Day some years ago, a dispute arose as to the team which gained the most hailes. The contention at length assumed such proportions that the captains were about to decide the point by an appeal to strength . . .

One of these captains, 'whom we shall call John', raised his caman to strike an opponent when he was frozen to the spot by the sight of a man walking quickly towards him. The man beckoned John to follow him to the strand. John pointed him out to his fellows, who could see nothing, but knew full well what John could see and left, terror-struck, for home. John proceeded to the first of many appointments with the figure, who told him that he was not to celebrate the New Year in so unseemly a fashion, predicted the place of his death at a ripe age, and identified himself as the spirit of a relative. 'We have suppressed the names of persons and places for certain reasons,' concluded A.B. MacLennan, 'but have no doubt our South Uist readers will readily recognise them.'

When Frederick Rea, the Birmingham man who served as head teacher at Garrynamonie School from 1890 to 1894 and from 1903 to 1913, wrote his memories of *A School in South Uist*, he made no mention of *iomain* or camanachd; although Kate MacPhee, the local woman who was a pupil and pupil-teacher at Garrynamonie in his time, remembered in her foreword to the book that 'the annual camanachd match played on New Year's Day by rival teams was eagerly welcomed by young and old alike'. But Rea may, unwittingly, have helped nail the old game's coffin. He described, with customary clarity, an event which occurred sooner or later in every parish in the Highlands and Islands: the introduction of the inflatable football.

Rea's brothers – 'great football players' – had arrived on Uist during leave from the army, bringing a football. Soon the wide sward of the machair was implanted with two sets of hastily improvised goalposts and the Rea family began to play.

> A number of figures appeared on the machair advancing towards us; more and more appeared on the sky-line coming from various directions, scores of them . . . the newcomer players became excited – then they would rush at the man who had the ball, catch hold of his coat and hold him . . . there were now fifty a side at least; some were tearing about the field looking for the ball or rushing at each other . . . News travelled fast on South Uist.

It certainly did. By the middle of the 1920s, when Rea came to write down his memories of that hilarious scrimmage on Garrynamonie machair, the game of football had established its hegemony in the Outer Hebrides. While Willie MacLean, Jimmy (the Slater) Fraser, and Bill Kennedy were helping the team which used to be Kiltarlity and was now Lovat win the northern trophy which had been put up in 1898, the MacTavish Cup; while the Argyllshire powers of Kyles Athletic, the Munros of Inveraray and Furnace took a tight grip on the Camanachd Cup, as well as on their own revived Celtic Society trophy; while nationally the game seemed to have recovered from the appalling losses it suffered during the First World War; in the heartland of Gaelic culture, the Western Isles, *iomain*, camanachd, the game which was as old as the language which they still used in preference to any other, was no more than a memory.

It was last known of on the sands of Laig, beneath the sheer cliff face which overlooks the Sound of Rhum, on the island of Eigg in the middle of the 1920s. Hugh MacKinnon, the scholarly, much travelled *seannachaidh* of that island, told Donald Archie MacDonald of the School of Scottish Studies in 1965 of the last New Year's Day game on this small island in the winter of 1925–26. Fifty or sixty men would gather there with camain of hazel, elm, oak, willow or birch cut from the woods, whittled and heat-bent in a peat fire, and a ball of hazel root. Two of the younger players would pick the sides and employ the familiar rituals of grasping a caman hand over hand, throwing it in the air to see, when it fell upon the sand, in which direction it indicated the thrower's side should play, and reply with 'Ligidh mi leat' to the challenge 'Buaileam ort!'. (It seems that, in Eigg, the latter invitation to play had been transformed over the years into 'Buail am port' – Strike up the tune!). Coilleagan, or goals of stone, were set up more than 200 yards apart between the mouth of Abhainn na Caime and Ceann Daoibhinn, and a game which had evolved a uniquely sophisticated set of indigenous rules took place. One score was not enough to count fully, it was known as a *leth-cluich* (half-play) only another hit between the stones below hip-height counted as a *cluich*. The ball passing either side of the goal, or *tuathal*, was out of play, and was the goalkeeper's to hit from his line.

Younger boys of school age were dissuaded from taking part, but there was no upper age limit. Hugh MacKinnon remembered one man:

> He was about eighty, and didn't have a stitch on but his trousers and his shirt. I remember it fine. It was a warm sunny day right enough. Oh yes, Gilleasbuig son of John son of Angus . . . And I can still remember, he was playing towards the south, over towards the Caime. And someone hit the ball from the other side and he saw it coming and the ball rose, going too high, about chest high and he stopped and stuck out his chest and that was how he stopped the ball . . . Ah, the poor man, and I think he died the next summer again.

In playing those day-long games, with the high Minch tide occasion-ally narrowing the width of their field to three or four yards, the people of Eigg were walking, 'gualainn ri gualainn' as their relatives in London might have put it, with their own history. As contemporary heavyweight boxing champions can claim to be linked directly by a series of blows to the chin to Bob Fitzsimmons, John L. Sullivan and Jem Mace; as cricket boasts the easy continuity of Grace having played with Rhodes, who played against Bradman, who played against Bailey; so the game of shinty can claim a lineage infinitely more ancient and involved. The Skye team which won the first MacTavish Cup Final in Inverness in 1898 included a notable player by the name of Billy Ross. Having survived the inferno at Neuve Chapelle, Company Sergeant

Major Billy Ross of the 4th Cameron Territorials was killed on the first day of the battle of Festubert, 17 May 1915. Ninety years after the MacTavish Cup victory, the great grandsons of Billy Ross were playing for Skye. Who knows which players might have been faced, birch camain in hand, with the forebears of Gilleaspuig, son of John, son of Angus, on the sands at Laig? We shall never know now: the imponderable agnation ended that winter in the middle of the 1920s when Hugh MacKinnon watched as 'they laid the camain aside and got out a football. That was what the young ones wanted.'

Even in Skye, which shares with Bute the distinction of being the only Scottish island to sustain to the present day an interest in competitive shinty at the highest level, the game died slowly in distant corners. The southernmost peninsula of Sleat, from which the high cliff walls of Eigg are clearly visible, was until the end of the 1930s one of the most productive shinty nurseries on the island. Its two west side villages of Tarskavaig and Achnacloich could raise, from not much more than thirty crofts, two teams to compete in the Sleat Shinty League for a trophy which had been provided in the early 1930s by a travelling whisky salesman named MacCowan. They played for this elegant three- handled quaich against sides from Aird, from Calligarry, from Ferindonald and Teangue, from Camus Croise, and occasionally from Broadford. They played on roughly hewn grounds at Ardvasar, at the Gillan in Archnacloich and on the flat land at Kinloch which had been cleared of its village in the eighteenth century and which is now a forestry plantation hemming-in the ground of the local football team. The village sides united annually to compete as a parish for the all-Skye trophy, the Robertson Cup, which had been provided in 1907 by R.C. Robertson MacLeod of Greshornish, against the pick of Bernisdale, Braes, Portree, Portree School and, before the First World War, Edinbane. And of course they played on New Year's Day, in Tarskavaig and on the grazings overlooking Cnoc Bay, with camain cut from the plentiful hazel in Sleat's wooded glens, and balls made of cork covered with wool.

Another Gilleasbuig, Archie MacDonald of Tarskavaig (the Gaelic forename of Gilleasbuig is translated into English as Archibald), remembers those matches where, outwith the remit of the Camanachd Association, national rules had nonetheless come to apply.

There were large crowds, all the locals came and watched, and there was much support locally in the form of dances and fund raising and travel – which was difficult in those days, we had to use an old car or lorry or bicycles.

It seemed to be on the up and up in those days. There was so much unemployment that people couldn't get jobs in the south, and that's why there were so many young men about. The ground below my house in Tarskavaig would be black. I spent every minute as a boy hitting the ball against the end of the house. With sheer practice you become like a golfer, you could more or less guarantee to land a ball inside a tin can at 20 yards: you became absolutely accurate, you would never miss a ball in the air – these are basic skills.

They are basic skills which were honed in village matches where two jackets or a pile of stones served as goals on a small strip of common grazing, in MacCowan Cup matches, where two posts would be erected and a rope crossbar strung between them, and in full, refereed matches for the Robertson Cup. In 1936, the year in which New-tonmore became the first side to win all three of the senior competitions open to northern clubs – the MacTavish Cup, the MacGillivray League, and, after a marathon replayed final against Kyles Athletic, the Camanachd Cup (in the course of which campaign they conceded only two goals) – and while the brothers Cumming, MacKenzie, Mac-Master and Keir were gearing themselves to mount the Caberfeidh club's eventually successful challenge to Badenoch supremacy, more modest by no less heartening success was being celebrated in Sleat as the parish team, which played under the name of its champion village, Tarskavaig, reached the final of the Robertson Cup.

They lost that final 1–0 to Portree School. The man who moved forward out of the School defence to lay on the winning goal for Peter Finlayson of Dunan a few minutes from time, a young teacher called Sorley Maclean, recalled the power and determination of the Sleat centre line and their constant pressure playing up a slight incline in the second half: pressure so intense that the School team, Maclean was always convinced, would not have survived extra time.

It could not have been predicted that, within a decade scarred by a second world war, the game of shinty in Sleat would be effectively dead – and that in Skye itself it would not long afterwards require urgent resuscitation. Tarskavaig reached the final of the Robertson Cup again in the following season, being beaten this time by Bernis-dale 4–1. In the season of 1938–39 they entertained Portree School to a

friendly game in Sleat and took belated revenge by beating the scholars
3–1 – no small achievement against a side whose home-grown talents
were enhanced by the presence of the brothers Willie and Peter
MacGillivray, Kingussie boys whose father had followed his calling in
the police force to Portree.

Then came the war, and after the war many of those who had
survived simply did not return, having sampled a new life and been
offered new opportunities away from the quiet crofts which stretch, as
neatly as a Department of Agriculture groundplan, north from Tarskavaig bay. Archie MacDonald recalls:

> I think we sent one team from Sleat to Portree in 1947. They tried to
> resurrect it after the war. There were men at home on leave, some
> finishing their service days, and they managed to rake up some of
> the old timers who were six, seven years older than they had been
> before the war, and that's the last team that played from Sleat. After
> that it died. The school population had fallen so much, and once the
> young people go there is no chance. Unless you get them young, it's
> no good.

The collapse of the popularity of the game of shinty in places such as
Lewis, Uist, Eigg and Sleat – and Sutherland and Caithness, and
Glenelg and Arnisdale, and innumerable other districts, islands and
townships where once no other outdoor sport was known of – has been
more than just a local private tragedy. Apart from the obvious
weakening of the spirit of a game which occurs when areas which
have known it since the beginning of recorded time cast the sport aside
in favour of another – or in favour of no other – the strength of the
material body of shinty has been relentlessly sapped since the start of
the twentieth century. Highlanders, clannish as any in their loyalties to
their own parishes at home, become a distinctly homogenous people
once away from the mountains and the sea. A Leodhasaich and a
Sgiathanaich are in Glasgow, Edinburgh or Ontario, neighbours, the
common ground between them easily crossing the division of twenty
miles of hostile Hebridean sea even if, as is occasionally the case, they
have no shared ancestry. Any erosion of that common ground chews
into the broad Highland identity. Once the game of shinty becomes no
longer a valid part of that expansive, ecumenical identity then shinty,
as well as the Highlander, is the loser. As the twentieth century drew to

*Calum Nicholson, one of the famous
Nicolson brothers of Kyles Athletic,
with the Camanachd Cup after beating
Newtonmore 2–1 in the 1927 final.*

a close, it was as common and regrettable to find two Gaels who could
not, upon meeting, while away an hour or two discussing the memories
and merits of shinty teams of the past and the present as it was to find
two Sgiathanaich who could not carry on a conversation in Gaelic.

Once, this homogenous body of Highlanders was distinguishable as
much, if not more, by its sports as by any other outward sign. The
London, Glasgow and Edinburgh camanachd clubs were speckled with
the surnames of a thousand Highland parishes. Any new arrival in
town, from Stornoway or Badenoch, Lochboisdale or Strathpeffer, was
justifiably considered as potential material for strengthening the squad.
And men did not have to travel that far to discover that shinty was
another large link in the binding chain. Many, such as Martin
MacInnes, a contemporary of Archie MacDonald's in the village of
Tarskavaig who enjoyed great success with Oban Camanachd, moved
easily into new shinty teams when their work took them to other parts
of the Highlands. The shinty record books are studded with the names
of people who found a welcome and success in the ranks of teams a
hundred miles from home. The Portree School team which won the
Robertson Cup in 1924–25 included a goalkeeper, Calum MacSween,
whose father was a mason from Scalpay, Harris; a half-back, John
MacKinnon, who was also from Harris; a centre, Tom Fraser, the son
of a minister with Uist connections; and it was captained by a youth of

Uist extraction, Lachie Boyd. The Glasgow Skye team of 1920–21 contained six players from the district of Braes. But by the end of the 1920s there were so few available players in Braes that the district had to merge with Bernisdale in order to compete in the Robertson Cup. When the Edinburgh University shinty team was restarted after the Second World War, seven of its twelve players were from Skye and most of these seven were from the outlying regions of the island: Bernisdale, Braes, Raasay, Tarskavaig and Elgol. Sorley Maclean, the young teacher who laid on that winning goal for Portree School in the 1936–37 Robertson Cup Final, whose shinty career was ended by shrapnel in the North African desert, and who went on to find unrequested acknowledgement as Scotland's greatest Gaelic poet (as well as achieving possibly more welcome acclaim for injecting new life into the game of shinty in Wester Ross while headmaster of Plockton High School in the 1950s and 1960s), remembered his

Giants from the south: the Inveraray squad which, with its usual sprinkling of Munros, beat Lovat 2–0 to win the 1925 Camanachd Cup in Inverness.

Players only! Back row (left to right): *A. Cameron, A. Munro, D. Campbell, R. Jenkins, D. Stewart.*
Middle row: *W. Jenkins, P. Munro, N. Munro, D. Munro, A. MacCaig. Front: A. Munro, N. MacGugan.*

The Edinburgh University team of 1929–30, with the Littlejohn Vase – 'a limited-entry prize as curiously valuable as the Calcutta Cup'.

Back row (left to right): *J. Fletcher, C. Mackintosh, M.C MacQueen, M. Macleod, N.A.S. Campbell.*
Middle row: *S. Maclean, D.J. Macrae (vice captain), T.N. Fraser (captain), A. Mackay (honorary secretary), G. Livingstone.*
On ground: *H. Maclean, W.E. Stuart.*

Nicolson grandfather's conviction that his Braes family was related to the famous Nicolson brothers of Kyles Athletic.

Over a period of forty years, in eight of these Nicolsons helped Kyles to nine Camanachd Cup finals and twelve Celtic Society Cup finals. No fewer than five of them were in the 1922 side which won the Celtic Society Cup and beat Beauly by 6–3 in the final of the Camanachd, refreshed, as always at half-time, by a pail of what was said to be oatmeal water delivered to the field by the wife of Hugh Nicolson. Two of them represented Britain at field events in the Olympic Games. Celly Paterson, who made his cup final debut for Kyles when they were beaten 2–1 by Caberfeidh in Inverness in 1939, who was still playing in goal twenty years later at Old Anniesland when Newtonmore, celebrating their twenty-seventh Camanachd Cup final appearance, ran riot to win 7–3, and who became chieftain of the Camanachd Association in 1985, was the son of the sister of the Nicolson brothers of Tignabruaich. Said Sorley Maclean: 'My Nicolson grandfather was not at all snobbish about being related to the chief of the Nicolsons but he would dearly have loved to have established his relationship with the strong men of Kyles.' Had the old man done so, he might have been able to explain once and for all the virtuosity of one of Skye's greatest players, big Hugh Nicolson from Braes, a six-foot-three-inch marvel who distinguished the Skye and Glasgow Skye teams in the years after the First World War. He may have shed light on why John Nicolson from Tighnabruaich was to be found coaching the Braes tug o'war team at the Portree Games in 1919; and on why a visit from Kyles Athletic is still acknowledged in Skye as an out-of-the-ordinary occasion.

This is the genealogy of Highland heritage, sketched on the team lists of shinty matches. Nicolsons of Tighnabruaich and Nicolsons of Skye, Munros of Inveraray, Frasers of Newtonmore, Cowies of Lovat and Skye, Murchisons of Skye and Lovat, Grants of almost every team and many others to be found in the ranks of the Glasgow and Edinburgh university and club sides, and on the pages of cup final programmes down through the decades, and all reduced each time a village or an island put aside its camain for the last time.

The competitive pressure which the game of shinty had to endure in Scotland as the twentieth century broke into a gallop cannot be overstated. The miracle may be not that it has survived with forty senior clubs, an active junior programme and many thousands of adherents, but that it has survived at all. As *Thomas the Tank Engine* and *Neighbours* beamed into Highland homes and beamed countless Highland children out of their native language, so the bright lights of Hampden Park, Ibrox, Parkhead, Tannadice and Pittodrie presented what should have been an irresistible challenge to affections which, in the years before a Scot developed the televisor and noctovisor, would automatically have been loaned to shinty. The game and the Gaelic language have not always taken the same road in the same districts over the last hundred years, but they have faced remarkably similar problems.

Unlike their relatives in the Republic of Ireland, neither have been given many of the benefits of governmental recognition and support. No such body as the Gaelic Athletic Association, with its openly nationalist fostering of indigenous Irish sports, has been allowed to Scotland or to anywhere else in the United Kingdom, where it is probably true that the only sporting body whose aspirations, difficulties and occasional crises have been shared at any time by government

Junior shinty – action from the 1985 MacKay Cup Final between Achnacarry and Kingussie Primary Schools. Kingussie won 3–2. (Donald MacKay)

is the Marylebone Cricket Club. No equivalent of the All-Ireland Hurling final, with its packed stadium and devout national media attention, has been considered feasible in this century by any administrator of the Camanachd Association, despite the bitter reflection that at the time of the Great Games between Strathglass and Glen Urquhart and of the first Camanachd Cup finals, Scottish shinty had taken at least a head start over Irish hurling. As the twentieth century showed

At a meeting of the Shinty-Players of the University of Abdn. held on the Links of Old Aberdeen on Saturday the ninth day of November Eighteen hundred and Sixty one Wm. John Murker Preses it was moved and seconded and carried unanimously that the said Shinty-Players do form themselves into a Club; and in order thereto Messrs. Murker Charles Fraser John Strachan, James Grant Senior and Alexander Thomson Grant were appointed as a Committee to draw up Rules & Regulations for the organization and management of the new Club.

(Signed) John Murker, Preses

Rules & Regulations of the Aberdeen University Shinty Club.

I. That the name of this Society be the Aberdeen University Shinty Club.

II. That
be the Patron of said Club and that the Office-bearers be a Captain, Secretary and Treasurer.

III. That the said Office-bearers be elected annually at the first meeting of the Club that shall take place after the commencement of the college Session, which meeting shall be summoned by the Secretary of the Club for the year preceding or failing whom by the other Office-bearers or any three of the members of the Club.

IV. That all Students of the said University shall be entitled to admission

The first page of the earliest rules and constitutions of a shinty club to have been written down in Scotland – at Aberdeen University in 1861.

no signs of slowing down, and as its media broke out of the semi-controlled gallop and into a maddened bolt, people with an interest in the well-being of shinty had good reason constantly to send up thanks for the deep roots which the game has sent down, and for the stout paling erected around its besieged trunk by a steady procession of dedicated, selfless administrators. They may also take heart from the probability that any game which did not possess in its own right a unique attraction to players and spectators alike would, like real tennis, quoits and Nine Men's Morris, have failed and withered long before the opportunity arose to renegotiate a sponsorship deal or the televising of a showpiece fixture.

Shinty's attraction as a spectator sport has become less dependent on rousing local loyalties and increasingly reliant on the ability of young men to develop and raise the quality of their game. Good players in

The Glasgow Skye squad of the early 1930s, which helped organise and supply most of the players for the 1932 international squad, the last Scottish select team to play Ireland for forty years.

Back row (left to right): *Iain Ross, Charlie Wilkinson, Donald Macleod, Iain MacLeod, John F. MacIntosh, John Nicolson, Alex MacKinnon.*
Middle row: *Willie MacIntosh, Archie MacPherson, Donald Grant, Angus MacLean, Alex Finlayson, Angus Young, Donald Grant, Jimmy Currie, John MacDonald.*
Front row: *F. MacLaren, John MacDonald, D.R. MacQueen, Kenny Beaton, D.J. Beaton, Vicky Ferguson, Hume Robertson*

The universities keep lines of communication open across the Irish Sea: Edinburgh University in action against Queen's University, Belfast, in the first post-war shinty/hurling clash in 1947. Archie MacDonald, Tarskavaig, on the ball, with Donald Neil Nicolson looking on.

any sport lift the standards of those pitted against them as well as of those who play with them, and if it is true that the years which prove an athlete are the years between the ages of eighteen and twenty-two, then there is reason to be grateful that when Archie MacDonald of Tarskavaig was demobbed from the Army, left a village which was shortly to be robbed of its interest in shinty, and went at last to Edinburgh University, he was able there to play the game.

The university sides are as old as organised shinty in Scotland. The Aberdeen University Shinty Club was constituted, complete with rules and regulations and a committee, on 9 November 1861; that was almost ten years before Edinburgh Camanachd, which has traditionally worn the laurels of shinty's elder statesman. On that day in 1861, thirty-eight students met on the links of Old Aberdeen and unanimously passed a motion that the shinty players of the university 'do form themselves into a club'. The mover of the motion, John Murker, was appointed with John Strachan, James Grant senior and Alexander Thomas Grant to draw up the club's regulations.

In order to secure a 'fair field', Messrs Murker and company also prepared 'bylaws towards the settling and preventing [of] all such points and disputes'. These bylaws are the earliest written rules of shinty to have come to light in the course of this writer's research. They were never broadly circulated and therefore could not claim the seminal effect of the Shinty Association's rules which were drawn up in Glasgow in 1877, or Archibald Chisholm's rules in 1880 (in the same way as a constituted club in Aberdeen, isolated north of the Mearns and east of the Grampians, could not exert the same influence on the bubbling shinty world of the north and west Highlands and of the Lowlands as could a club constituted in Edinburgh or in Strathglass); but if posthumous awards are to be handed out for bold innovation and initiative, John Murker and his band of Grants, Strachans, Frasers, MacDonalds, MacPhersons, Gordons and Grahames deserve their share.

They were of course fairly basic rules: no more than five in all; and rather than offering a legislative blueprint, they tell us of how the game was played on the links of Old Aberdeen. No player was to throw his caman at any other during the course of a game, nor was he to clutch or push with the hand, nor was he to trip another player. The ball could not be lifted off the ground (presumably by hand). Any new arrival during the course of a match should not immediately attach himself to a side, but should 'await the end of the game when the Drawees shall draw for new comers under the auspices of the umpire for that occasion'. Within this loose and friendly framework the game of shinty was played in happy solitude for almost three decades on the links. Twice a week (including Saturdays) during the winter session the students braved the cold north wind, unaware, it must be assumed, that John Murker's competent pen had written, in their name, a bit of shinty history.

There is no record of the Aberdeen University Club facing outside opposition until December 1889, when they travelled west to face Inverness Railway Club on a field belonging to Angus Bethune at Seafield. The students lost 4–0 and told their opponents that it was their first-ever match. Two months later the mechanics were invited back to Duthie Park in Aberdeen and this time they won by just 2–1, explaining upon their return home that the university side had played according to different rules. Who knows what changes had been moved, seconded and ratified by fully appointed club meetings on the links of Old Aberdeen since 1861?

Shinty/hurling internationals resumed: Scotland v Ireland at the Bught Park, Inverness, in June 1974. The game was played, and scored, under composite rules, and Ireland ran out winners by 3–8 and 1–6. (Donald MacKay)

Not until three decades later did the students of Edinburgh University follow the example which had been set in the north, and form their own club. Edinburgh's *Student* magazine of 1921–22 suggests that their club was 'inaugurated about 1850', but while there cannot be any doubt that students in Edinburgh had played the game since that year and before, their club was not formed until November 1891. Professor John Stuart Blackie, the distinguished classicist, translator of the *Iliad* and founder of the Chair of Celtic Studies at Edinburgh, became their first president, expressing his delight at being able to accept the post, as during his own youth in Aberdeen shinty, not golf, had been the game. Hugh Gunn, the club's moving force, quickly organised a match at Inverleith Park 'between teams of twelve men a side, representing Arts and Medicine'.

More than thirty players had signed up when Edinburgh took a deep breath and challenged Aberdeen in November 1892. Released at last from confinement, Aberdeen ran riot, scoring thirteen times without reply. A month later, Edinburgh bravely travelled north for a return and lost by just 5–3. By 1894 the inter-university match had become an annual fixture, with Aberdeen thus far continuing to hold the upper hand. In the December of that year 'skilful tactics and quick passing' by MacDonald and Beaton was rounded off by the sure touch near goal of MacKay and MacLennan to give them a 4–0 victory. Two years later, in 1896, Edinburgh achieved their first result – a 2–2 draw at Aberdeen.

In 1901 Glasgow University completed the triad. Angus John MacVicar arrived to study for the ministry and, following his boyhood in North Uist and schooldays at Kingussie, was disappointed to find that his chosen seminary had no shinty club. 'It was a question which I frequently discussed with other Highland students,' he wrote.

> One evening at the beginning of the 1901 session I happened to meet in the town Murdo MacRae and Murdo MacKenzie, two medical students from Ross-shire. On our way home to our lodgings we dropped into a public house at the corner of Park Road and Gibson Street. Over a drink in the taproom we discussed the possibility of forming a University shinty team and there and then decided to call a public meeting of all the Highland students so that the matter might be put to them. We approached Walter Shaw, a native of Sutherland and well- known in University circles, and he agreed to preside.

The meeting was packed to standing room only, the motion that the shinty club be formed was 'carried with acclamation', office-bearers were appointed and MacVicar was elected captain. Their first game was against Glasgow Cowal at Strathbungo. 'We were defeated,' recalled MacVicar, 'but not disgraced.'

One by one, the student clubs affiliated with the Camanachd Association and, in the case of Glasgow and Edinburgh, entered for the southern competitions – the revived Celtic Society Cup and the newly formed Dunn League – wherein, pitted against teams of considerable experience and continuity of players, the young, constantly changing university sides enjoyed a great deal of travel and little success. They did not, fortunately, have long to wait for a competition that would recognise their unique place in the game, and for a trophy which may never have been the most prestigious in shinty, but which remains one of the most remarkable artifacts in the game.

Alexander Littlejohn was a London stockbroker with a passion for the classical civilisations, in whose number he counted not only the

Greeks, Romans and Etruscans, but also the Celtic cultures of Europe. At the end of the nineteenth century he bought the extensive Invercharron Estate in Easter Ross and took for himself the estate's proprietory title. In 1905 Littlejohn of Invercharron approached the Aberdeen University Atheletic Club (AUAC) and offered to them a 'Challenge Vase', for the 'encouragement of manly sport and good fellowship among students attending the University of Aberdeen and more particularly for continuing the interest in the Ancient Celtic Game of Shinty'. When the AUAC accepted Littlejohn's kind offer, they can hardly have anticipated the nature of the gift. The Littlejohn Vase, when it arrived, turned out to have been modelled in silver on a fourth century BC sculpted container which had been discovered in 1770 in a lake by a Roman villa at Pontinello. It was accompanied by a tract, bound in leather, scripted, illustrated, and adorned with gold leaf and tartan inset, in the style of a promising medieval calligraphist who has been woofed through seven centuries and given a planchette, a lot of money and a late-Victorian sentiment for the Highlands. The manuscript offered a scholarly treatise on the history of the game of camanachd by Alexander MacBain, some notes on the Littlejohn family and the articles of the deed of gift. It makes the *Book of the Society of the True Gael* look like a penny pamphlet.

Aberdeen University could not keep this magnificent piece of baroque to themselves. Within a year it was on offer to the winner of a three-cornered (and occasionally, when St Andrews have entered, four-cornered) competition between the Scottish university shinty clubs – or, at least, the Littlejohn Vase was on offer. The manuscript remains under lock and key in the archives of the Queen Mother Library. Glasgow won the trophy in 1906 and since then it has passed regularly around the triangle, a limited-entry prize as curiously valuable as the Calcutta Cup.

The university game has done more than add an extra dimension of competition to Scottish shinty. Although its successes in the wider world of senior shinty may well be limited to Glasgow's occasional lifting of the Skeabost Horn and Aberdeen's three Strathdearn Cup triumphs in the 1970s, many of the game's finest players have appeared in the ranks of the student teams when they were at the peak of their ability and when, if they had not been able to develop that ability for three or four crucial years, they might have been lost to the game. When the Schools Camanachd Association was started in 1937 (under the presidency of yet another Provost of Kingussie, Donald Cattanach), offering first the MacPherson and then the MacKay, MacBean and Wade Cups to different age-groups of schoolchildren and offering a network of advice and assistance to teachers in areas where shinty was strong and where it was not, it continued that necessary spread of the game into the education system of the twentieth century. The activities of such men as Sorley Maclean at Plockton High School and D.R. MacDonald at Portree, where both helped to revive an ailing game in two of its proudest areas, were building upon the groundwork laid by John Murker, Hugh Gunn and Angus John MacVicar. And they were tacit acknowledgement of the enormous changes which shinty had now to confront if it was not to fade as swiftly from sight throughout the Highlands and Islands as it had already faded from the machair, strands and common grazings of Uist, Eigg and Tarskavaig.

The universities were to be thanked for another accomplishment. During a period of some forty years they kept open a thin line of communication between Scottish shinty and its thriving brother across the Irish Sea.

One bright day in 1897 could have seen the beginning of a long and mutually rewarding relationship between shinty and hurling. On the Saturday afternoon of 5 June that year, two hurling teams were simultaneously in action against Scottish shinty clubs. In Glasgow, Cowal were beating Dublin Celtic Hurling Club at Parkhead by 11–2, while in London a large crowd was watching the Ireland United Hurling Club draw 4–4 with London Camanachd at Stamford Bridge. Some of the Beauly players who were in town as Scottish champions turned out to help London ward off the Irish threat. After Beauly had themselves demolished their metropolitan opponents, an argument started about the respective merits of the Irish team and the Scottish champions. Beauly confidently offered a £50 wager. The Irishmen refused to match it and no contest took place.

Cowal returned the fixture by visiting Dublin two months later, again emerging victorious, this time by 2–0, from a game which was refereed by Michael Cusack, the uncompromising founder and first secretary of Cumann Lúthchleas Gael (the Gaelic Athletic Association), and that match on 17 July 1897 was the last contest between the two codes for twenty-seven years. In 1905 an inter-provincial hurling competition was held at Liverpool and in 1913 hurling teams from Kerry and Kilkenny performed exhibition matches at Liverpool and

Glasgow, but not until 1924 were the two styles of camain seen again on the same ground. In the August of that year the Tailteann Games were woken from a sleep of 850 years and the Camanachd Association was invited to send across an international squad to join in the celebrations.

The 1920s were dominated in Scotland by Argyllshire teams and this was reflected in the squad which strode on to the field before 14,000 Irish spectators. No fewer than six of the twelve were from Kyles Athletic, including Andrew Nicolson and Allan MacFadyen. The goalkeeper was Dick Cameron of Brae Lochaber and there was a representative from each of Mid-Argyll, Glasgow University, Cowal and Skye. Two substitutes were from the Furnace Club and the other, Colin Murchison, from Skye. The referee was a well-kent Argyllshire figure of Skye extraction – John 'Kaid' MacLean. The result was devastating for the hurlers – the Scottish side won. As the *Irish Times* reported:

> The stick used in shinty is slighter than the broad caman of the hurlers. The advantage of the latter was counterbalanced by the use in this match of a smaller ball than is usually employed in hurling. The Irish Hurling team played an open game, sending the ball on long high passes, but shooting rather wildly at goal; while the Scottish team, though getting the ball less frequently to their forwards, dribbled it neatly towards the objective. In the result the Scottish team gained two goals; the Irish team but one.

Smaller, unfamiliar ball or not, Irish hurlers had yet to defeat a Scottish shinty team. It could not and did not last. Scotland sent no squad to the 1928 Tailteann Games, but in 1932 a team consisting mainly of players from the Glasgow Skye Club, with a leavening of talent from Mid-Argyll, Glasgow Inverness and Cowal, travelled in hope and returned at the wrong end of a 6–1 scoreline. Two players survived the eight-year gap, John Gemmill of Cowal and Alec MacDonald, who had left university and in 1932 was on the books of Glasgow Inverness. The Skye captain in the first game, D. MacLachlan, refereed the second. These were the last Tailteann Games and, coincidentally, the last official contact between shinty players representing the Camanachd Association and hurlers representing the Gaelic Athletic Association for forty years.

In 1933 a number of meetings took place between representatives of the Camanachd Association and the Gaelic Athletic Association (GAA), which culminated in the drawing up of a set of compromise rules to be used whenever shinty met hurling. These rules were never tested on the field of play. Word reached the government offices of Edinburgh and Whitehall that an international fixture had been provisionally scheduled for the Easter of 1934 and discreet approaches were made to the officials of the Camanachd Association which resulted in the announcement from Inverness that as the Gaelic Athletic Association had an 'anti-British political flavour' the Camanachd Association had been advised by 'one in high authority' to 'have nothing to do' with international hurling/shinty matches. And that was that. With no explanation as to how it had taken the Association fifty years to learn that the GAA had its origins in the struggle for Irish independence and had always seen its sole reason for being as the promotion of native Celtic sports to the exclusion and ostracism of all imported athletic pursuits (whose introduction it regarded as 'an alien policy of racial demoralisation'), and apparently with no questioning of the right or the motivation of people 'in high authority' to dictate policy to a small sporting body in the north of Scotland, the Camanachd Association slashed the twine and let the rope bridge fall. If there were losers in the years which followed this strange episode, they were not to be found in Ireland. Hurling teams travelled the world, performing before huge crowds in New York and Australia, establishing outposts of their game and their Association as far away as Argentina and South Africa; while shinty, the oldest surviving version of the Gaelic stick-and-ball game, remained locked in self-imposed solitude in the country to which the Irish had introduced it 1,500 years before.

But even if it had wished to do so, the Camanachd Association could not prevent individual clubs from stretching hands across the sea, and after the Second World War the university clubs began to make contact with the hurling fraternity. Edinburgh led the way in 1947 with a memorable fixture against Queen's University, Belfast, at Edinburgh's new ground in East Fettes Avenue (Queen's won 3–2). In 1950 Edinburgh went over to Belfast and the Camanachd Association made tentative approaches to the Gaelic Athletic Association which came to nothing. In 1952 Glasgow University played Dublin University College and by 1957 the Scottish and the Irish Associations were talking again – only, yet again, to fail to reach an agreement. In 1964 the Camanachd Association once more pronounced itself to be firmly against any links and its members were asked not to patronise shinty/

hurling internationals. In the same year students from Aberdeen University attended a hurling coaching course in Ireland and instituted a series of exchange matches which continued through the 1960s.

When the ice was finally melted, it was, fittingly, a group of shinty players from the schools who first applied the torch. In the Easter of 1971 a hurling team from the Blessed Oliver Plunkett School travelled from Dublin to play Oban High School. In October Oban returned the visit and by that time two new presidents of the two Associations, Padraig O'Fainin of Waterford and Ken MacMaster of Strathpeffer, both of whom acceded to office in 1970, were talking. Their discussions bore fruit on 5 August 1972, when an international squad from Ireland strode on to the Bught Park to meet fourteen Scottish shinty players – forty years, almost to the hour, since six Glasgow Skyemen and some of their Argyllshire acquaintances stepped out at the Tailteann Games and delighted the *Irish Times* with their use of Gaelic on the field of play. The compromise rules in 1972 included the Irish points and goals system and at half-time the Scots appeared once again to be on the verge of an unlikely victory when they led by 4–3 to Ireland's 2–2, but the visitors ran out winners by 6–4 to 4–5. On the previous day, the boys from Blessed Oliver Plunkett had been back to Oban again and had won by 3–2. Internationals have taken place irregularly since 1972, Scotland's best performance coming at Old Anniesland in 1976, the year that the goals-points scoring system was again removed. A 5–5 draw resulted after a stirring contest. Despite the Camanachd Association's chronic – and, beside the riches of the GAA, saddening – poverty, which has caused the fixture to be postponed, the two Associations were in 1989 talking in a friendly and constructive manner.

That would have pleased Kaid MacLean, the Scottish referee at the 1924 triumph who wrote after that occasion:

> No longer are we troubling
> About the grand old game
> Since we have seen in Dublin
> Both countries play the same.
> Those camans told of days of old
> Of muscle, brawn and brain,
> So let us strive to keep alive
> Our grand old fathers' game.

8

The End of Spring

'What is a *kayman?*

If the results of international fixtures are to be seen as a reflection of the state of health of Scottish shinty, then those within the game would have had little reason to be optimistic for fully sixty years. The golden years, it would have to be said (as it doubtless is said, by some), faded with the Beauly and Cowal sides of the 1890s and the Argyllshire teams of the 1920s. But that is evidently not true. Shinty has thrown up, and continues to throw up, gloriously skilful and successful club teams. When Kingussie entered 1989 with a two-year run of unbeaten games behind them, they were raising no new standard. Newtonmore had known such dominant success, as had Kyles Athletic, Caberfeidh, Inveraray, Oban Celtic and many others who, to a greater or lesser degree, reigned over the game for a period of time, setting new standards and leaving behind a sackful of exhilarating memories and cheerful stories. Innumerable great players, heroic centre lines and irresistible teams have flourished on Scottish turf, untested on the international stage.

Prior to 1971, when they visited Dublin's Na Fianna Hurling Team, no Newtonmore player had met an Irish hurler on the field of play. But Newtonmore's record in shinty is incomparable. Before being stripped of their mantle in 1987 by a Kingussie team which had been carefully nurtured to that end by a latter-day Alexander MacKellar, a former Highland League footballer from Badenoch called Donnie Grant, Newtonmore had won the Camanachd Cup on no fewer than twenty-eight occasions since that first time at the Dell, Kingussie, in 1907, when they beat Kyles Athletic 7–2. At times their dominance of the opposition was dismaying. In 1908, 1909 and 1910 they defeated

Furnace in three consecutive Camanachd finals by 5–2, 11–3, and 6–1 respectively, led into the overwhelming assault by 'Nelson' Cattanach and by the great Dr Johnny Cattanach, who found the Furnace net on eight occasions in Glasgow in 1909. The comparatively lean years which followed saw Furnace take revenge by 2–0 in the 1923 final; but by 1929 (following a brief, unsuccessful amalgamation with Kingussie) Newtonmore were back on course. Four MacDonald brothers, Angus, John, Duncan and Alastair, featured in the teams which lifted the Camanachd Cup in 1929, 1931, 1932 and 1936.

They won the cup again on its first resumed season after the Second World War, beating a combined Lochfyneside squad 4–0 at Oban in 1947. One of those brothers, Angus MacDonald, was moved from full back to full forward in that season and celebrated by hitting fifty goals, including two in the Camanachd final. Angus MacDonald got a hat-trick the following year at Inverness, when Newtonmore held the cup, 4–2, against the Ballachulish challenge. They saw off the quality of Kyles Athletic and the Campbells of Oban Camanachd between 1957 and 1959, suffered a lean decade in the 1960s, then bounced back at the dawn of the 1970s, beating Kyles 7–1 in two consecutive Camanachd finals and proceeding to dominate the game until, in the middle of the 1980s, Donnie Grant's young Kingussie side matured and slipped up as if unseen to mug their neighbours and bag the championship.

In fact, Kingussie had not, in the post-war years, been complete strangers to success. They had won the northern cup, the MacTavish, on a respectable number of occasions; and they had dominated the northern MacGillivray League between 1980 and 1982, lifting the title for three successive years. But the crux of the matter was that since 1921 the name of Kingussie Shinty Club had been etched onto the grand trophy, the Camanachd Cup, on just one occasion: and that had been in 1961 when they beat Oban Celtic 2–1. By 1983, when the Camanachd Cup was rid of the geographical divisions which had guaranteed a representative from the north and from the south in the final and made a truly open competition, the previous sixty-one years, which had seen the first holders of the trophy triumph just once, had been dominated by Kyles Athletic with fourteen wins and – more painfully for Kingussie – Newtonmore with twenty-two.

That first 'open' year of 1983 looked, at one crucial stage, to have made not an iota of difference to the Old Firm. With Kyles already in the final, Newtonmore were obliged to go through the formality of

The modern greats: typically titanic struggle between Newtonmore and Kingussie at the Eilan, Newtonmore, in 1980. (Donald MacKay)

dismissing Strachur, the small Lochfyneside team who had never made an appearance in the final, in the semis. The result was one of the greatest upsets in shinty history: Roddy Leitch and Donald MacPhail scored in the second half to put the holders out, and those who had predicted a northern domination of the cup if regionalising was abandoned were obliged to sit back and watch an all-south final.

They were almost obliged to watch another wound inflicted on the pride of one of the game's grand masters. Kyles took the lead in the final through Billy Paterson, but John MacDonald and Roddy Leitch put Strachur 2–1 ahead and to within three minutes of victory before Robert Baxter and Donald MacRae took advantage of forced errors in their defence to steal the match.

It took the north no more than twelve months to regain its pride. In 1984 Newtonmore and Kingussie met at Oban in the final. It was, remarkably, the first time that the Badenoch sides had played each other for the Camanachd Cup, and it turned out to be the benchmark in Kingussie's carefully planned campaign to turn the tables on their neighbours. While Newtonmore were beginning to talk of rebuilding their team, Kingussie had already started, under the magisterial eye of a veteran player with experience as a Highland League footballer: Donnie Grant.

Grant took the field at Oban that day, along with his son Ross, and after just three minutes he may have been regretting the decision as Kenny MacIntosh put Newtonmore ahead. But Davie Anderson equalised before half-time, and when the Kingussie 'keeper Rab Muir, who had defied Newtonmore for the first hour of the game, saved a penalty in the second half, Grant's boys took the game by the scruff of the neck, scoring three times before the end through Ally Dallas, Anderson and Dallas Young, to run out 4–1 winners and return in jubilation to Kingussie.

Newtonmore were not, of course, knocked from their perch so precipitously. The following year they won both the northern league and the Camanachd Cup, the former by two points and the latter by 4–2 over Kingussie. In 1986 they won the Camanachd again, beating Oban Camanachd 5–1; but in 1987 Kingussie were ready to embark on a record-breaking run of galloping success. With the league already under their belts, they beat Newtonmore by the odd goal in seven in one of the greatest-ever Camanachd Cup finals, and in 1988 they strolled unde-feated through the league and found themselves facing, in the Camanachd Cup final at the Bught Park in Inverness, a team which had chosen this venue to write their name in the history of shinty more than a century earlier but which had never taken part in a Camanachd Cup final.

Like Strachur in 1983, Glenurquhart were thrillingly unlikely finalists, and like Strachur they had no intention of simply making up the numbers. The very presence of Glenurquhart in a Camanachd Cup final was enough to stir the imagination, and when they had taken the lead twice through Ron Fraser and led 2–1 at half-time (Kingussie having responded through the ever-dangerous Stephen Borthwick), bonfires may not have been prepared at Delshangie, but the disbe-lieving eyes of the crowd were alight. The dream result for Glenur-quhart was not to be: Davie Anderson, Kevin Thain and Steven Borthwick robbed them of all but their pride in the second period; and the cover of that year's *Shinty Year Book* was free to depict a cartoon of a Kingussie player running away with a sackful of trophies.

But as Strachur and Glenurquhart had proved in 1988, 1983 and 1887, the game of shinty is no groveller before reputation, however hard-won. Like all great team sports, it produces its dominant sides and, like all great team sports, those sides are there to be toppled by an adverse run of form, by an unsuitable pitch, by complacency, by simple bad luck, or by a better team on the day.

By the first Saturday of May, 1989, Kingussie had gone sixty-three matches without defeat. It had been a barnstorming run, leading some to suggest nervously that they might be in a league of their own. They travelled on that day to Oban, to face in the final of the MacAuley Cup a team with no small reputation of their own to uphold. Kyles Athletic – who had not even won the southern league that year – wasted little time in making their historic point. Neil Nicolson put them ahead after eleven minutes, Fraser MacDonald added to the lead, and Peter Briggs made it 3–0 shortly after half-time. Kevin Thain and David Borthwick pulled two back, but a Peter Moebeck strike in the seventy- eighth minute meant that not even another Borthwick goal six minutes from time could really lift Kingussie's chances. Not for the first time, a trophy which should by rights have found its way to Badenoch was hijacked by a determined band of men from the shores of Loch Fyne. It is the sheer dynamic quality of such teams in full flow which leads one of the game's respected contemporary administrators, Jack Richmond of Newtonmore, to talk about the possibility of sporting achievement which is available to Highland shinty teams. 'In the national and international context', says Richmond, 'to what level is football, or rugby, played in the Highlands?' The answer is, to a very low level. But Highland shinty players are capable of elevating their native game to a spectacle so fast, thrilling and skilful that the most dispassionate observer must be moved and entertained.

The lengthy absence of shinty from the international stage has contributed to keeping the entrancing sight of such as the Frasers of Newtonmore away from the national gaze, and thereby to obstructing the national recognition of the game that would inevitably have followed. It has given the film and print media, which have historically been reluctant to afford time and space to the game of shinty, a ready excuse for regarding it as a parochial sport of little interest to people outwith the villages of Badenoch and Lochfyneside. It has helped bring about the cruel irony of Scottish ice hockey teams receiving regular, live, peak-viewing television coverage while shinty has struggled at times to win edited, shoddily filmed reports of the Camanachd Cup final broadcast on the Sunday after the event – a day on which many of the game's most loyal adherents will not, because of their faith, turn on the television.

At times, even those poor scrapings have been withdrawn. In 1978, the BBC, which had traditionally sent a camera or two to the

Camanachd final, withdrew at the last minute from the Newtonmore–Kyles Athletic clash which had been scheduled for Fort William on 27 May to suit the convenience of the outside broadcast units. Due to an oversight, the Corporation admitted, their units had been treble-booked on that day for the conference of the Scottish National Party at Edinburgh, the Golden Fiddle Awards in Aberdeen and the Camanachd Cup final. There was, obviously, never any question about the loser.

In 1983 a superb final between Kyles Athletic and Strachur was never filmed, there being a General Election in progress at the time. Such behaviour does much to explain the response which the sports commentator David Coleman elicited from contestants on the BBC's quiz programme *A Question of Sport*, when he asked 'What is a *kayman?*' Baffled not so much by the expert's mispronunciation, athlete after athlete failed to answer, until an Irish rugby internationalist said that it was a hurling stick. Coleman, slightly dubious, awarded him the point.

The hiding of the game's light has left it with little political clout. The Inverness MP Sir Russell Johnston, a man with a genuine affection for shinty, has at times tried and failed to win some small concessions from government, such as the exemption from VAT of increasingly expensive camain. The sport's few other encounters with politicians since those days in the 1930s, when somebody in Whitehall thought it timely to advise the Camanachd Association to have nothing to do with the nationalists of the Gaelic Athletic Association, have bordered on the bizarre. In 1964 a large crowd which had assembled at Strachur Park for the Sutherland Cup final between Kyles Athletic and Boleskine was interested to see Sir Fitzroy MacLean, then the MP for North Ayr and Bute and a Conservative with a celebrated, idiosyncratic interest in the affairs of Eastern Europe, march up to the field in the company of the Soviet foreign secretary Gromyko, Prime Minister Kosygin and the son of Nikita Kruschev, who was at the time the editor of *Pravda*. The Soviets enjoyed the match (which Boleksine won 4–0) and each left with a caman under his arm. In 1984 a small row broke out over the behaviour of Mrs Winifred Ewing before the Camanachd Cup final between Kingussie and Newtonmore at Oban. Mrs Ewing, who was conducting an eventually successful Euro-election campaign as Scottish National Party candidate for the Highlands and Islands, apparently considered herself to be upstaged by the presence of rival candidate Russell Johnston as an official guest of the Camanachd

Association, and, wearing SNP colours, ran on to the field before the start of the game to kiss several players. The Secretary of the Association, Donald MacKenzie later stated: 'The Camanachd Cup final should not be used as a political arena . . . It would appear that Mrs Ewing had little regard for shinty but used the final for her own means.' These were curious incidents which went not one step along the road to giving shinty the command over political affection and respect which is enjoyed by the Marylebone Cricket Club and the Gaelic Athletic Association.

In the 1970s and the 1980s the shinty community grappled with its identity and role in the modern sporting world. At the end of April 1974, shortly after relations had been resumed with Ireland, sixty delegates from nineteen clubs attended a Shinty Forum at the Balavil Arms Hotel in Newtonmore. They spent two days at the foot of the Monadhliath mountains, just a couple of miles from the birthplace of the Camanachd Association, looking into the game's past and wondering about its future. They heard recorded messages from Angus MacPherson, recalling the 1880s and the 1890s and that controversial final of 1899 between Kingussie and Ballachulish, and from Reverend John Sellar, who had played in Newtonmore's 1907 Camanachd Cup-winning side.

They disagreed about the present state of the game. Sandy Russell of Newtonmore argued that 'it is in a healthier state than ever it was', while Iain Cameron insisted: 'We play as ineffectually, and accepting as low a standard, as we do in organising the game.' Cameron laid the blame for this decline squarely at the door of the Camanachd Association. Shinty, he said, 'has been in a state of stagnation for years largely through the failure of the governing body to fulfil its aim to foster and develop shinty'. But the forum heard of the difficulties experienced by the majority of clubs in finding keen and competent administrators of their own; in raising money for travel and equipment; in attracting players to training and coaching sessions; even in finding a suitable piece of ground on which to play. Delegates pondered on the fact that the Scottish game had no central home, no 'Hampden of shinty', and no full-time administrator. They listened as their collea-gues spoke of the difficulties which they had experienced in attracting the interest of the media. Peter English, a descendant of the 'Ally Ban' MacDonald who had scored the winning goal for Glen Urquhart against Strathglass in 1888, and who had himself three years earlier launched the *Shinty Year Book*, the annual communications lifeline for the game, confessed that he saw 'no easy answer' to the question of attracting widespread media interest in shinty. 'We must project,' said Ian MacInnes at the end of an exhaustive two days, 'a new image of the game, otherwise we will go to the wall.'

On 19 April, 1980, the Camanachd Association, beset by a shortage of funds despite the recent injection of sponsorship money from the whisky distillers MacDonald & Muir, wrote to the Gaelic Athletic Association in Dublin to convey its decision that the annual internationals which had been recommenced in 1972 would have to be cancelled. Ireland had won the previous two matches, in Fort William in 1978 and on the Isle of Man in 1979.

Five months later, in October, 1980, a committee of eighteen under the chairmanship of Jack Richmond was appointed by the Camanachd Association to examine the future of shinty. The Committee met, debated and formalised proposals for twenty working hours on three different occasions in November and December. 'There was', they reported,

Highland genealogy, written on the team lists of shinty matches . . . this shot, of the challenge match between Glenurquhart and Kyles Athletic, held in August 1985 to celebrate the former club's centenary, shows Billy MacLean (left) of Glenurquhart and Donald MacRae of Kyles. MacLean had two great-grandfathers in the original Glenurquhart team; and MacRae has followed in the footsteps of his father and his grandfather by winning a Camanachd Cup winners' medal. (Donald MacKay)

keen awareness by all concerned that what they were doing could
easily produce more harm than good. They knew that the game, an
important part of Gaelic society for many hundreds of years, has
strong traditions and that to tamper with these could offend. Nonetheless, the pressure for the enquiry had come from a mounting
conviction that the sport of shinty must examine itself to see how it
stands in the modern world for the sake of its own continuing
existence.

The committee's many recommendations, some of which were
promptly adopted, included an upgrading of the secretarial role in
the Camanachd Association, the restructuring of the Association's
executive, the need to investigate the possibilities of generating more
income from sponsorship and other sources (the Camanachd Association had, in 1980, £700 in a current bank account and £1,000 on
deposit), and a greater emphasis on youth and schools games and on
coaching programmes. It was also recommended that a national league
be introduced and that the shinty/hurling internationals be continued.
Donald Skinner, the president of the Camanachd Association, told the
committee at one stage in its deliberations that shinty had no divine
right to an assured future. 'If all in the game adopt a fiery cross
approach,' he said, 'we will go on having, and deserving, a sport second
to none in the world.'

By the spring of 1989 the Camanachd Association was attracting
£30,000 a year in sponsorship. The old northern MacGillivray League
and the southern Dunn League had become the Marine Harvest leagues.
Marine Harvest, a subsidiary of Unilever, pioneered the salmon farming
industry which mushroomed in the Highlands and Islands of Scotland in
the late 1970s. Glenmorangie (whisky) and the Bank of Scotland had
appended their names to the MacTavish Cup, the Glasgow Celtic
Society Cup, the Sutherland Cup and the Camanachd Cup.

Discussions with the Scottish Sports Council had resulted in the
shelving of any idea of making the Bught in Inverness the Hampden Park
of shinty. Instead, the Bught was to share the Camanachd Association's
major occasions with An Aird at Fort William and Mossfield at Oban, and
over £200,000 had been spent on bringing these three venues up to an
acceptable late twentieth century standard. Plans were under-way to
mount a major exhibition of archival material in 1993 to mark the
hundredth anniversary of the Camanachd Association.

Eye on the ball . . . Johnny MacKenzie, helping Newtonmore to win the 1978 Camanachd Cup Final at Fort William. This photograph, by Donald MacKay, was selected as 'Scottish sports picture of the year' in the Scottish Sports Council's annual competition.

On the field of play, London Camanachd had re-entered the
Camanachd Cup and sides with briefer histories enjoyed small successes and saddening failure. At Easter weekend the County Clare
champions, Scariff Hurling Club, visited Inverness to play a North of
Scotland select. The game resulted in a creditable 2–2 draw, with a
Murchison from Skye and a Ross from Kingussie putting their names
on the Scottish scoresheet. Doors which might never have been shut
were slowly opening again, as throughout Scotland shinty players
awaited the beginning of summer and the end of another season of
camanachd.

9

A Third Century

The Camanachd Association's centenary in 1993 passed with a season of celebrations from Kingussie to Edinburgh Castle. As befitted the occasion, they looked mostly backwards. Few people at the time might have realised that the succeeding ten years would encompass more institutional change for the game of shinty than had the previous hundred.

Two games in particular demonstrated the theme of the year. On 3 April 1993 a squad of shinty players representing the old heroes of Glasgow Cowal disembarked from the north-bound train at Kingussie Station and – as their predecessors had done exactly a century earlier – made their way to the Eilan to face the locals. The final scoreline and the rules were different, but the atmosphere and the crowd – notably those ladies of Badenoch who had taken the trouble to step into late-Victorian bustles and strap on bonnets – might have been little changed.

Later in the year a team of hurlers representing the cream of the Irish game arrived in Inverness for another revival of the full international fixture, and what happened next was truly remarkable.

By 1993 the two branches of the camanachd family had enjoyed such different fortunes that for every single player of Scottish shinty, there were 100 hurlers in Ireland. The composite-rules shinty/hurling internationals, as we have seen, had since 1924 reflected that disparity. But in 1993 the form-book was turned on its head. A Scottish team managed by Donnie Grant of Kingussie, and reinforced throughout by the stalwarts of his club, completely outplayed the men of Ireland at the Bught Park and won by 6–4.

There were, at long last, reasons other than sentiment and the pull of history to continue this fixture – reasons which were suddenly

*The Scotland shinty squad. The revived full shinty/hurling interaction between
Scotland and Ireland in 1990 proved an astonishing success, not least for a
Scotland squad which went unbeaten for most of the decade.* (Willie Urquhart)

reconnected with competition and sporting pride. The Irish tipped
their hats to Scottish superiority and vowed to redress the balance.
Donnie Grant pointed out that winning in Inverness was one thing;
beating the Irish in Ireland would be quite another.

A year later, on a field at Athenry, the two teams drew 3–3. The year
after that, in 1995, Scotland won again on a wet and windy day in Fort
William when Ireland felt the full thrust not only of the Highland
climate but of another force of nature: Kingussie's young striker
Ronald Ross, who was busily rewriting the goal-scoring record books
in domestic competition.

Scotland would not in fact be beaten again by Ireland until the year
2000, by which time the boys in blue had become not only the most
successful international shinty squad of all time, but also arguably the
most successful modern Scottish international team in any sporting
discipline. The spirit of "Kaid" Maclean hung over them.

The centenary year celebrations of 1993, which were chaired by the
formidable and media-friendly Kenny Thomson, had offered the game
a fresh momentum both on and off the pitch. New sponsorship deals
were struck. State funding was found for youth development initia-
tives. Prime Minister John Major had been given a caman and Sports
Minister Sir Hector Munro had hosted in Edinburgh Castle a recep-

tion for numerous representatives of the game. Shinty's public profile had by the middle of the 1990s possibly never been higher. The time seemed right to adjust its league competition from regional to national. This task would pre-occupy the six years in office of Ken Thomson's successor at the Camanachd Association.

Few presidents of the Camanachd Association steered the game through such a dramatic period of change as Duncan Cameron, who took the job in 1994, twelve months after centenary year. While Thomson seemed never more at home than when charming the great and the good in Edinburgh receptions, Cameron stalked the land, trotting throughout the winter months from one village hall to another, persuading recalcitrant shinty clubs to sign up for national league competition.

The most likeable of men, he was difficult to refuse. One interesting result of this charm offensive was that some shinty representatives found themselves saying one thing in public and another on the ballot paper. This disturbed Duncan Cameron not a whit: the national eight-team Premier Division scraped through and became a reality in 1995. It was such a close-run thing that few imagined that Cameron would press on, before the end of the century, with introducing another national division – effectively bringing all major first teams in Scotland out of their local regimes.

That was to underestimate Duncan Cameron. Press on he did, immediately following his re-election to a second three-year term as president. What happened next almost split shinty in two. For a few weeks in 1999, when all four of the southern qualifiers looked set to reject National Division One, shinty seemed close to taking five steps back, right into the 1890s, when south was south and north was north and never the twain would meet. Calming those troubled waters, holding the game together – and, as no mean afterthought, getting National Division One launched with a full body of teams on time – was probably Duncan Cameron's greatest achievement as president.

Kingussie won the first National Premier Division, and Kingussie continued to win the title throughout the 1990s and into the new millennium. Between 1996 and 2000 the Badenoch side actually went unbeaten for ninety-six senior competitive matches. They did not taste defeat between an extraordinary Camanachd Cup final on 1 June 1996, when Oban Camanachd's Gordon MacIntyre – who the previous year

Kingussie play Fort William, one of the few teams in Scotland to offer a challenge to the Badenoch club's dominance of club shinty in the last years of the twentieth century. (Willie Urquhart)

had lost an eye in a shinty injury – scored the winner in the west coast side's 3–2 victory, and a fateful meeting with Fort William in the spring of 2000. Their brilliant, record-defying run distorted competitive club shinty. Of that there can be no doubt. At a time when the game at both national and international level took great strides forward, the simple unavoidable fact of one club being so far ahead of all its rivals was not especially good for shinty's image. It became difficult to explain to neutrals, to potential supporters, that this extraordinary hegemony had been the result more of one outstanding team than of a series of lacklustre also-rans. When the game needed competition, it suffered under a monopoly. Every little victory for every other side was just that: a small achievement; a semi-final conquest; with always the black cloud of mighty Kingussie waiting like nemesis at the end of the road.

Lochcarron v. Inveraray. National premier leage shinty – Lochcarron, from the old north of shinty, take on Inverness, from the old south, in the national league in the summer of 2004 (Willie Urquhart)

None of that, of course, was Kingussie's fault. It was more than their right, it was their duty to put out the strongest and best prepared shinty team available to them. If the rest of Scotland was not capable of beating them, the fault did not lie in Badenoch. And there were positive spin-offs, not least the phenomenal success enjoyed by a Scottish national side built around a Kingussie backbone. Perhaps most of all, Scottish shinty could celebrate the fact that they were for a decade and more in the presence of one of the greatest shinty teams.

Two generations of players arrived in that team, each one as devoted to success and to a high standard of play as the last. That was the real achievement. Usually when a single sports club establishes an arm-lock on a team sport, it is for just one generation of players. Then it fades and they are replaced. Kingussie approached their third successive generation to hold sway over Scottish shinty. In the course of those years, that shinty club delivered several excellent contests, even more astonishing one-sided masterclass performances, and at least one player – the goal-scoring Ronnie Ross – who went down in anybody's list of all-time shinty greats.

There was one further adjustment to be made. In the summer of 2004, shinty ceased for the first time in its history to be a winter sport. Following chronic fixture pile-ups and futile experiments with a midwinter lay-off, the Camanachd Association decided that from the year 2004 onwards the season would run from spring to autumn, rather than the other way round. The start of summer would still have resonance. It would merely represent a beginning rather than an end.

Appendix 1

Rules of the Game

33.1 The Field of Play

(33.1.1) Dimensions

The Field of Play shall be rectangular, its length being not more than 170 yards (155 metres) nor less than 140 yards (128 metres) and its breadth not more than 80 yards (73 metres) nor less than 70 yards (64 metres).

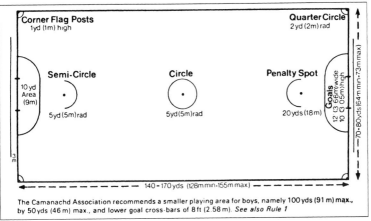

The shinty pitch, showing dimensions.

(33.1.2) Marking
The Field of Play shall be marked with distinctive lines, the longer boundary lines being called the side-lines and the shorter the bye-lines.

(33.1.3) The lines across the goals joining the goalposts shall be called the goal-lines.

(33.1.4) A flag on a post not less than 3 feet 6 inches (1 metre) high and having a non-pointed top shall be placed at each corner.

(33.1.5) The centre of the field shall be indicated by a suitable mark and a circle of 5 yard (5 metre) radius shall be marked round it.

(33.1.6) Ten Yard Area (Nine Metre Area)
In front of each goal a line shall be drawn, 12 feet (3.66 metres) long, parallel to and 10 yards (9 metres) from the goal-line. The line shall be continued each way to meet the bye-line by quarter circles, having the inside of the goalposts as centres. The space enclosed by this line, and the bye-line, shall be known as the Ten Yard Area (Nine Metre Area).

(33.1.7) Corner Area
From each corner flag-post a quarter circle, having a radius of 2 yards (2 metres), shall be drawn inside the Field of Play.

(33.1.8) Penalty Spot
At each end of the Field of Play, a suitable mark shall be made in front of the goal, 20 yards (18 metres) from the mid-point of the goal-line. These shall be the penalty-hit marks. A semicircle of 5 yard (5 metre) radius shall be drawn behind each penalty-hit mark.

(33.1.8) The Goals
The goals shall be placed on the centre of each bye-line and shall consist of two upright posts, equidistant from the corner flags and 12 feet (3.66 metres) apart (inside measurement), joined by a horizontal cross-bar, the lower edge of which shall be 10 feet (3.05 metres) from the ground. The width and depth of the uprights and the cross-bar shall be not more than 4 inches (10 centimetres) and not less than 3 inches (7.5 centimetres).

(33.1.9) The goals shall be provided with nets attached to the uprights and cross-bars, and fixed square with the goals at a distance of not less than 3 feet (1 metre) behind the goal-line and cross-bar.

(33.1.10) All lines, with the exception of the goal-line, should be a minimum of ½ inch (4 centimetres) and a maximum of 3 inches (7.5 centimetres) wide.

(33.1.11) The goal-line shall be the same width as the depth of the upright.

(33.1.12) The field of play shall be fenced off at a distance of not less than 6 feet (2 metres) outside the bye-lines and side-lines.

(33.1.13) Where it is not possible to protect the whole of the field of play with a fence, both goals must be protected in the rear by a fence of wood, wire or rope over a minimum distance of 15 feet (5 metres) from either side of the goalposts and not less than 6 feet (2 metres) from the parallel to the bye-line. Only the goal-judges shall be permitted between this line and the bye-line during play.

(33.1.14) The cross-bars and uprights must be made of wood or metal and shall be painted white. They may be square, rectangular in shape, and no bar, strut or board, except at the top, shall connect the uprights and the posts supporting the goal-nets.

33.2 Number of Players

(33.2.1) A match shall be played by two teams, each consisting of not more than twelve players, one of whom shall be the goal-keeper.

(33.2.2) Substitutes, up to a maximum of three per team, shall be permitted during a match, except in representative and Under 14 matches, where the maximum permitted shall be four per team. The Referee shall be informed of the names of substitutes (if any) before the change is made.

Punishment
(33.2.3) If, without the Referee being notified, a player or a named substitute changes places with the goal-keeper during the game, or at any interval during the game in which extra time is played, and then handles the ball within the Ten Yard Area (Nine Metre Area), a penalty-hit shall be awarded.

Decisions of Interpretation
(33.2.4) A competitive match shall not be considered valid if there are fewer than eight players in either team.

(33.2.5) Names of substitutes must be included in team lines, any two of whom shall be eligible to play.

(33.2.6) A player who has been replaced shall not take any further part in the game. The Referee must be informed if a player is to be substituted and this is done by the Referee receiving a card from the player coming on, informing him of the player's name and number, and the name and number of the player coming off.
  A substitute may only be permitted to enter the field of play, at the mid-point of either side-line, during a stoppage in the game and after he has received a signal from the Referee authorising him to do so. A substitute shall be deemed to be a player and shall be subject to the jurisdiction of the Referee whether called up to play or not.

33.3 The Ball

The ball shall be spherical – the interior shall be cork and worsted, the outer cover shall be of leather or other approved material. The circumference of the ball shall be not more than 8 inches (20 centimetres) and not less than 7'½ inches (19 centimetres). The weight of the ball, at the start of the game, shall be not more than 3 ounces (85 grams), nor less than 2'½ ounces (70 grams). The ball shall not be changed during the game unless authorised by the Referee.

33.4 Players' Equipment

(33.4.1) Teams shall play in distinguishing colours and goal-keepers shall wear colours which distinguish them from outfield players and the Referee.
  Goal-keepers and outfield players' jerseys shall be numbered to correspond with team lines.

(33.4.2) A player shall not wear anything which is dangerous to another player, nor shall a player use a caman which is in a condition which is dangerous to another player.

(33.4.3) Boots must conform to the following standard:

a) Studs must be of solid construction and made of leather, rubber, plastic, aluminium or similar material. Where studs have a metal seat for screw type studs, the metal seat shall not be visible.

b) Studs with a metal tip are permissible provided they do not have a pointed tip, and there are no sharp or ragged edges which could be dangerous to other players. Studs moulded to the boot are permissible.

(33.4.4) Helmets must conform to the following standard. Helmets worn shall preferably be the same colour in any one team and matching the team colours.

(33.4.5) Secondary Shorts must conform to the following standard. Secondary shorts shall be the same colour as the team shorts, except in specific instances when they are worn on medical advice with no matching colour available.

(33.4.6) The caman must conform to the following standard:

a) The head of the caman must not be of a size larger than can pass through a ring of diameter of 2 inches (6.3 centimetres).

b) No plates, screws, or metal in any form shall be attached to or form part of the caman.

c) No equipment should be used in any competition run under the auspices of the Camanachd Association unless first approved by the Executive Council.

No liability shall be attached to the Camanachd Association on equipment so approved.

Decisions of Interpretation

(33.4.7) A player whose caman is broken during a game may play the ball before obtaining a replacement caman, providing the broken caman is not in a condition which is dangerous to himself or another player. A player changing his caman must do so at the side-lines or bye-lines.

33.5 Referees

(33.5.1) A Referee shall be appointed to officiate in each game. His authority and the exercise of the powers granted to him by the Rules of Play commence as soon as he enters the Field of Play. His power of penalising shall extend to offences committed when play has been temporarily suspended, or when the ball is out of play.

His decisions on points of fact connected with the play shall be final, so far as the results of the game are concerned.

(33.5.2) He shall:

a) Enforce the Rules of Play.

b) Refrain from penalising in cases where he is satisfied that, by doing so, he would be giving an advantage to the offending team.

c) Keep a record of the game; act as timekeeper and allow the full or agreed time, adding thereto all time lost through accident or other cause.

d) Have discretionary power to stop the game for any infringement of the Rules and to suspend or terminate the game whenever, by reason of the elements, interference by spectators, or other causes, he deems such a stoppage necessary. He shall stop the game and call the two captains into the centre circle, informing them of his decision and the reasons for abandoning the game. In such a case he shall submit a detailed report, which should be in the Executive Officer's hands not later than the fifth day following the match.

e) From the time he enters the Field of Play, caution any player guilty of misconduct, ungentlemanly behaviour or the use of foul or abusive language and, if he persists, suspend him from further participation in the game; send off the Field of Play any player who, without any previous caution, is guilty of violent conduct or serious foul play. In such cases the Referee shall send the name of the offender to the Executive Officer not later than the fifth day following the match, in accordance with the provisions of the Disciplinary Machinery.

f) Allow no person other than the players, Goal Judges and Linesmen to enter the Field of Play without his permission.

g) Stop the game if, in his opinion, a player has been seriously injured, have the player removed as soon as possible from the field of play, and immediately resume the game. If a player is slightly injured, the game shall not be stopped until the ball has ceased to be in play.

h) Signal for recommencement of the game after all stoppages.

Decisions of Interpretation

(33.5.3) The Referee shall report to the appropriate authority misconduct or any misdemeanour on the part of the spectators, officials, players, named substitutes, or other persons, which takes place either on the field of play or in its vicinity at any time prior to, during, or after the match in question so that appropriate action can be taken by the authority concerned.

(33.5.4) In no case shall the Referee consider the intervention of a Goal Judge if he, himself, has seen the incident and, from his position on the field, is better able to judge.

(33.5.5) The Referee can only reverse his decision so long as the game has not been restarted.

(33.5.6) If the Referee has decided to apply the advantage clause and to let the game proceed, he cannot revoke his decision if the presumed advantage is not realised, even though he has not, by any gesture, indicated his decision. This does not exempt the offending player from being dealt with by the Referee.

(33.5.7) The Referee shall not allow any person to enter the Field until play has stopped, and only then if he has given them a signal to do so. This applies to club trainers, etc.

(33.5.8) In the case of serious injury, the Referee should exercise extreme care before removing the injured player from the field and, if possible, seek the opinion of any qualified medical person in attendance.

33.6 Goal Judges

(33.6.1) Two Goal Judges shall be appointed, whose duty (subject to the decision of the Referee) shall be to indicate:
a) When a goal is scored.
b) When the ball is out of play over the bye-line and whether a bye-hit or a corner should be awarded.
c) When an attacking player is off-side.

(33.6.2) They shall assist the Referee to control the game in accordance with the Rules.

In the event of undue interference or improper conduct by a Goal Judge, the Referee shall dispense with his services and arrange for a substitute to be appointed. (The matter shall be reported by the Referee to the appropriate authority.)

Decisions of Interpretation
(33.6.3) Goal Judges, where neutral, shall draw the Referee's attention to any breach of the Rules of Play of which they become aware if they consider that the Referee may not have seen it; but the Referee shall always be the judge of the decision to be taken. Goal Judges shall not change ends at half-time.

33.7 Linesmen

(33.7.1) Two Linesmen shall be appointed where available, whose duty (subject to the decision of the Referee) shall be to indicate when the ball is out of play, over the side-lines, and which side is entitled to the hit-in. Each Linesman shall be responsible for one side-line.

Decisions of Interpretation
(33.7.2) Linesmen shall not change over at half-time.

33.8 Duration of the Game

(33.8.1) The duration of the game shall be two equal periods of 45 minutes, subject to the following:
a) Allowance shall be made in each period for time lost due to injury.
b) Time shall be extended to permit a penalty-hit being taken at or after expiration of the normal period in each half.
c) The half-time interval shall not be of more than ten minutes' duration.
d) The ball must be in play when each half is terminated.

Decisions of Interpretation
(33.8.2) The duration of the game may be less than 90 minutes if a shorter period is mutually agreed upon and it is permissible under the Rules of the Competition. The agree time shall be divided into two equal periods.

33.9 Start of Play – The Throw-up

(33.9.1) At the beginning of the game, choice of ends shall be decided by the toss of a coin.

(33.9.2) The Referee, having blown his whistle, shall start the game by throwing up the ball to a minimum height of 12 feet (4 metres) between two opposing players standing at the centre spot, at least 3 feet (1 metre) apart, with their camans crossed above head level. The players shall not shift their stance until the ball is struck in the air, or touches the ground. No other player shall be within 5 yards (5 metres) of the centre spot until the ball has been played. A goal scored direct from a throw-up shall count.

(33.9.3) After a goal has been scored, the game shall be restarted in like manner.

(33.9.4) After half-time (when restarting after half-time), ends shall be changed and the game restarted in like manner.

(33.9.5) After any temporary suspension (when restarting after a temporary suspension from any cause not mentioned in these Rules of Play, provided immediately prior to the suspension the ball has not passed out of the Field of Play), the Referee shall throw the ball up at the place where it was when play was suspended.

Decisions of Interpretation
(33.9.3) If the ball, when thrown up by the Referee, strikes one or both of the camans, it shall again be thrown up to the required height by the Referee.

(33.9.4) If the two centre players are one left-handed and the other right-handed, each shall have choice of his side in the throwing up for one half of the match.

(33.9.5) If one player should use his caman to hold his opponent's caman and prevent his opponent playing the ball, or shift his stance, he shall be penalised by the award of a free-hit to his opponent.

(33.9.6) If the ball is within the Ten Yard Area (Nine Metre Area) when play is temporarily suspended, the Referee shall restart the game with a throw-up outside the area at the spot nearest to where it was when play was suspended.

33.10 Method of Scoring

(33.10.1) A goal is scored when the whole of the ball has passed over the goal-line and under the cross-bar, except when resulting directly from a free-hit or when it has been kicked, carried or propelled by hand or arm by a player of the attacking side.

(33.10.2) The team scoring the greatest number of goals during a game shall be the winner; if no goals, or an equal number of goals, are scored, the game shall be termed a 'draw'.

Decisions of Interpretation
(33.10.3) The method of scoring (above) defines the only method according to which a match is won or drawn; no variations whatsoever can be authorised. A goal cannot be allowed if the ball has been prevented by some outside agency from passing over the goal-line. If this happens in the normal course of play, other than

at the taking of a penalty- hit, the game must be stopped and restarted by the Referee throwing up the ball outside the Ten Yard Area (Nine Metre Area) at a point nearest to where the interference took place.

33.11 Ball In and Out of Play

(33.11.1) The ball is in play at all times from the start of the match to the finish including:
a) If it rebounds from a goalpost, cross-bar or corner flag-post into the field of play.
b) If it rebounds off the Referee.
c) In the event of a supposed infringement of the Rules of Play, until a decision is given.

(33.11.2) The ball is out of play
a) When it has wholly crossed the goal-line, bye-line or sideline, whether on the ground or in the air.
b) When the game has been stopped by the Referee.

33.12 Fouls and Misconduct

(33.12.1) A player who intentionally commits any of the following offences shall be penalized by the award of a free- hit, to be taken by the opposing side at the place where the offence occurred.
a) Kicks the ball.
b) Kicks or attempts to kick an opponent.
c) Jumps at an opponent.
d) Charges an opponent from behind.
e) Charges an opponent in a violent or dangerous manner.
f) Uses his caman in a violent or dangerous manner.
g) Pushes an opponent.
h) Trips an opponent, i.e. throwing or attempting to throw him by use of the legs or caman.
i) Strikes or attempts to strike an opponent with his hand, arm or caman.
j) Strikes or impedes an opponent's caman, except to 'block' or 'hook' a caman which is within striking distance of the ball.
k) Throws his caman.
l) Attempts to participate in the game without his caman in his hand.
m) Holds an opponent or an opponent's caman.
n) Obstructs an opponent, i.e. running between the opponent and the ball or interposing the body so as to form an obstacle to an opponent.
o) Handles the ball, i.e. carries, strikes or propels the ball with his hand or arm. Note – the goal-keeper is permitted to stop and slap the ball with his open hand within the Ten Yard Area (Nine Metre Area).
p) Heads the ball.

Decisions of Interpretation
(33.12.2) Should a player of the defending side commit one of the aforementioned offences within the Ten Yard Area (Nine Metre Area), he shall be penalised by the award of a penalty-hit.

(33.12.3) A penalty-hit can be awarded irrespective of the position of the ball, if in play, at the time an offence is committed within the Ten Yard Area (Nine Metre Area).

(33.12.4) A player may stop the ball with one foot provided that it is at rest on the ground at the moment of contact.

(33.12.5) A player may stop the ball with both feet while he is moving, provided that both heels are together at the moment of contact. If both feet are off the ground at the moment of contact, the Referee shall be the sole judge of whether or not the player intentionally kicked the ball.

(33.12.6) A player is allowed to play an opponent's caman with his own caman only to 'block' or 'hook' the swing of a caman which is within playing distance of the ball, except in the case of blocking an opponent about to strike the ball or in shielding the ball while in possession.

(33.12.7) If, in the opinion of the Referee, a player deliberately hits the ball out of play to waste time, the Referee shall caution the player for ungentlemanly conduct and award a free-hit.

(33.12.8) Hitting the ball with one hand on the caman is not a foul, unless in the opinion of the Referee the caman is being swung in a dangerous manner.

(33.12.9) Hitting the ball while lying on the ground is not a foul, unless in the opinion of the Referee the player is endangering himself when attempting to play the ball or he is swinging his caman in a dangerous and reckless manner while still lying on the ground.

33.13 Cautionable Offences

A player shall be cautioned if:
(33.13.1) He is guilty of reckless or dangerous swinging of the caman.

(33.13.2) He is guilty of obstruction involving dangerous bodily contact.

(33.13.3) He is guilty of charging an opponent in a violent or dangerous manner.

(33.13.4) He is guilty of adopting a threatening or aggressive attitude.

(33.13.5) He is guilty of feigning injury.

(33.13.6) He is guilty of deliberately tripping an opponent.

(33.13.7) He is guilty of inflammatory action.

(33.13.8) He uses foul and abusive language.

(33.13.9) He persistently infringes the Rules of Play.

(33.13.10) He shows, by word or action, dissent from any decision given by the referee.

(33.13.11) He is guilty of ungentlemanly conduct in the following manner
a) Shirt pulling.
b) Time wasting.
c) Encroaching.
d) Gesticulating in front of an opponent taking a free-hit.
e) Deliberate handball.
f) Entering or re-entering the Field of Play without first having received a signal from the referee to do so.
g) Any other offence deemed misconduct.

33.14 Sending Off Offences

A player shall be sent off the Field of Play if:
(33.14.1) In the opinion of the Referee he is guilty of violent conduct or serious foul play.

(33.14.2) He uses serious foul or abusive language.

(33.14.3) He is guilty of serious violation of any of the above cautionable offences.

(33.14.4) He is guilty of a second cautionable offence after receiving a caution.

33.15 Off-side

(33.15.1) An attacking player shall be off-side if he is within the Ten Yard Area (Nine Metre Area) when the ball enters that area either on the ground or in the air.

Note
The Ten Yard Area (Nine Metre Area) includes the goal area between the goal line and the nets.

Punishment
For an infringement of this rule a free-hit shall be taken by a player of the defending side from the place where the infringement occurred.

Decisions of Interpretation
A player is considered to be off-side if any part of his body or stick is within the Ten Yard Area (Nine Metre Area) before the ball enters that area. A player who steps over the bye-line to avoid being off-side shall not be allowed to enter the field of play while the ball is within the Ten Yard Area (Nine Metre Area).

33.16 Bye-hit

(33.16.1) When the whole of the ball passes over the bye-line, either in the air or on the ground, having been last played by one of the attacking side, it shall be hit direct into play from a point within the Ten Yard Area (Nine Metre Area).

(33.16.2) The striker shall not play the ball a second time until it has touched or been played by another player. No player shall be within 5 yards (5 metres) of the striker when the hit is being taken.

(33.16.3) A goal from such a hit shall count.

Punishment
(33.16.4) If a player taking a bye-hit plays the ball a second time before it has been played by another player, a free- hit shall be awarded to the opposing team, or, if the infringement occurred inside the Ten Yard Area (Nine Metre Area), a penalty-hit shall be awarded to the opposing team.

33.17 Corner-hit

(33.17.1) When the whole ball passes over the bye-line, either in the air or on the ground, having last been played by one of the defending team, a member of the attacking team shall take a corner-hit from the quarter circle at the nearest corner flag-post, which must not be removed. A goal may be scored direct from a corner-hit.

(33.17.2) No player shall be within 5 yards (5 metres) of the striker when the hit is being taken. The striker shall not play the ball a second time until it has touched or been played by another keeper.

Punishment
(33.17.3) If a player taking a corner-hit plays the ball a second time before it has been played by another player, a free-hit shall be awarded to the opposing side.

33.18 Hit-in

(33.18.1) When the whole ball passes over the side-line, whether in the air or on the ground, it shall be hit into play, by an overhead hit, by a player of the team opposite to that of the player who last touched it.

(33.18.2) In taking the hit the player shall stand outside the side-line, facing the Field of Play, with both feet on the ground and in a position square to the side-line. The caman shall be withdrawn directly overhead and at the time of contact both the ball and the caman shall be directly overhead. If the player taking the hit misses the ball entirely, the opposing team shall be awarded the hit-in. The striker shall not play the ball a second time until it has touched or been played by another player. No player shall be within 5 yards (5 metres) of the striker when the hit is being taken.

(33.18.3) A goal may be scored direct from a hit-in.

Punishment
(33.18.4) If the ball is hit-in improperly the hit-in shall be taken by a player of the opposing side.

(33.18.5) If a player taking a hit-in plays the ball a second time before it has been played by another player, a free- hit shall be awarded to the opposing team.

33.19 Free-hit

(33.19.1) A free-hit is awarded for any infringement of the Rules, except by a defending player within the Ten Yard Area (Nine Metre Area) and shall be taken by the opposing side, from the place where the offence occurred.

(33.19.2) The ball must be struck by the club, or scooped, and it shall not be deemed in play until it has travelled the distance of its own circumference.

(33.19.3) No player shall be within 5 yards (5 metres) of the striker while the hit is being taken. The striker shall not play the ball a second time until it has touched or been played by another player. A goal from such a hit shall NOT count.

Punishment
(33.19.4) If a player taking a free-hit plays the ball a second time before it has been played by another player, a free-hit shall be awarded to the opposing team.

Decisions of Interpretation
(33.19.5) The Referee has the discretionary power to refrain from awarding a free-hit if, in his opinion, it will benefit the offender.

(33.19.6) If any player stands within 5 yards (5 metres) of the striker when the hit is being taken, the Referee has the discretionary power to order the hit to be retaken.

33.20 Penalty-hit

(33.20.1) A penalty-hit is awarded for any infringement of the Rules by a defending player within the Ten Yard Area (Nine Metre Area) and shall be taken by the opposing side from the penalty-spot. When the hit is being taken, all players, with the exception of the player taking the hit and the defending goal-keeper, shall be within the Field of Play but outside the 5 yard (5 metre) semi-circle behind the penalty spot.

(33.20.2) The defending goal-keeper must stand, without moving his feet, on his own goal-line until the hit is taken.

(33.20.3) If the ball on being struck does not reach the goal-line or bye-line, the hit shall be held to be a bye.

(33.20.4) The player taking the hit shall not play the ball a second time until it has touched or been played by another player. If necessary, time of play shall be extended at half-time or at full-time to allow a penalty-hit to be taken.

(33.20.5) A goal from such a hit shall count.

Punishment
For any infringement of this Rule:
(33.20.6) By the defending team, the hit shall be retaken if a goal has not resulted.

(33.20.7) By the attacking team other than the player taking the hit, if a goal is scored it shall be disallowed and the hit retaken.

(33.20.8) By the player taking the hit, committed after the ball is in play, a player of the defending side shall take a free-hit at the place where the infringement occurred.

Decisions of Interpretation
(33.20.9) If a retake has been awarded, a change of penalty taker is permissible.

(33.20.10) Rules for Penalty Play-off
When it is necessary to decide a tie after extra time, the following rules shall operate for a penalty play-off:
a) At the end of extra time, the Referee should call both captains together and ask for the names of penalty takers.
b) A team shall nominate five penalty takers.
c) A team may not change the nominations after they have been made.
d) The Referee will decide by the toss of a coin which team will strike first. Each team will take five penalties alternatively.
e) If no decision is made after five penalties each, a sudden play-off will take place, with each team taking it in turn to hit one penalty shot in the same player sequence until one team has scored more goals than the other after an equal number of shots.
f) All players not involved in the play-off will be ordered to the sideline at the half-way line.
g) Any player taking part in the play-off, but not in the striking side, should be in the centre circle with a Goal Judge.
h) Only players on the field at the end of play will take part in the play-off.

33.21 Rules for Schools Competitions

Provided the principles of these rules be maintained, they may be modified in their application to players of school age as follows:

(33.21.1) Size of playing pitch.

(33.21.2) Size, weight and material of ball.

(33.21.3) Width between goalposts and height of cross-bar from the ground.

(33.21.4) The duration of the periods of play.

33.22 Variations applying to Youth Shinty

(i.e. all competitions, whether Schools Camanachd Association or Camanachd Association organised, for players eligible for juvenile or younger competitions. This rule does not apply to Under 18 or Under 21 matches which play to senior rules.)

(33.22.1) Under 14 Competition
a) *Team Lines*
Team Lines containing full names, addresses and dates of birth of all players and substitutes shall be handed to the Referee prior to the commencement of each match. All team lines will be forwarded to the keeper of the player register after each match.

b) *Pitch Dimensions*

The length of the pitch will not be more than 130 yards and not less than 120 yards. The width of the pitch will not be more than 80 yards and not less than 70 yards.

c) *Goal Dimensions*

The goals will be twelve feet wide by eight feet high.

d) *Results*

Results of all matches should be passed to the area Fixture Co-ordinator by the Secretary of the home club within 24 hours of the match.

e) *Rules of Play*

Apart from the minor amendments stipulated above, the competition will be governed by the Rules of Play and Rules of Competition laid down by the Camanachd Association.

(33.22.2) Duration of games

Juvenile Under 16: 40 minutes each way.
Under 14: 35 minutes each way.
Primary Under 12: 30 minutes each way.

(32.22.3) Player endangering himself.

Interpretation

The rules already allow a Referee to prevent injury by stopping play and penalising a player for endangering himself. In the junior context Referees are asked to be particularly aware that this may occur and to be ready to stop play if a dangerous situation is developing.

(33.22.4) Kicking the Ball

Interpretation

Referees are asked to interpret the rules relating to stopping the ball with the feet as for the senior game, i.e. with no leniency.

© The Camanachd Association

Appendix 2

The Camanachd Association Challenge Cup

Final Results and Venues

1896	Kingussie 2, Glasgow Cowal 0. At Inverness.
1897	Beauly 6, Brae-Lochaber 0. At Inverness.
1898	Beauly 2, Inveraray 1. At Inverness.
1899	Ballachulish 2, Kingussie 1. At Perth.
1900	Kingussie 1, Furnace 0. At Perth (after drawn game at Inverness).
1901	Ballachulish 2, Kingussie 1. At Inverness.
1902	Kingussie 3, Ballachulish 1. At Inverness.
1903	Kingussie awarded Cup after drawn game at Perth, with Inveraray, who refused to play at Inverness.
1904	Kyles Athletic 4, Laggan 1. At Kingussie.
1905	Kyles Athletic 2, Newtonmore 0. At Inverness.
1906	Kyles Athletic 4, Newtonmore 2. At Inverness.
1907	Newtonmore 7, Kyles Athletic 2. At Kingussie.
1908	Newtonmore 5, Furnace 2. At Inverness.
1909	Newtonmore 11, Furnace 3. At Glasgow.
1910	Newtonmore 6, Furnace 1. At Kingussie.
1911	Ballachulish 3, Newtonmore 1. At Lochaber. (In first game at Inverness, Newtonmore won 3– 2, but protest granted to Ballachulish.)
1912	Ballachulish 4, Newtonmore 2. At Perth.
1913	Beauly 3, Kyles Athletic 1. At Kingussie.
1914	Kingussie 6, Kyles Athletic 1. At Glasgow.
1915–19	No competition, owing to First World War.
1920	Kyles Athletic 2, Kingussie 1. At Glasgow (after drawn game, 0–0, at Inverness).
1921	Kingussie 2, Kyles Athletic 1. At Inverness.
1922	Kyles Athletic 6, Beauly 3. At Oban.
1923	Furnace 2, Newtonmore 0. At Inverness.
1924	Kyles Athletic 2, Newtonmore 1. At Kingussie (after drawn game, 3–3, at Glasgow).
1925	Inveraray 2, Lovat 0. At Inverness.
1926	Inveraray 3, Spean Bridge 2. At Oban.
1927	Kyles Athletic 2, Newtonmore 1. At Inverness.
1928	Kyles Athletic 6, Boleskine 2. At Glasgow.
1929	Newtonmore 5, Kyles Athletic 3. At Spean Bridge.
1930	Inveraray 2, Caberfeidh 1. At Oban.

1931	Newtonmore 4, Inveraray 1. At Inverness.
1932	Newtonmore 1, Oban 0. At Glasgow.
1933	Oban 3, Newtonmore 2. At Keppoch, Lochaber (after drawn game, 1–1, at Corpach, Fort William).
1934	Caberfeidh 3, Kyles Athletic 0. At Inveraray.
1935	Kyles Athletic 6, Caberfeidh 4. At Inverness.
1936	Newtonmore 1, Kyles Athletic 0. At Spean Bridge (after drawn game, 2–2 at Oban).
1937	Oban Celtic 2, Newtonmore 1. At Keppoch, Lochaber (after drawn game, 2–2, at Inverness).
1938	Oban 4, Inverness 2. At Oban.
1939	Caberfeidh 2, Kyles Athletic 1. At Inverness.
1940–46	No competition, owing to Second World War.
1947	Newtonmore 4, Lochfyneside 0. At Oban.
1948	Newtonmore 4, Ballachulish 2. At Inverness.
1949	Oban Celtic 1, Newtonmore 0. At Glasgow.
1950	Newtonmore 4, Lochfyneside 2. At Oban.
1951	Newtonmore 8, Oban Camanachd 2. At Inverness.
1952	Inverness 3, Oban Celtic 2. At Glasgow.
1953	Lovat 4, Kyles Athletic 1. At Fort William (after drawn game, 2–2, at Oban).
1954	Oban Celtic 4, Newtonmore 1. At Inverness.
1955	Newtonmore 5, Kyles Athletic 2. At Glasgow.
1956	Kyles Athletic 4, Kilmallie 1. At Oban.
1957	Newtonmore 3, Kyles Athletic 1. At Spean Bridge.
1958	Newtonmore 3, Oban Camanachd 1. At Inverness.
1959	Newtonmore 7, Kyles Athletic 3. At Glasgow.
1960	Oban Celtic 4, Newtonmore 1. At Oban.
1961	Kingussie 2, Oban Celtic 1. At Fort William.
1962	Kyles Athletic 3, Kilmallie 1. At Inverness.
1963	Oban Celtic 3, Kingussie 2. At Glasgow.
1964	Kilmallie 4, Inveraray 1. At Fort William.
1965	Kyles Athletic 4, Kilmallie 1. At Oban.
1966	Kyles Athletic 3, Newtonmore 2. At Inverness.
1967	Newtonmore 3, Inveraray 0. At Glasgow.
1968	Kyles Athletic 2, Kingussie 1. At Oban (after drawn game, 3–3, at Fort William).
1969	Kyles Athletic 3, Kilmallie 1. At Oban.
1970	Newtonmore 7, Kyles Athletic 1. At Kingussie.
1971	Newtonmore 7, Kyles Athletic 1. At Inverness.
1972	Newtonmore 6, Oban Celtic 3. At Glasgow.
1973	Glasgow Mid Argyll 4, Kingussie 2. At Fort William.
1974	Kyles Athletic 4, Kingussie 1. At Oban.
1975	Newtonmore 1, Kyles Athletic 0. At Fort William (after drawn game, 3–3, at Kingussie).
1976	Kyles Athletic 4, Newtonmore 2. At Inverness.
1977	Newtonmore 5, Kyles Athletic 3. At Glasgow.
1978	Newtonmore 3, Kyles Athletic 2. At Fort William.
1979	Newtonmore 4, Kyles Athletic 3. At Oban.
1980	Kyles Athletic 6, Newtonmore 5. At Kingussie.

1981	Newtonmore 4, Oban Camanachd 1. At Glasgow.
1982	Newtonmore 8, Oban Celtic 2. At Inverness.
1983	Kyles Athletic 3, Strachur and District 2. At Fort William.
1984	Kingussie 4, Newtonmore 1. At Oban.
1985	Newtonmore 4, Kingussie 2. At Kingussie.
1986	Newtonmore 5, Oban Camanachd 1. At Glasgow.
1987	Kingussie 4, Newtonmore 3. At Fort William.
1988	Kingussie 4, Glenurquhart 2. At Inverness.
1989	Kingussie 5, Newtonmore 1. At Oban.
1990	Skye 4, Newtonmore 1. At Fort William
1991	Kingussie 3, Fort William 1. At Inverness
1992	Fort William 1, Kingussie 0. At Glasgow
1993	Kingussie 4, Oban Camanachd 0. At Fort William
1994	Kyles Athletic 3, Fort William 1. At Inverness
1995	Kingussie 3, Oban Camanachd 2. At Oban
1996	Oban Camanachd 3, Kingussie 2. At Inverness
1997	Kingussie 12, Newtonmore 1. At Fort William
1998	Kingussie 7, Oban Camanachd 3. At Oban
1999	Kingussie 3, Oban Camanachd 0. At Kingussie
2000	Kingussie 3, Kyles Athletic 1. At Fort William
2001	Kingussie 2, Oban Camanachd 0. At Glasgow
2002	Kingussie 3, Inveraray 2. At Inverness
2003	Kingussie 6, Fort William 0. At Fort William
2004	Inveraray 4, Fort William 0. At Oban

Bibliography

Barron, R., *Some Unrecorded Words and Meanings in the Gaelic of Badenoch* (paper to Gaelic Society of Inverness, 1950)

Boswell, James, *The Journal of a Tour to the Hebrides* (1786)

Campbell, J.F., *Popular Tales of the West Highlands* (1861)

Campbell, John Lorne, *Highland Songs of the Forty-Five* (1933)

Carswell, Catherine and Carswell, Donald, *The Scots Weekend* (1936)

Chalmers, Robert, *The Picture of Scotland* (1830)

The Columban Record, Hurling: Some Notes on the History of the Game (1914)

Dillon, Miles and Chadwick, Nora K., *The Celtic Realms* (1967)

Dunlop, Annie I., 'Scottish Student Life in the 15th Century', in *Scottish Historical Review* (Month 1947)

English, Peter, *Glen Urquhart* (1985)

Fairweather, Barbara, *Highland Heritage* (1984)

Finlay, Ian, *Columba* (1979)

Fraser, Alexander, *The Royal Burgh of Inveraray* (1977)

Grant, Elizabeth, *Memoirs of a Highland Lady* (1988)

Grant, Isabel F., *Highland Folk Ways* (1961)

Lady Gregory, *Cuchulin of Muirthemne* (1902)

Grieve, Symington, *The Book of Colonsay and Oronsay* (1923)

Howell, Nancy and Howell, Maxwell, *Sports and Games in Canadian Life* (1969)

Hunter, James, *For the People's Cause* (1986)

Inverness Field Club, *The Hub of the Highlands* (centenary volume, 1975)

Johnson, Samuel, *A Journey to the Western Islands of Scotland* (1775)

Kinvig, R.H., *The Isle of Man* (1944)

Logan, James, *The Scottish Gael* (1843)

MacCulloch, J.A., *The Misty Isle of Skye* (1905)

MacDonald, Alexander, *Shinty: Historical and Traditional* (address to the Gaelic Society of Inverness, December 1919)

MacDonald, Colin S., *West Highland Emigrants in Eastern Nova Scotia* (1959)

MacDonald, Rev. J. Ninian, *Shinty: A Short History of the Ancient Highland Game* (1932)

MacDougall, Rev. J., *Folk and Hero Tales from Argyllshire* (1891)

MacKay, John G., *Life in the Highlands a Hundred Years Ago* (address to the Gaelic Society of Glasgow, 1890)

MacKay, John G., *West Highland Tales* (1940)

MacKay, William, *Olden Times in a Highland Parish* (1893)

MacKenzie, Rev. George, *Student Life at Aberdeen Two Centuries Ago* (1892)

McKerral, Andrew, 'West Highland Mercenaries in Ireland', in *Scottish Historical Review* (April 1951)

MacKinnon, Donald, *The Prose Writings of Donald MacKinnon* (1956)

MacLagan, Robert Craig, *The Donald Games and Diversions of Argyllshire* (1901)

Macleod, Dr Norman, *Caraid nan Gaidheal* (1867)

MacLeod, Rev. Roderick, *The Bishop of Skye* (paper to Gaelic Society of Inverness, 1983)

Macnab, P. A., *The Isle of Mull* (1970)

MacNeill, F. Marion, *The Silver Bough* (1961)

MacPherson, Alexander, *Church and Social Life in the Highlands* (1893)

MacPherson, Angus, *A Highlander Looks Back*

Martin, Angus, *Kintyre, The Hidden Past* (1984)

Martin, Martin, *A Late Voyage to St Kilda* (1698)

Mercer, John, *Colonsay, Gigha, Jura* (1974)

Murray, W.H., *The Islands of Western Scotland* (1973)

Nicolson, Alex, *History of Skye* (1930)

O'Curry, Eugene, *Manners and Customs of the Ancient Irish* (1873)

Ó Maolfabhail, Art, *Camán: 2,000 Years of Hurling in Ireland* (1973)

Pennant, Thomas, *A Tour in Scotland, 1769* (1774)

Prebble, John, *Culloden* (1961)

Prebble, John, *The Highland Clearances* (1963)

Rea, Frederick, *A School in South Uist* (1964)

Redmond, Gerald, *The Sporting Scots of Nineteenth-Century Canada* (1982)

Rees, Alwyn and Rees, Brinley, *Celtic Heritage* (1961)

Rogers, Rev. Charles, *Social Life in Scotland* (1884)

Roughead, William, *Glengarry's Way* (1922)

Scott, Sir Walter, *The Highlanders of Scotland* (1893)

Stewart, Col. David, *Sketches of the Highlanders of Scotland* (1822)

Thompson, Francis, *The Supernatural Highlands* (1976)

Thompson, Rev. Thomas, *History of the Scottish People* (1894)

Young, A.J. 'Sandy', *Beyond Heroes: A Sport History of Nova Scotia* (1988)

Index